TUMHARI AUQAAT KYA HAI, PIYUSH MISHRA

TUMHARI AUQAAT KYA HAI, PIYUSH MISHRA

PIYUSH MISHRA

TRANSLATED FROM THE HINDI BY
SHILLPI A SINGH

HarperCollins *Publishers* India

First published in India by HarperCollins *Publishers* 2025
HarperCollins *Publishers* India, Cyber City,
Building 10-A, Gurugram, Haryana – 122002, India
www.harpercollins.co.in

2 4 6 8 10 9 7 5 3 1

Copyright © Piyush Mishra 2025
English translation copyright © Shillpi A Singh 2025
Pictures on pages 230 and 245 © Avani Rai

P-ISBN: 9789373077222
E-ISBN: 9789373070407

The views and opinions expressed in this book are the author's own and the facts are as reported by him, and the publishers are not in any way liable for the same.

Some names and identifying details have been changed to protect the privacy of individuals.

The book is based on real events, recreated through first-hand accounts and/or narrated anecdotes. In instances, names have been changed, events compressed and dialogues have been recreated by the author for reliability.

Piyush Mishra asserts his moral right
to be identified as the author of this work.

All rights reserved. No part of this publication may be reproduced, stored in a retrieval system, or transmitted, in any form or by any means, electronic, mechanical, photocopying, recording or otherwise, without the prior permission of the publishers.

Without limiting the exclusive rights of any author, contributor or the publisher of this publication, any unauthorized use of this publication to train generative artificial intelligence (AI) technologies is expressly prohibited. HarperCollins also exercise their rights under Article 4(3) of the Digital Single Market Directive 2019/790 and expressly reserve this publication from the text and data-mining exception.

Typeset in 10.5/12.5 Garamond Premier Pro
by HarperCollins *Publishers* India Pvt. Ltd

Printed and bound at
Thomson Press (India) Ltd.

This book is produced from independently certified FSC® paper
to ensure responsible forest management.

HarperCollins *Publishers*, Macken House, 39/40 Mayor Street Upper, Dublin 1,
D01 C9W8, Ireland

समझदार तो फँसा रहा ये सोचे क्या ये मुमकिन है
और मूरख साला कर गुज़रा यूँ जोड़े-जोड़े हर तिनका
फिर बाद किसी ने बतलाया ओ मूरख भैया मालूम है?
जो कर गुज़रे हो सच्ची बोलूँ वो साला नामुमकिन था!

The wise one was caught up wondering whether it could be.
The fool, on the other hand, went along with it, stacking twig upon twig.
Only later, someone said, O fool, did you know?
What you have achieved had once seemed impossible.

Priya, my life, my heartbeat. If you had not been, I could not have been either!
My two golden boys, Josh and Jai—make me proud in the future, bey!
Little Vini, you are so adorable!

To those I betrayed and later regretted doing so.
To those who betrayed me and made me learn the great quality of forgiveness.
And to all my bloody friends, who are too many to thank ...

TWO WORDS

I don't have the courage to write an autobiography. Neither do I have the temperament. Nor the mood.

So I am writing a novel. And I would urge you to read it as one too.

It is a particularly itchy task to adapt an autobiography (or even a life) into a novel. There is a fierce clash between imagination and reality. An almost compulsive need to give wings to the imagination. That has happened here as well.

Now, for the convenience of my readers, let me tell you one thing … that the main character of this novel … Santap Trivedi alias Hamlet … is yours truly.

Thanks to my friends Nishant Agarwal and Rahul Gandhi, who gave this book the most perfect title—*Tumhari Auqaat Kya Hai, Piyush Mishra*!

Thanks a lot to Kamal Ahmed sahab, who typed it out well despite my poor handwriting.

दरबदर की ठोकरों का लुत्फ़ पूछो क्या सनम
आवारगी को हमने तो अल्ला समझ लिया
ज़िन्दगी से बात की इक कश लिया फिर चल दिये
ज़िन्दगी को धुएँ का छल्ला समझ लिया|

Ask me about the thrill of wandering around, my love
Wandering itself became sacred to me
I talked to Life, took a puff and moved on
Life passed by, like the wispy rings of smoke.

The rest after you read it …

—Piyush Mishra

Fear is a bitch—for some reason it clearly cannot be a dog. Fear comes blazing, boiling, and barrelling. Its arrival is inevitable—because when fear comes knocking, not even its maker can hold it back.

Fear is brutal, dangerous, foreboding and sometimes, exhilarating. Fear sends tendrils of anticipation down our spines, before it strikes; teasing us with its unsettling thrill.

Fear comes bursting, trembling, fluttering ... suddenly shattering the serenity, peace and joyfulness of a seemingly normal life, leaving it in shambles.

Every character born from a writer's imagination has fear etched in their hearts. Be it King Lear or Macbeth, Kalidasa or Vilom, Stanley Kowalski or Willy Loman ... even Savitri or Mahendranath ... fear has ruled over everyone. Then how could Hamlet remain free from fear?

It was with fear that he entered the National School of Drama and it was with fear that he left. But they kept saying: What an extraordinary person he was! He lived life on his own terms ...

All his friends moved away to Bombay, but look at Hamlet, he never went to Bombay.

HAMLET NEVER WENT TO BOMBAY

Hamlet often wondered why he never went to Bombay.

JUST NUMB YOUR MIND. IS THERE A WAY TO DO THAT? DRINK ALCOHOL. WHY? ARRE YAAR! AT LEAST THIS DAMN FEAR WILL VANISH INTO THIN AIR!

But more than Hamlet himself, there were those who claimed to know him better than *he* knew himself, those who seemed most concerned about him. There was the media, which heralded Hamlet as the Che Guevara of Indian theatre—his departure would leave Delhi's theatre scene desolate, they said.

Then there were those who celebrated Hamlet as a hero who had sacrificed everything for the sake of theatre. And then there were others who said that theatre was Hamlet's life, and he couldn't survive without it.

Now, how many of them were right ... nobody knew. The truth was that Hamlet also hungered for fame and glory, even if these desires had been pushed down somewhere deep within his being. As for the question of theatre being his life, well, life cannot be compared to anything else but itself ... not even theatre.

Life was passing him by, and Delhi's Mandi House was slowly emptying out. Everyone Hamlet knew had migrated to Bombay. In fact, in time, some of them also found their footing in the city. They beckoned him to join them, too. 'Join us,' they said. 'Bombay is waiting for you ...' But he refused to oblige. What held him back?

It was because despite having strong wings, Hamlet had chosen not to fly. By choice—but was this a wise choice?

It's hard to tell.

But then, did Hamlet love Delhi that much? Who could say anything about Delhi ... but he definitely loved Mandi House more than any other place. He was the king of Mandi House (or ... at least he thought so). It did not seem right to him to forsake his kingdom and move to Bombay. Or, was he just worried about losing his kingdom or something more?

In which corner of Mandi House hadn't he rehearsed? Could he leave all this behind? But then, wouldn't he miss all these memories?

Indeed! These damn 'memories' haunted him incessantly. In fact, he felt that he was particularly troubled by the bouts of being haunted by them. Didn't others have memories too? So why did they feel so oppressive only to him?

Arre yaar! How exhausting. If only a person didn't have to *think* so much, how happy they'd be. But there's a lot of difference between 'thinking' and 'remembering'. Do memories come tracing the steps of thought?

So, what then? Nothing, yaar.

Just numb your mind.

Is there a way to do that?

Drink alcohol.

Why?

Arre yaar! At least this damn fear will vanish into thin air!

Indeed! This damn fear. This fear had become Hamlet's constant companion, drinking whatever he drank and eating whatever he ate; always by his side. But didn't others feel the pangs of this fear, too? So, what then? Well, it simply means this fear haunted Hamlet more than others. Or would it be better to say that this fear was innate to him? Reason? Who knows?

So, what to do? One can always drink more alcohol ... It'll drive the fear away ... at least temporarily. But on its own time—even when briefly driven away—

fear returns, always. So, Hamlet ultimately resigned himself to the fact that his fear was a puzzle, and he did not have the courage to unravel it, no matter how hard he tried.

In his outgoing speech at the National School of Drama, Hamlet had pompously declared that he'd go to Bombay, make movies, and work for television! He had been unabashedly confident. Four years later, he'd discovered he was the only one from his batch still doing theatre ... and that too in Delhi! Like an ox! Alone! He was the only one still doing theatre. All his batchmates had moved to Bombay. Yes, he felt that he was gradually becoming more isolated.

And often, this isolation turned into an overwhelming loneliness.

He didn't mind being alone ... but sometimes, he couldn't sleep. He enjoyed solitude ... as long as it wasn't excessive. He loved being alone ... but not at the cost of nightmares. But what he didn't know was that loneliness was his strength, something that he was born with ... loneliness was his madness, his passion, something in which he would occasionally drown himself in, to find himself rejuvenated ... and loneliness was his destination, a path he had to keep making progress on, gradually. But that time was yet to come. And waiting for it was even more terrifying.

TUMHARI AUQAAT KYA HAI SANTAP TRIVEDI?

'That dude is wild, uncivilized, an alcoholic, womanizer, difficult to work with ... he's a self-obsessed beast!'

A voice filled with hatred echoed.

'He's extremely ambitious. Saying otherwise would be a lie,' another voice boomed.

'What features, yaar! I'm smitten,' a shy smile floated in the air.

'There's a diffidence in his eyes ... but he has a glad eye.'

'I cried buckets at his wedding,' said a journalist from *The Times of India*.

'One must marry as per their parents' wishes,' Jia said, sobbing uncontrollably.

'His *Hamlet* is a masterpiece! Splendid!' read the headline in *The Indian Express*.

'He's atrocious ... very undisciplined!' the National School of Drama commented.

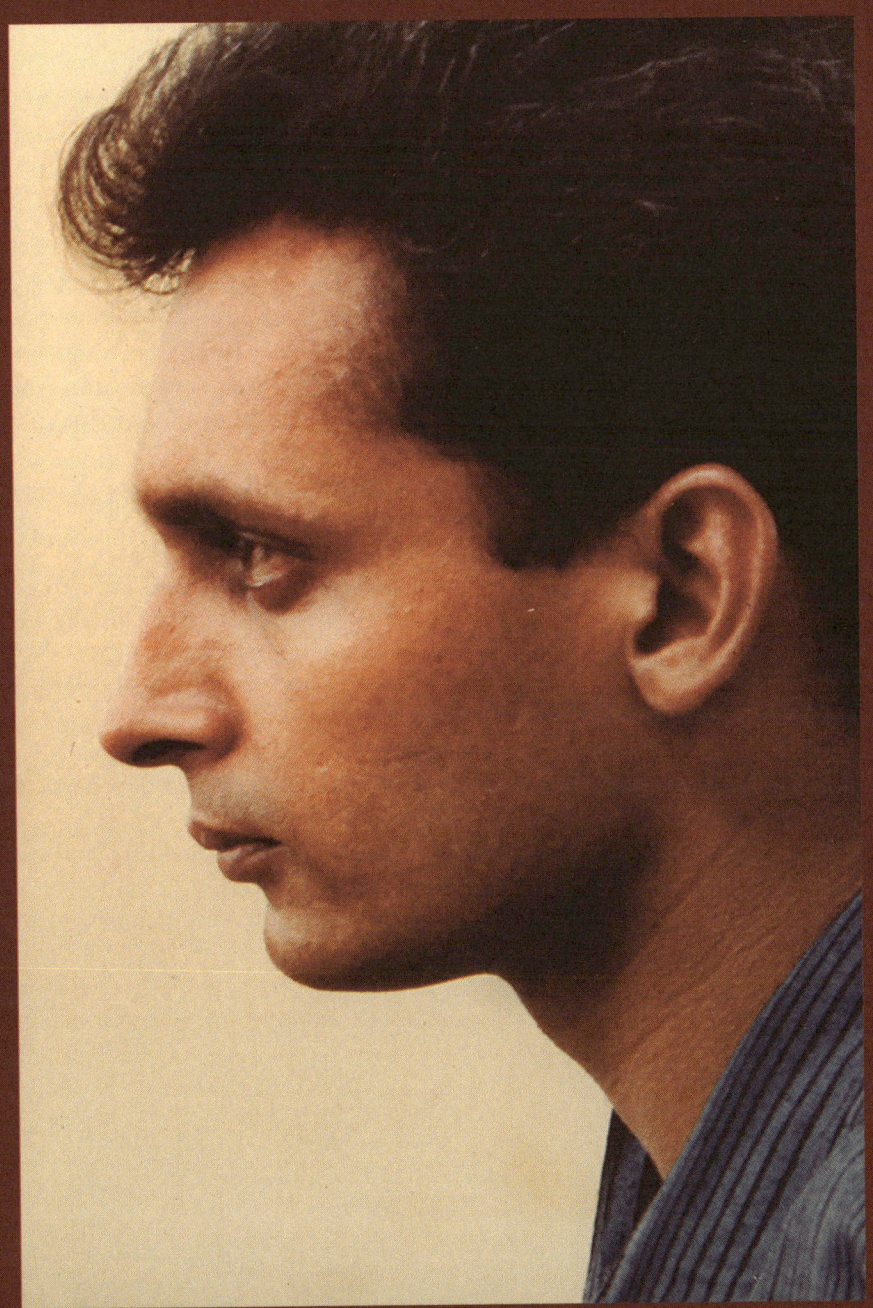

'Every indiscipline has a discipline. You need the right perspective,' Vishnoi said, his tone serious.

'You think you can act without me, moron? Let's see you try,' Pandit roared.

'I want to reach the micro level of the art of acting ...' he mumbled.

'You didn't leave Gwalior to perform in some nautanki!' Pramad Dube said sarcastically.

'I'll spend my entire life with her,' he said with conviction.

FROM ITO TO FEROZ SHAH ROAD, AND FROM INDIA GATE TO CONNAUGHT PLACE

... I'M THE KING HERE. I FIRE MY GUNS HERE, AND THE ECHOES REACH DIBRUGARH

'You can't stay with anyone for too long,' Marathe remarked seriously.

'This system is rotten. It needs to be reformed,' he had howled into the microphone, addressing a crowd of four lakh people at India Gate.

'There's something about your songs. They tug at the heartstrings,' Comrade Khushhal Singh from the Politburo remarked.

'You come to Bombay. You are awaited here,' Samar Bajpayee had said, placing his hand on his.

'Absolute bastard!' Nadeem Shah growled venomously.

'Yaar, have you done everything in your life?' In Matheran, Padam Kapoor's sharp remark was followed by a burst of mocking laughter from the people around.

'If this continues, it'll be difficult to get work in the film industry,' warned Sambal Bhardwaj in a serious tone.

'You're my God, Santap bhai,' Aniket Kashyap said, his voice trembling with overwhelmed emotion.

PIYUSH MISHRA

MANDI HOUSE

Delhi's cultural hub, Mandi House, was bustling with activity. A rippling buzz was in the air. Omi's chaat stall, located at the end of Bhagwan Das Road near Bahawalpur House, was brimming with large crowds—almost eighty to ninety per cent of them chhichore theatre folk.

At the Alka tea stall, the vendor's fingers flew as he brewed tea for the wannabe actors who lined up on the pavement. The buzz of chatter, swirling cigarette smoke, and a constant flow of people created an atmosphere accented by jokes, wisecracks, sideways glances, and sarcastic looks amidst the noise, chaos and madness that prevailed.

Mrs Kirti Jain had recently taken over the reins at the National School of Drama, which helped the institute get back on track. Academic activities were in full swing once again.

Alkazi sahab had also made a thunderous comeback to the theatre scene. He had established his school, Little Theatre, on Copernicus Marg.

Occasionally, the stormy plays of Habib Tanvir sahab and B.V. Karanth were staged, resulting in a frenzy for tickets at Shri Ram Centre and Kamani Auditorium. Energetic performances of Punjabi plays at Sapru House coexisted with small and large theatre groups rehearsing in every nook and corner of Mandi House. The sweet laughter of girls from the Kathak Kendra hostel floated through the air, their sharp glances leaving the young men of the National School of Drama completely besotted. Meanwhile, countless theatre artists wrestled with lights and sets, their hands moving deftly to breathe life into their creations. This scene was mesmerizing and Delhi theatre enthusiasts were willing to bet everything on it, even the most enchanting moments of their lives.

Hamlet wandered through these iconic lanes. Alone. Clad in a black overcoat, his pockets stuffed with everything from his toothbrush to his shaving kit.

He drifted and swayed, carefree, defiant, fearless, rugged and aimless.

'Why go to Bombay? What's so special about that city? I sow my own seeds and reap them too ... I'll find my own success in my 12-by-10 foot room at 1/6, Pant Nagar, Bhogal. This is my territory, and these are my guns. From ITO to Feroz Shah Road, from India Gate to Connaught Place ... I'm the king here. I fire my guns here, and the echoes reach Dibrugarh.

Is Bombay the gold standard for judging one's talent? Samar Bajpayee went to Bombay. Let him go. He was a great actor. Ayush Vidyarthi also left. Not a bad actor himself. I wish him the best in Bombay. Sambal and Surekha Bhardwaj also left. They were a great couple. Good luck to you too, friends. Hundreds have left ... So what's the point? Should I leave too? Bombay is like the dust on my shoes! I wash them daily, and it comes off quickly. Instead of running to Bombay, buggers, you should focus on honing your acting skills ... nothing else will save you when He asks about what you were sent to do and what you ultimately accomplished.

Drinking won't solve your problems ... (He would pause, staring at the bottle of rum mixed with Coca-Cola in his hands. Then he would shake his head.) 'I mean, I drink too ... but ... ugh you're just here for this endless fuckery, you bastards ...'

Just a few days ago, he had narrowly escaped losing his left eye in a scooter accident in Nizamuddin. He would touch his left eye and move on.

As he passed, people bowed their heads and stepped aside; some out of fear, some out of respect, and most out of admiration.

He sat next to the fountain on Bhagwan Das Road and shouted, 'Abey, just act, you fool! Life is too short. You won't find salvation so easily!'

A bout of laughter erupted from him, echoing across Mandi House. People turned in shock because talking to oneself was perceived as madness even back in 1996.

But actually, all of this didn't start here.

He didn't know this madness was a manifestation of his growing fear.

AN OLD MEMORY

IT ALL BEGAN ON 1 JANUARY 1985. THERE WAS AN ELECTRIFIED FRENZY at the National School of Drama—squeals of amazement and applause filled the air. 'Yaar, this is wonderful! I have never seen or heard anything like this before.' The teachers were mesmerized, the students wide-eyed and the audience stunned. 'This is incredible ... simply incredible.'

1 January 1985 was a historic day. On this day, Rajiv Gandhi's government had assumed power following Indira Gandhi's assassination. A shell-shocked nation had suddenly found itself being led by a handsome, young prime minister.

'Finally, things will return to normal.'

Streets were abuzz with anticipatory relief. And then there were girls crushing on his looks, calling him 'smarty'. Who knows whether and to what extent Rajiv Gandhi was impressed by all that attention ... But there was a thrilling excitement

in the country for sure. The situation, however, remained as it was. Punjab was burning in the flames of terrorism. The situation in Kashmir was even more dire. Meanwhile, people were beginning to see a new saviour in Amitabh Bachchan, who had defeated Hemwati Nandan Bahuguna by a massive margin and ascended to Allahabad's seat of power.

It was during this time that the International Film Festival kicked off at Vigyan Bhavan with great fanfare. The torchbearers of Parallel Cinema (many of whom would later become 'popular' or massy directors) arrived with their jholas from Bombay and various other parts of the country to Delhi. Ketan Mehta, Saeed Akhtar Mirza, Govind Nihalani, Shyam Benegal (a central figure in Parallel Cinema) Kundan Shah (whose recently released film *Jaane Bhi Do Yaaro* had created a stir at the box office), Prakash Jha and others wandered through Delhi, shouldering the burden of cinematic intellectualism in the country. Undeniably, the cultural milieu of the nation was in a state of flux.

> 'TO PORTRAY A CLASSICAL CHARACTER WITH SUCH FINESSE, AND AT JUST 22 ... IT MEANS FOR THE REST OF HIS LIFE, SANTAP WILL WALK LIKE HAMLET, TALK LIKE HAMLET, POOP LIKE HAMLET AND EVEN PEE LIKE HAMLET!'

However, the ongoing commotion at the National School of Drama had nothing to do with these activities. It had to do with the student production presented by the second-year batch—*Hamlet*—which once witnessed, embedded itself in the audience's hearts, evoking astonished glances, a frenzy of madness and thunderous applause.

Santap had landed the role of Hamlet. His eyes were wide with wonder as he looked around, soaking it all in; utterly bewildered. The hands of his teachers patting his back... his friends hugging him tight and the girls extending their shaky hands towards him for an autograph. For him, the entire universe had turned upside down. Until now, even the stray dogs in his city had not acknowledged his presence with a bark. But now here he was, with everyone clamouring for his attention.

'Fantastic! Fantastic!' People were congratulating him with trembling hands. Diplomats, bureaucrats and Delhi's crème de la crème of intellectuals and artists. All of them were going berserk.

Actually, this was the first time that the National School of Drama had staged

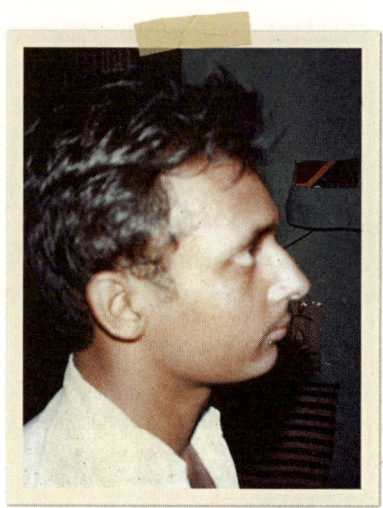
a full-length production of *Hamlet*. That, too, directed by the ruthless German director Fritz Bennewitz, infamous in the acting community on account of being a monstrous taskmaster. His direction was brutal, and his actors often suffered from suicidal tendencies. Before his arrival in the rehearsal room, they often felt their hearts skip a beat, wondering who would be subjected to his wrath that day. Bennewitz was well known in the Asian theatre landscape and was considered a world-renowned expert on Shakespeare, Goethe and Brecht.

Under his direction, however, Santap had delivered a stunning performance. Sudhir Kulkarni, his makeup teacher, had remarked in his characteristic style, 'Johnny, Santap is done for! To portray a classical character with such finesse, and at just 22 ... It means for the rest of his life, Santap will walk like Hamlet, talk like Hamlet, poop like Hamlet and even pee like Hamlet! Look at Manohar bhai. He still goes around behaving like Tughlaq.' (Santap later discovered this notion was far from true after watching Manohar Singh's performance in *Sandhya Chhaya*.)

For some reason, Santap had invited his folks from Gwalior. His father had come to watch the play.

After the performance, he stood still for a long time, holding Santap's hand. He was speechless.

'That was superb, yaar. Truly superb!'

Hamlet stood there with his head bowed.

Later, he had introduced his father to the school's director, Mohan Maharishi.

'Sir, my father, Prabhash Sharma,' he forced the words out of his mouth with painful effort.

'I won't say much, Prabhash sahab. If he stays grounded, he'll touch the sky.'

His father's knees seem to buckle under him. Who knew, even in that profound moment, where had Hamlet been looking. He seemed distant, removed from the moment.

That night, in room number sixteen of the National School of Drama's boys' hostel on Vakil Lane, Hamlet lay in bed. He suddenly woke up. Prabhash was sleeping beside him. Hamlet turned to look at him. He saw his father's frail face and sunken eyes that appeared to be buried in their sockets.

Hamlet remained motionless for a while, listening to the creaking of the ceiling fan. Then he got up and sat by the window, gazing outside.

The whole city was silent, including Vakil Lane.

He sat there for a long time, gazing into the darkness. He realized that merely staring wouldn't change anything.

Actually, the story hadn't begun here either.

GWALIOR/A MUCH OLDER MEMORY

It all began on 12 July 1977, in Gwalior.

Hamlet quietly entered his house.

Inside, silence prevailed. The house seemed desolate. Occasionally, the sound of his mother rearranging the utensils broke the lull. The scorching June heat wave only amplified the middle-class blandness of the house. Every now and then, a tempo would honk outside, breaking the usual stillness. But other than these interruptions, the very air was dense with an unsettling quietness, largely due to Jidda's absence. Otherwise her bellowing reigned supreme in the house.

Hamlet walked into the drawing room. The furniture was neatly arranged and appeared to have been dusted recently. His father was seated in his black armchair, which always held a place of pride in the room. On the side table rested an empty teacup. He held the morning newspaper, its newness and news already old. His father sat in his characteristic style, feet up and eyes half-closed.

Hamlet moved forward, fidgeting with his marksheet.

The faint rustling startled Prabhash, who opened his half-closed eyes and gazed at Hamlet. He continued to stare without saying anything, as was his habit.

Then, a bit later, he asked, 'Yes?'

Hamlet handed him the marksheet.

'What's this?' Prabhash asked as he took it.

'It's my class ten board exam marksheet,' Hamlet mumbled.

'Oh! It was supposed to arrive today, wasn't it?' Prabhash straightened up.

He opened the envelope calmly. Hamlet stood there, silent and stiff.

'Compartment in two subjects,' he said, taking a deep breath. It was another one of his habits.

'SANTAP TRIVEDI? WHO IS HE?' SHE ASKED, LOOKING AT HER SON. BY THEN, PRIYANSH HAD COMPOSED HIMSELF, HIS EYES FIRM. 'IT'S ME. THIS IS MINE. I GOT MY NAME CHANGED.'

Then he turned away. 'Hmm! What are you going to do now? These marks won't get you a seat in the Science College, and without science life is pointless.'

Hamlet remained silent; his eyes still fixed on his own feet.

His father took another deep breath. 'What can I say now? Go, do whatever you want.'

Hamlet stood rooted in his spot, unmoving.

'This is how you'll waste your life, and eventually you'll realize your father was right.'

Hamlet's gaze remained locked at his feet.

'Now go, what are you staring at?' his father said weakly before turning away again.

Hamlet continued standing there.

The real storm was yet to arrive.

Right at that moment, his mother entered the living room, drying her hands with a rag.

'What happened?' she asked, looking first at Prabhash and then at Santap. 'What's wrong?'

The members of this household were adept at sensing the tension floating in the air. Prabhash inhaled deeply once more.

'He has got compartments in two subjects. He will have to sit for the exams again.'

His mother took the marksheet from Prabhash's hand and examined it, turning it this way and that, as though she could magically change the compartment grades into an 'A'.

'What will you do, Priyansh? Your father is getting old. Speak up …' She looked at Priyansh's face.

'Say something, will you? This …' And then she was jolted by surprise; she suddenly stopped speaking. Seemingly her *rural* instincts had alerted her to something that Prabhash had missed.

'Whose marksheet is this?' She looked at him.

'It's his,' Prabhash replied, matter-of-factly. Priyansh stood there silently.

'But it has some other name?'

Prabhash took the marksheet back from her hand.

'Santap Trivedi? Who is he?' she asked, looking at her son.

By then, Priyansh had composed himself, his eyes firm.

'It's me. This is mine. I got my name changed.'

'You changed your name? Why? What was wrong with your old name?'

'People started calling me Priya, Priya. I didn't like it. Besides, I was adopted by Jidda, so my surname had to change anyway. I changed my name too.'

'I had chosen your name with such love ... Anyway.' Prabhash took a deep breath. 'If only you could change to good grades that easily along with your new name. But fine.'

He turned to the other side of the chair, implying his desire for solitude. His movement also signalled the end of the conversation.

His mother stood where he was for a moment. Then she went away.

Hamlet stood there for a while and then stepped out of the house. The scorching sun beat down on him, and the sky seemed to be raining fire. A tempo drove by on the deserted road, the noise of its honking scattered through the silence. Hamlet looked around, unsure where to go or whom to talk to. All his friends were celebrating their exam results. He stood there, silent and still.

Then he took a step forward, letting his feet guide him, wherever they might take him. Now, wherever did his feet take him that day ... who could say? He barely remembers himself ... Perhaps because that's not where his story had started either.

FROM THE BEGINNING

IT BEGAN ON 13 JANUARY 1963, WHEN HE WAS BORN IN THE RENOWNED city of Gwalior.

For the uninitiated, Gwalior district is located in the central region of Madhya Pradesh, which is also the birthplace of notable figures like Javed Akhtar, Nida Fazli, Madhavrao Scindia and Tansen. Shamsher Singh Tomar and Shambhudas Gadariya were also born here. (By the way, the last two names were synonymous with locally made guns, knives and pistols.) Back then, the Tomar Building in the city had the reputation of being seen as a laboratory for regional devastation, where various innovative inventions, including pistols and bombs, were developed.

The majestic Tomar dynasty fort, a symbol of architectural excellence, housed not only the prestigious Scindia School, but also the Gujari Mahal, along with various other buildings, which allowed the city's young boys and girls to sneak

PIYUSH MISHRA

away from their parents to indulge their mischievous desires and murmur sweet nothings like 'Oho, stop it now!' to each other.

In those days, in that city crowned by Maratha domes, a unique symphony played out. The melodic waves of music blending well with the sharp clangs of knives and daggers.

In those days, if one were to travel from Patankar Bazaar to Shinde's cantonment in Gwalior, one would pass by a press that printed the daily, *Dainik Aacharan*. Next to it stood a yellow house that has since been demolished. Right in front of it, a park was constructed after overcoming significant challenges. The residents had developed a strange liking for uprooting the gates and pillars of the earlier structure and selling them off as scrap. It was in that now-demolished house that Hamlet was born.

In this very city of Gwalior, Hamlet's family and the entire related community had nurtured a ferocious dream that he would grow up to attend a medical college, become a doctor, and, after dissecting a patient's body, vomit in the corner before stepping outside, gasping for air.

After that, he would marry the sixteen-year-old daughter of a high-born Brahmin and bring her home, treating her occasionally to chhole bhature or masala dosa from a street vendor in Kampoo. Then at night, with great skill, he'd wrap her in his arms in their bedroom, while taking care to muffle each other's groaning and moaning so effectively that even the flies in the room wouldn't be aware of their presence. After all, any untoward, loud sounds like these would inevitably invite Jidda's screaming.

'For god's sake, go to sleep, you wretches!' Jidda often howled at night even now.

Hamlet had observed his parents adhering to Jidda's instructions word for word.

'She raised us, son. Who else will we listen to if not her?'

Hamlet had committed this unconditional obedience to his memory.

It was October and the neighbourhood was abuzz. The scene was set on the chabootra outside Hamlet's house. The characters were Jidda and Panditain ji. (Panditain ji was a fifty-year-old, slender woman who lived in the neighbourhood and would inexplicably appear, out of nowhere, as soon as Jidda sat down outside on the chabutra.)

An absolute silence ... before Jidda uttered these immortal words: 'Arre Panditain ji, I pooped today.'

The rustle of the leaves paused, the birds stopped chirping, and even the passing traffic seemed to come to a screeching halt.

This might have brought comic relief to a few passersby. Some might have even stifled a laugh, pressing their palms to their mouths. But Panditain ji and Prabhash Sharma's entire family, including his forefathers, did not dare to laugh at Jidda's words. Jidda's word was the absolute, almost sacred truth.

'Yes, sister, it happens,' Panditain ji replied.

'If only this damned poop could pass every day, I would go and take a holy dip in the Ganga!' Jidda said, referring to her struggles with constipation.

This was just a brief sneak peek into the daily life of Hamlet's family.

SCENE TWO

The courtyard of the house. Evening time.
THE CHARACTERS: *Bhole chacha, Amma, Jidda and little Pinni.*

CRACK!

Jidda's sarauta struck Bhole chacha's forehead with lightning speed. He immediately recoiled, almost arching backwards in pain.

Amma, who was working nearby, looked up briefly before returning to her task.

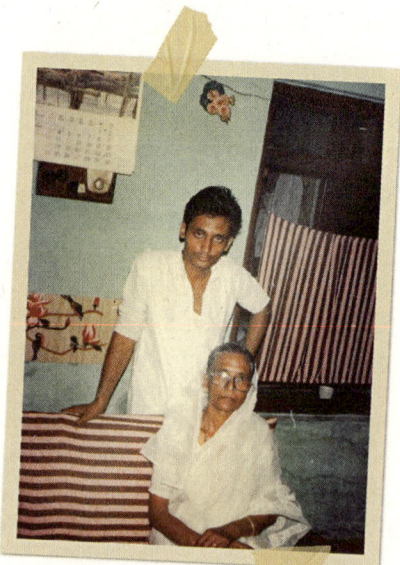

Little Pinni was too young to make sense of all that was happening around her.

'Did you wash the paandaan?' Jidda's howl echoed.

'Arre, I washed it with my own hands, Jidda!' Bhole chacha cried out, still writhing in pain.

'Why is there still so much lime on it?' Jidda fumed.

'I don't know. I'll wash it again,' chacha uttered, struggling through his pain.

'You bet, it has to be washed again. Servants need to be reminded of their position constantly.'

Cut ... thus the second scene concludes too.

The real issue was that Jidda came from the so-called Diwan family of Mahendragarh, Haryana. (The term Diwan must have some association with deewana—a lunatic.) Many moons ago, she was married into Gwalior. Her husband was thirty-two years older than she was; this was his second marriage. (Such absurd things were fairly common back then.) Now, one condition of the marriage was that her two brothers would accompany her. (Perhaps this is what they referred to as dowry.) So, her two brothers came. And then Jidda's husband passed away. The couple had no children. She made sure that her brothers were educated. Prabhash completed his education but Satbir remained uneducated (he had a learning disability and behaved like a child even as an adult). Prabhash got married, and had a son named Priyansh. Jidda's booming declaration that she would adopt and raise the child could not be refused. After all, the house itself belonged to Jidda. When Priyansh grew up, he changed his name to Santap Trivedi. (But that's a story for later.)

Bhole chacha had joined their household when he was just a child. He was born into a Thakur family and was adept at mechanical work, and took care of all the household chores too. He was especially fond of the children—much like a Ramu kaka in the movies. As time passed, everyone at home grew up. Then Pinni was born, followed by Reva. Then the 1971 war was fought, which, well ... came and went. All in all, it had been a while since 1973; much had happened since then. Such is the way of the world.

Now, that's also when the Bania had arrived.

Fear has no caste. Fear has no creed. Fear has no religion. Fear enters our lives like an unwelcome guest and it overstays like one too.

As for when Hamlet had his first encounter with fear ... he has no recollection. But he recalls how in the first standard, during the countless hours he spent waiting for his mother in the eerily silent premises of the school after it had ended—that is when he used to feel a lot of fear. (To this day, he hasn't understood the concept

> FEAR HAS NO CASTE.
> FEAR HAS NO CREED.
> FEAR HAS NO RELIGION.
> FEAR ENTERS OUR LIVES LIKE AN UNWELCOME GUEST AND IT OVERSTAYS LIKE ONE TOO.

of attending tuitions in the first standard.)

His mother used to bring milk to him at school. A deserted school, and that too a convent. Mothers and sisters of the convent shuffled about in their habits. Birds chirped as dusk settled. The school stood vacant, deserted.

In the evening, Bhole chacha used to come to pick him up, it was only then that Hamlet breathed a sigh of relief. He would return home with chacha, only to find Jidda growling. She never used to growl at Hamlet, but nevertheless someone was always at the receiving end of her wrath. It could be said that growling was a hobby for her. If the dal was not salted properly, she would growl; at the raised voices of the tenant, she would growl; if pita ji was visiting Trishala aunty, she would growl. Who knows, maybe she was born after having done a crash course in growling ... or perhaps it was a skill developed during her husband's time (the latter seemed more likely). Whatever the reason, her growling was relentless, unabated.

She was from an aristocratic family that had no bank balance to speak of. But they continued to exist in the faded glory of their once-illustrious lineage.

In the evening, after finishing dinner, Hamlet would head to the rooftop to listen to the sounds of vehicles passing by, with an imli tree towering above him. Then, deeper into the evening, his father used to take him for a cycle ride. At times, they would ride past Mandre ki Mata, occasionally stopping at Chhatri or travelling along Mahal Wali Road. On their return journey, he was often gifted a sweet paan from Pandit's at Ghoda Chowk. In exchange, he had to diligently recite a table in English, daily, on the spot. This was his favourite recreational time during the day. Afterwards, they would return home to find Jidda growling again, as usual.

She would make him sleep next to her, clutching him tightly. He wasn't allowed to show affection to anyone, not even his mother. Jidda would snap fiercely if she ever even suspected it.

'She may have given birth to you, but I raised you!'

So it was that life carried on at its own pace.

It was around that time that the Bania entered the lives of the Trivedis.

TUMHARI AUQAAT KYA HAI, PIYUSH MISHRA

AND THE BANIA ARRIVED

Even though the Bania coming to their house was nothing unusual, an uncanny air took over the house every time before his arrival. Hamlet's mother would wipe and dry her hands and stand at the living room door in anticipation. (Most of her time was spent in the kitchen.) Bhole chacha would gently stroke Pinni's hair as she lay down. (Pinni was diagnosed with enlarged liver disease as a child.) Jidda would sit quietly in the living room with her paandaan. (It was impossible to imagine Jidda without the paandaan; much like Goddess Kali without her garland of severed heads!) Father would sit

> 'DO YOU EVER GET SCARED?' 'SCARED? SCARED AS IN?' SIYAL REPLIED. 'SCARED, AS IN FRIGHTENED. YOU KNOW, THIS FEELING THAT YOU FEEL INSIDE ... FEAR OF FLOWERS, LEAVES.'

upright in his black chair. And Hamlet would usually cling to the wall of his room while the adults talked outside.

The Bania always came around the fifteenth of every month. Donning a prim white kurta-pajama with black sunglasses and shiny shoes. A white cap on his head. Hamlet thought he looked like a crow.

Silence spread through the neighbourhood.

'So, Sharma sahab, how are you?'

Prabhash remained silent. Jidda was quiet as well. Mother appeared to press closer against the door.

'Even I don't like coming here so often, but I'm forced to. What choice do I have?'

Still, Prabhash remained quiet. Jidda was to be usually found gazing downwards; the prestige of her family was on shaky ground after all.

'I heard you have now been transferred to Simco. The salary must be good there, isn't it?'

Prabhash still remained silent, his eyes downcast. Jidda glared at him.

'Arre, say something? I didn't come here to see your face.'

The Bania suddenly burst into peals of laughter. Maybe he was drunk, even though it was only the afternoon. (Later, Hamlet discovered that what is acceptable to consume during the day is called beer.)

'Look, Charan sahab,' his father said in a stifled voice.

'Arre, *show* me,' the Bania laughed again, looking around at everyone as if he sought the invaluable opinion of the Trivedi family on the hilariously original joke he had cracked.

'I can't give anything anymore, Charan sahab. I've given too much already.' Prabhash's voice broke.

'Arre, I'm not asking for someone else's money, right? It's my own. And if you couldn't repay it on time, why did you borrow it in the first place?'

Jidda kept glaring at Prabhash. Family secrets are best kept behind the family walls.

'See, I need to educate my son and run the household, too.'

'So do it ... When did I stop you?'

'How long can I keep giving?' His voice sounded liquid. As if he would burst into tears anytime.

'Keep giving. I'll continue taking as long as you keep giving. I'm not even asking for the principal amount, just the interest.'

Prabhash's father broke down, saying, 'I can't give any more, Charan sahab. This repayment burden is backbreaking.'

Jidda's gaze seemed fixed elsewhere. Mother stood frozen against the door. Hamlet's ears remained glued to the living room wall.

'Then you shouldn't have borrowed the money in the first place, no? Now that you have, you'll need to return it. Okay tell me, when should I come next?'

Prabhash's father had perhaps folded his hands, pleadingly.

'This won't work, Sharma ji. If I start waiving off everyone's debts, I'll go bankrupt. Now answer my question. When should I come again?'

The living room was pregnant with silence. Some questions, perhaps, have no answers.

'Alright, I'll come in fifteen days. Maybe make some arrangements in the meantime, at least? In the future, you should consult me before borrowing from anyone else, okay? I will suggest some tricks. Okay, I'm leaving now.'

The chair creaked; the Bania was getting up.

Then he heard the door open. Maybe the Bania had left.

Hamlet took a deep breath and stepped away from the wall. Now the brewing storm would be let loose, he knew. Hamlet held his breath tight.

Suddenly, a loud sound of a plate breaking shattered the silence. Pinni could be heard crying. Hamlet sat on the bed and plugged his ears with his fingers. Then, Jidda's shriek thundered and Pinni's wailing grew louder. Despite the heat, Hamlet pulled the sheet up to his neck. At that time, Hamlet was in class five.

Sorry! He was in the *fifth standard*. His father had enrolled him in a convent school. He was going to become an I.A.S., I.P.S., or I.F.S. officer, his father had been certain. Perhaps he had forgotten about the prime minister's position.

The next day, Hamlet had asked his classmate Rajendra Siyal—

'Do you ever get scared?'

'Scared? Scared as in?' Siyal replied.

'Scared, as in frightened. You know, this feeling that you feel inside ... fear of flowers, leaves.'

'How can anyone be scared of flowers and leaves?' Siyal laughed.

'I mean, like, fear of the imli tree or a moving tempo.'
'Abey, have you lost it? Why would anyone be scared of a tempo?'
'No, I mean, like, fear of Chand Khan or Ishak Ali?'
'Abey, who are these people? Are they your neighbours?'
'Answer my question first, na. I mean, like, are you scared of going to the school or returning home?'
'Abey, why would anyone be scared of going to school? We have so much fun. And home is, well, home. What's there to be scared of? Are you scared of being there?'
'I ... I don't know! Maybe yes, maybe no.'
Siyal laughed at him and said, 'Abey, that's why everyone calls you Priya-Priya! You need to relax and have fun, man. That's what life is all about.'
Before Hamlet could understand the meaning of life, Pinni passed away.

As Einstein had once said, the only thing that can run faster than light is human thought. Hamlet had inherited this speed as a legacy. He would ride on a shining white horse every night (and sometimes during the day), laughing and carrying Pinni behind him. He'd take her on a ride through the skies, shaking hands with the stars, bidding farewell to the moon and warning the sun: burn a bit less violently, bey.

His flights would transcend Delhi (which he would visit later), Bombay ... hell, in fact India itself! He would fly to places as far as America and England. His father's collection of books greatly contributed to these adventures.

'Will you read this?' Prabhash asked, tossing a new issue of *Chandamama* in front of him. Hamlet devoured it within an hour.

'When will you get the next issue?'

'Next month. It's a monthly magazine,' Prabhash replied with a chuckle.

Then Hamlet went on to read *Parag, Nandan, Lotpot* (*Champak* was launched during this time), *Indrajal* comics, *Betaal,*

> **HAMLET REALIZED THAT PEOPLE ULTIMATELY DEPART. BUT WHERE DO THEY GO? THIS QUESTION EXPLODED WITHIN HIM, AND THE PURSUIT FOR ITS ANSWER WOULD LEAVE HIS FUTURE BURNING IN HELL AND REDUCE IT TO ASHES.**

Rex, Baba Mauj, Tom Tom, Mandrake, Hojo, Diana Palmer, *Narada* and what all and what not. He developed a taste for reading in Hindi. He even read the Mahabharata, Ramayana and Puranas at a young age.

His father was a good-looking man. He stood tall at five feet ten inches and was athletic in build (he was quite fit back then). When he returned from his office at J.C. Mills on his bicycle, Hamlet thought he was the most handsome man in the world.

He proudly told his friends, 'My dad has studied till the sixteenth class.' (This was his favourite story.)

AS EINSTEIN HAD ONCE SAID, THE ONLY THING THAT CAN RUN FASTER THAN LIGHT IS HUMAN THOUGHT. HAMLET HAD INHERITED THIS SPEED AS A LEGACY.

PIYUSH MISHRA

WHEN PINNI LEFT THEM

HIS ATHLETICALLY BUILT FATHER SAT STILL, HIS SHOULDERS DROOPING. It was around 2 a.m.

In between, mother's sobs could be heard. The daughters of the Khanvilkar family—who were their tenants back then—stepped in to manage the kitchen. Bhole chacha sat cradling Pinni's body in his arms, his eyes swollen and burning red.

Hamlet sat quietly, tightly enveloped in Jidda's arms. He forcefully freed himself and headed straight to Pinni's room. Pinni lay with her eyes closed. Amma sat beside Pinni, looking desolate and shaken. A couple of women from the neighbourhood placed their hands on her shoulders as her sobs erupted occasionally. Hamlet continued to stare at them before stepping out.

The entire neighbourhood was shrouded in darkness. A heavy silence hung in the air.

Pinni is no more.

Hamlet couldn't comprehend it. Pinni had been here just yesterday. So why isn't she here today? How did that happen? Is she free to decide how long to stay, and leave as and when she pleases?

Manju Khanvilkar came out and placed her hand on his head.

'Come, let's go inside.'

Hamlet gazed at her, and then suddenly tears filled his eyes. He went inside and started to sob uncontrollably.

'Arre, now the child is crying too. Take her away, now,' Jidda said in a burnt voice, pulling him into her lap.

Pinni's body was being taken away. Her father sat like a statue. Amma's wailing grew louder. Wrapped in Bhole chacha's arms, Pinni bid adieu to the house and left for ever.

On that day, Hamlet realized that people ultimately depart. But where do they go? This question exploded within him, and the pursuit for its answer would leave his future burning in hell and reduce it to ashes. (But that was many days or perhaps even years later.)

He tried to understand. Would Pinni return? The answer: no.

Why did she leave, then? And why did she come in the first place if she had to leave? Did she have the power to come and go as she pleased? *Where* did she go? He was told that God had called her. Now where does this *God* live? He was told that God lives in the sky.

For many dark nights, Hamlet tried to look at the sky closely. He could see nothing but the moon and stars. Eventually he grew tired, so he lowered his gaze. Yet this question had already taken root in his young mind at that tender age: *Where do we ultimately go?*

The following day, a fight broke out between Chand and Ishaq in the neighbourhood. One struck the other with a hockey stick, splitting his head. Blood spilled. Hamlet felt frightened.

Why are they fighting? Both of them are Muslims. He was told that Hindus and Muslims fight with each other, but Muslims don't fight among themselves. So why were these two fighting with each other?

He suddenly remembered his childhood friends, Qamar and Bhaiyye. He never had a fight with them, right?

Why has the imli tree stooped so low? What shape does it resemble? Hamlet was terrified and ran downstairs.

Why was the house screaming in silence? Why does everyone look so grim?

Why does the tempo make so much noise while passing by on the street? Why-why-why?

He was so tiny. What if a grown-up slammed him?

This city? This neighbourhood? These people?

Uff! He held his head in his hands.

He was struggling to understand the ways of the world.

His days followed a mundane routine: going to school and then back home. There was no peace there, however. But then others around were at peace, clearly. His school friends. They played hard. They laughed heartily. He would sit under a tree and watch them. The basketball made a loud noise as it went into the hoop. He was startled. And people looked at him and laughed.

'Are you daydreaming, bey?' Jazoo shouted.

Hamlet tried hard to smile.

Similar things happened in the class, too.

'What is the passive voice of "I gave him this book"?' Hamlet remained silent.

'I'm asking you, Priyansh,' Mrs Roberts's voice echoed.

He was jolted awake. The people seated around him burst into laughter.

Soon, he earned the nickname 'Khoya Khoya Chand' in the convent.

He loved the Hindi classes. He had a keen interest in the language, and he was good at it, too. There wasn't a single question that Mrs Katju asked that he couldn't answer.

But it was certain that a strange quest had begun within him. Who are we? Where do we come from? Where are we going? At such a tender age, questions like these were sprouting in him, which couldn't be answered by the world outside.

So he began to look within himself—into his inner self—without realizing that being introverted and self-reflective at this age were considered terrible things.

God only knows whether this resulted from Amma's constant prayers at gods' feet or a blessing of nature that the Bania stopped visiting them.

'I won't come again, Sharma ji. But from now on, if you take money from anyone, please think carefully before borrowing.'

A kind of silent peace had descended upon the family. Now, he was a little older too—he was in the seventh grade.

And suddenly, Santo chachi appeared, and his flat, bland life seemed to burst with the colours of spring.

SANTO CHACHI

Where did Santo chachi come from, how did she come, and why did she come? He found the answers to his first two questions almost immediately. For the third, he had to wait until Santo chachi had left.

She had come from Chittorgarh, Rajasthan, by train, and arrived with a flourish.

Santo chachi was radiant, shiny and sparkling!

Her arrival seemed to fill the house with immense joy. A steady stream of visitors, mostly men from the neighbourhood, hungered for her attention. The news spread like wildfire in the community that the same feisty woman was back at Jidda's home (Jidda was Jidda for the entire Gwalior). To be sure, the eyes of all the Arjunas and Duryodhanas of the community brimmed with excitement ... and along with them, all the Dhritrashtras too adjusted their blindfolds, eager to peek into their home.

> 'WHAT ARE YOU LOOKING AT?'
> 'YOU. YOU'RE VERY NICE.'
> 'OH REALLY? YOU'VE GROWN UP SO MUCH NOW THAT YOU HAVE STARTED TO FIND WOMEN ATTRACTIVE?'

Santo chachi was the darling of the children. She would roam around the house care-free, the tinkling of her anklets like music in the air, leaving the women of the neighbourhood frowning in disgust.

'Oh my ... has anyone ever seen a widow jingling her anklets like this? This is the height of shamelessness.' (Her husband had died in a road accident five years ago.)

Her face was always lit up with laughter, her tongue quick with witty comebacks, and her constant stream of playful jokes filled the whole house with mirth.

This time, she had brought a harmonium for Hamlet from Chittorgarh. 'This belongs to my aunt in Bhilwara, Jidda. She gave it to me. It was lying around in the house, rotting. I thought Priyansh could use it. His voice is very good. Mark my words, he will grow up to be a famous singer.' (Her prediction turned out to be true years later.)

She wore a veil only in the presence of elders. Otherwise, with her face uncovered, she was usually seen frolicking with the children. If not with the children, she could be found at the kachori shop of S.S. in Kampoo, sometimes at Bahadura's laddoo shop in the new market, sometimes at the aloo samosa shop near the Ram temple, and sometimes swaying around the ice-candy vendor's crusher next to the rabdi shop at Jhansi Rani.

Thirty-five-year-old Santo chachi had a special fondness for Priyansh. She would take him out with her, sometimes in a tempo, sometimes in an auto rickshaw. They wandered all day, and neither of them felt like returning home in the evening. One day, they were sitting in Phool Bagh. To their side, the majestic rear facade of the Gwalior Fort rose into the sky. On the other, the lush greenery of Phool Bagh's trees and plants exuded an indescribable serenity. Occasionally, the rumble of traffic passing by on the nearby road could be heard.

There was a comforting silence all around.

'You should stay here only, chachi.'

Santo chachi giggled, sounding like a chorus of hundreds of silver bells. She stroked his head affectionately.

'Then who will stay in my house?'

'Why? Don't you have a family?'

'That's why. Someone has to take care of the family, too.' Her fingers were entangled in his hair.

'Who all live in your house?'

'My mother-in-law, father-in-law and sister-in-law.'

'Who is a sister-in-law?'

'She's my husband's sister. Like Jidda is to your mother. She also has to be married. My brother-in-law is still young.'

'You take care of so many people all by yourself?'

'What's wrong with that? I go to teach, return from school and cook food. After that, I teach my brother-in-law. By then, Rajni is home from college. I talk to her, then make dinner and go to sleep.'

Hamlet was observing her keenly, but then his gaze wandered elsewhere. Santo chachi's fingers continued to play with his hair.

'Why are you a widow?'

Her fingers stopped. Hamlet looked at her as she sat silently.

'Tell me. Why are you a widow?'

She smiled silently. 'Because I don't have a husband.'

'He's not there? What do you mean?'

She murmured quietly, 'He's gone to be with god.'

Hamlet was irritated.

'Pinni's also gone to be with god ... what's the matter?'

She smiled at him.

'Grow up a little. In time, you'll get all the answers!'

'I am a big boy now. I'm in the seventh grade.' He felt slighted.

She giggled again. A strand of her hair slipped and hung near her cheek.

'Arre, wah re, my babbar sher. You've really become a big man.'

Hamlet was looking at her, completely entranced.

'What are you looking at?'

'You. You're very nice.'

'Oh really? You've grown up so much now that you have started to find women attractive?' Her giggles continued.

'No, seriously. I feel very happy when you visit. Otherwise, my house feels so empty.'

She became serious.

'Jidda … Does she still get angry?'

'Why does she get so angry, chachi?'

'While her husband was around, no one uttered a word to chastise her … and now, no one dares to speak up.' She sighed deeply. 'But she loves you so much. Why are you sad?'

'What can I do with this kind of love, soak it in honey and suck it up like a lollipop?'

Then she laughed heartily. Her face shone in the warm sunlight.

'Aa, ee, ee! Why are you biting me?'

'I'm just feeling so much love for you right now.' She removed her finger from his cheek.

'Really … did your husband ever lose his temper with you?'

She stared at him intently, her gaze piercing.

'Why are you talking about him?'

'Why shouldn't I?'

She fell silent.

'Shall we go now?'

'You haven't answered my question.'

'Not everything has an answer, Priyansh …' She turned away. The lone tear in her eye had been wiped away by the time she turned back again.

As the day ended, they returned home. Everyone was sitting in the living room.

'Arre Santo, why are you so late? I was worried.'

'Arre, I was accompanied by this full-grown man. What did I have to worry about, Jidda?' she said with a laugh.

Priyansh pulled his hand away and went into his room.

'Don't be too harsh with him now, Jidda. He's all grown up now.'

Bang! Priyansh slammed the door of his room. Inside his room, he could still hear everyone's laughter. The next day, the courtyard buzzed with activity. Mother was cooking while Santo chachi ground chutney on the sil-batta. Hamlet sat nearby, engrossed in *Indrajal* comics.

'What are you reading?'

'*Indrajal* comics.'

'What is this?' she asked as she ground the chutney.

'This features the magician Mandrake and also includes Lothar.'

'Who are these people?'

'He is a very famous magician.'

'Oh, really? How famous?'

'Very famous.'

'What does he do?'

'You should ask what *can't* he do.'

'Oh?'

'He can conjure storms, halt trains, uproot trees and reduce whole mountains to rubble!'

'Oh, is that so? And?'

'He can even bring Indira Gandhi here. He can take you on a tour of Chittorgarh while you sit here. And if he wants, he can even reunite you with your husband.'

Her grinding stopped. She kept staring at him intently. Her gaze had hardened.

'Tell me? Do you want to meet him?'

Silence. Then came a sound of 'Uff'. Suddenly, Amma rushed in.

'Arre, what are you doing, Santo?'

She took her crushed finger in her hand.

'Arre, it's badly crushed. Wait a minute. I'll get the medicine. Be careful while you're grinding.' Amma hurried inside.

'Nothing to worry about, bhabhi. It's just a small injury,' she said quietly, putting her finger in her mouth. Her eyes remained fixed on Hamlet.

From that day onwards, she started distancing herself from him.

He would hold her hand, but she would pull it away and leave.

'Look, chachi. This is Betaal and accompanying him is his horse.'

She would focus intently on the *Indrajal* comics, ignoring him completely.

Annoyed, he stormed off to his room while she sat quietly outside.

Hamlet used to look at her in confusion and she used to gaze back at him silently.

'Leave it! I'll never speak to you again!' he exclaimed one day, scrunching his nose before retreating into his room. A little while later, he stepped out and she was still seated there.

'Did you get angry with your husband like this as well?' Hamlet asked. She continued to look at him in complete silence.

It was a sweltering summer afternoon. A scorching loo was blowing outside. (That scorching loo—dry, hot winds—had a significant impact on Hamlet's life.)

Everyone in the house had gone to watch a movie.

'Yadav Talkies is just around the corner. Why do we need a tonga?' Jidda stepped outside, signalling everyone else to follow her on foot. She was a huge movie buff and a hard taskmaster.

Soon, everyone had left. The house was silent. After an hour, suddenly, there was a knock at the door.

Hamlet opened the door to find Santo chachi standing outside, her face flushed red from the sun.

'Where is everyone else?' Hamlet stepped aside. 'They're watching a movie. I have a headache.'

Santo chachi said as she entered, 'You go to sleep!'

And as they say in the world of cinema, cut to ...

Hamlet writhed, he tried to wriggle his way out. But his body had been pinned under Santo chachi's weight.

Hamlet had tried to scream.

'Shh ...' and a strong Rajasthani hand muzzled his mouth. 'I'll cut you into pieces if you make any noise ...'

There was a fierce hiss in her voice, like a snake.

He made a last attempt to get away.

'I said, quiet.' The vegetable knife she had brought from the kitchen flashed before his eyes.

'Why won't you let me live, you bastards? What have I done to deserve this?' Her voice cracked.

And Hamlet realized that the string of his pajamas had snapped with a loud crack. He mewled loudly one last time.

Suddenly, his body stiffened, and a blood-curdling scream escaped his lips, which was muffled by Santo chachi's palms.

Cut to ... an hour later ...

The doorbell rang. Santo chachi opened the door. Jidda's voice came through.

'Arre, what a great movie, Santo. Rajesh Khanna and Asha Parekh looked like Shankar and Parvati. How are you feeling now?'

'I'm better, Jidda. My head hurts a little.' Santo chachi moved away.

His mother came inside. Hamlet was lying curled up like a bundle of clothes left out for a wash.

'What's wrong, Priyansh? Are you feeling alright?'

He coiled up tighter, frozen in place.

She placed her hand on his forehead.

'Arre, you are running a fever?'

'I'll take care of him, bhabhi. You go.' Chachi's voice echoed.

And that night, Santo chachi slept with Hamlet.

In the same bed. (He saw that his torn, blood-soaked pajamas had been washed and hung out for drying.) Hamlet looked at them with fear in his eyes. His entire face was drenched in tears.

'Satvanti has a special affection for children, like a mother to her own. Only a widow or a childless woman can understand the pain of not having a child.'

The next day, Santo chachi left, and went back to Chittorgarh.

'Arre, you said you'd stay for ten days? Why are you leaving so soon?'

'Jidda, I had left my insurance policy formalities incomplete. It would lead to an unnecessary waste of money,' she replied.

Her autorickshaw had arrived by then.

After touching everyone's feet, she looked at Hamlet. He shivered and hid behind his mother, but as he turned, he saw a tear welling up in Santo chachi's eye.

And with that, Santo chachi left, leaving him alone and forsaken. And maybe even lonelier than before.

PIYUSH MISHRA

FIRST SPIRITUAL EXPERIENCE

Hamlet's life had taken a turn.

He sat on the rooftop, silent and still. The sound of passing tempos seemed strange to him, and the imli tree looked ghostly.

'Look, the latest issue of *Chandamama* is here.'

He quietly extended his hands to take it.

'Want some more chapatis?' his mother asked from the kitchen.

'Okay.'

'What has happened to you? You've forgotten how to smile, you wretched fellow.' Jidda pulled him close, clutching him tightly in an embrace. He gave in helplessly.

There had been another fight in his neighbourhood. This time, Chand had smashed Ishaq's head.

He heard himself shouting, 'Kill each other, haramzaadon. Cut each other up.'

And then he realized that he had cussed for the first time in his life.

When Qamar and Bhaiyye came, he refused to meet them.

'They're Muslims. They'll kill me.'

'What are you saying, Priyansh? Where did you learn to talk like that?' Bhole chacha chided him gently.

Life continued to become crueller.

And then one day, something strange happened—he didn't know what it was. Was it magic, sorcery, or a miracle ...

The suddenness of it all left him stunned.

There was a library on the third floor of the convent. He was leaving after borrowing a book when his feet suddenly froze. He stood still, unable to move. He tried to look around but couldn't move his head. He should have been scared, yet there was no fear. He could see the students passing by, but they seemed distant. Suddenly, a light burst forth in his eyes and seemed to spread around him. It was as if he was bathed in its warmth.

No, he wasn't feeling hot. It was more like a cool shower inside him. His body and mind glowed from within. He saw himself smiling and felt different, distant and detached from everyone around him.

He stood in that reverie for almost a minute before someone shook him. Startled, he returned to his senses. It felt like he had opened his eyes for the first time. And he realized he was standing in the corridor, dazed, surrounded by students who had gathered around him.

Girish Malpani, who had jolted him from his stupor, asked, 'What happened? Are you okay?'

He returned to himself slowly, the crowd of students grew larger around him every passing minute, gawking at him in astonishment.

'What's going on, bey? Why are you just standing there like that?' Girish asked.

He looked around in surprise. Behind him was the library door and before him, the descending stairs.

'Where am I?' he heard himself say.

And the people around him started laughing.

'Dude, have you started daydreaming while standing now? You've been here for a minute, standing still as if you had seen a ghost. Where did you vanish?' Jaju said.

'Nowhere!'

'You're slowly becoming moony, bey, Khoya Khoya Chand, wandering in your own world. Dude, where did you get lost?' Rajesh Bansal

> **HIS BODY AND MIND GLOWED FROM WITHIN. HE SAW HIMSELF SMILING AND FELT DIFFERENT, DISTANT AND DETACHED FROM EVERYONE AROUND HIM.**

asked.

'What happened?' Sister Rene came running up the stairs.

'Nothing, Sister. He was just lost, as usual. Daydreaming.'

And everyone laughed.

He didn't know this rare miracle would happen to him many more times.

Years later, he heard Vishnoi say, 'Every indiscipline has a discipline. You just need to have the right perspective. What we don't understand, we call it a miracle. If we open our eyes and look, we'll realize it's a reality.'

It was this incident that gave Hamlet everything he had been searching for. But before that, there was something else, too.

FIRST PAINTING

'You'll get food later ... but you have to do something else first.'

Kanchan didi removed the plate in front of him, laughing.

Seth Madanlal Garg owned a mansion in New Market. He was the wealthiest man in town, possessing countless riches—and was particularly passionate about the arts. He adored the artist community. Every artist who came to the town would stay at his place. Parveen Sultana, M.F. Husain, Ramdhari Singh Dinkar! Numerous renowned artists had enjoyed his hospitality. And today, a truly extraordinary personality was present at his home.

'So, what will you recite?' Pandit ji turned to ask him.

It was a robust gathering. Despite the cavalier mood, everyone looked alert and watchful.

'What's your name?'

'My name is Priyansh. Priyansh Sharma,' Hamlet replied, trembling.

'Please accept this laddoo, Pandit ji. These laddoos are from Bahadura. They are a specialty of Gwalior.'

Pandit Ravishankar picked one up and turned.

'What will you sing? What's wrong? You barely speak.' Sweat started to trickle down Hamlet's forehead.

> HAMLET KEPT READING THE PLAY AGAIN AND AGAIN, ENDLESSLY. HE FELT THAT SOMETHING WAS HAPPENING TO HIM

Ravishankar was sitting across him. *The* great Ravishankar! *The* Ravishankar, Pandit Ravishankar. The name synonymous with the sitar in the world.

Sahni said, 'He's nervous, sir.' Pravesh Sahni was a year older than Hamlet. He was a dear friend. Pradeep Garg was Sahni's friend and this was Pradeep Garg's mansion.

'Who wouldn't feel nervous?' Madanlal ji laughed, and so did many others.

Hamlet cleared his throat and started singing a ghazal.

'*Aaj jaane ki zidd na karo ...*'

The ghazal went on. The audience listened in rapt attention.

A thunderous applause made him realize that he had finished his ghazal. Taken aback by the reception, he suddenly became self-conscious.

'Incredible!' Pandit ji exclaimed, clapping his hands. 'A voice like this at your age? You'll go far. What charisma!'

'He's just in the eighth standard, Pandit ji,' Kanchan didi said with a laugh.

'That's wonderful,' said Pandit ji. He turned around and added, 'There's something special about Gwalior. At every Tansen Samaroh here, we discover a new talent.'

When he returned downstairs, Pravesh Sahni grabbed him again.

'Abey, now that Pandit Ravishankar has praised you, you can do it finally!'

'Yaar guru, I've never even touched a brush.'

'Yaar, you're an artist. You can do anything.' Pradeep Garg said, bursting into peals of laughter.

> 'EVERY INDISCIPLINE HAS A DISCIPLINE. YOU JUST NEED TO HAVE THE RIGHT PERSPECTIVE.'

The thing was, Pravesh Sahni was the casanova of the convent. He was always in love with women; whether they were students or teachers, that made little difference to him. This time, his heart was set on Gita Kanwar from the ninth grade. The beautiful Gita had recently entered Pravesh's life, and as always, he was apparently *very serious* about her. There was a painting exhibition at the school, and she was a painter. She had painted a brilliant piece, but despite not having any skill with paints and not even a proxy painter who could create a piece for him, Pravesh challenged her, claiming that *his* painting would certainly be better than hers. Gita laughed and accepted the challenge. Now, he was frantically searching for an artist, and his eyes locked on Hamlet.

Pravesh had purchased canvas, oil paints and brushes for Hamlet and had stored them at his home.

'Just start. Let's see what happens,' his father laughed.

And so Hamlet began to paint.

Certainly, the painting gradually took shape.

Hamlet was astonished. The painting was finished.

Hamlet stared blankly at the brush in his hand and then at the colours on the canvas. This was his first painting and it was stunning.

He added some final touches and there it was—all done! Now, where it stood in comparison to Gita's, who knows. He didn't know either, but he realized that day that he could paint, too.

And so it was this incident that gave Hamlet everything … everything he had been searching for.

AND SO THE FRENZY BEGAN

Recess at the convent. Everyone was having lunch. There was noise, chatter and buzz all around.

Hamlet was sitting in class 8-B, eating a snack from his tiffin. Vijay Jaju, Girish Malpani, Shailesh Srivastava, Anil Gupta and Fukhhe (whose real name was Praveen Parashar) made up his gang.

The next period was free. Professor Raj was absent today.

Suddenly, Mary appeared at the door.

'Sister Repreta's messenger has arrived!' Jaju remarked in his humorous tone. Everyone burst out laughing. 'Miss Katju and Miss Vijayan would like to see you,' she said in her broken Hindi, gesturing at Priyansh.

(It was customary in the convent to call all teachers 'Miss', regardless of their age.)

Answering the summons, Hamlet entered the staff room. Lunch was over and everyone was packing up.

'Yes, Priyansh,' Mrs Katju turned to him.

'Good afternoon, Miss. Good afternoon, teachers.'

She handed him a book, saying, 'Read this.'

Priyansh took the book from her absent-mindedly.

'It's a play from *The Arabian Nights—Who Died First?* ... You'll be playing the main role.'

Hamlet flipped through the book, utterly confused.

'But I've never acted before!'

'When would you have done it? In your past life?' Mrs Rao remarked and everyone laughed.

'I've observed you speak. You'll do a great job.'

'Don't worry. We are with you,' Mrs Vijayan smiled.

Hamlet stepped outside with the book.

When he got home, he told his father, who was overjoyed to hear the news.

'I've heard you speak. You have a wonderful way of telling stories. You can definitely do it.'

Immediately after saying this, he went to his room.

Hamlet used to find this habit particularly strange. His father used to frequently turn away from him during conversations and retreat to his room instead.

Well, that was that ... He began reading the play and then kept reading it, again and again.

The story is about Qasim and Nauzyatul, servants of the king and queen of an Arab country—both are frequently short on money, and their earnings from work are insufficient. Naturally, they are always considering hacks to earn more.

They devise a plan. Qasim suggests that he would pretend to be dead first: 'You go to the queen and say you need money for the funeral. You bring the money. Then I will go to the king and inform him that Nauzyatul, my wife, is no longer alive. I will take the money from him. Then we will both enjoy.'

Now that is exactly what happens in the story. First, Qasim pretends to be dead, and Nauzyatul goes to the queen and takes the money on the pretext of arranging his funeral. Then Nauzyatul pretends to be dead, and Qasim goes to

the king and takes the money for Nauzyatul's funeral. Both are quite happy about how their plan has worked out and spend the money lavishly.

Meanwhile, the king and queen meet in the palace and they discuss recent events. The king states, 'Nauzyatul is dead,' and the queen replies, 'Qasim is dead.' They argue over the matter and ultimately decide to go to the couple's house and see for themselves.

As they are approaching their house, Qasim and Nauzyatul are terrified that their lies will be exposed and so they wonder what to do. In that moment, they decide to lie down under a blanket, pretending to be dead.

When the king and queen enter the house, they find two dead bodies inside it. Seeing these bodies, they argue again about which one of the two died first. Unable to decide it on their own, they announce a reward of a hundred dinars for anyone who could tell them. Hearing about the hefty reward, Qasim and Nauzyatul quickly get up. Qasim claims that he had died first, and Nauzyatul vehemently nods in agreement.

The king and queen are astonished. They realize the foolishness of their actions and burst out laughing. They forgive Qasim and Nauzyatul and announce a reward of a hundred dinars for each. And so, they all live happily ever after.

Who Died First? Indeed ...

Hamlet kept reading the play again and again, endlessly. He felt that something was happening to him. First, he saw Qasim's face, then Nauzyatul's, then the king's and finally the queen's. Next, he saw the king's palace, the servants, the furniture, the dome and the palace's architecture. Then, he stepped outside the palace.

Then he saw all of Arabia: people dressed in colourful clothes, walking through the markets, camels sauntering along, and cashews, raisins and dates displayed for sale in the lanes.

Then he also began to think about the aspects that were not included in the play.

'I wonder if Qasim had two friends.'

'Qasim?' Varsha Kala inquired, raising an eyebrow. She was a year older than him and was portraying the role of Nauzyatul in the play.

'Yes, Qasim's. Their names are Qamar and Bhaiyye.'

'Who are they? They're not mentioned anywhere in the script?'

'Not everything is written in the script.'

'I just want to deliver my lines properly ... only that much I'll do. Who has got the time to think so much?'

But Hamlet's thoughts had already taken flight. He was soaring.

'Today, the queen's sheera was scalding, and she burned her mouth eating it,' he murmured while sleeping at night.

'Which queen?' Jidda asked, lifting her head.

'She's stunningly beautiful. She's Nauzyatul's employer.' He laughed.

'Shut up! You're dreaming in your sleep,' she rebuked him.

'In Arab countries, people stroll in the streets in the evening, and the king rules over them with severity. But he also has a soft heart.'

He was completely unaware of the profound impact his efforts would have in the future—how they would become his trademark values that everyone would respect.

'I want to understand the art of acting at a micro level.'

He started to enjoy rehearsals, remaining engrossed even in the most dreaded subject—mathematics—knowing all too well that after this boring class, he had to go for drama rehearsals.

At home, he would affectionately hug and play with Reva. (Reva was born after Pinni and was seven years younger than him.)

Over time, the terrifying atmosphere at home had dissipated as well, making way for tenderness. A smile sometimes escaped Jidda's lips, softening even her most intemperate outbursts.

His fingers began to fiddle on the harmonium. (Despite the painful memory of Santo chachi fresh in his mind.)

Pravesh Sahni had brought him a Seydel harmonica.

> **'I WANT TO UNDERSTAND THE ART OF ACTING AT A MICRO LEVEL.'**

'Play this. You'll play it well.'

'Let us also take pride in having an artist friend,' Pravesh Garg had said. Hamlet and Pravesh were always together.

The world opened up for him, and everything around him was blindingly beautiful.

Finally, the day of the play arrived. Despite the chaos of the rehearsals, he was experiencing immense joy.

The room was crowded. Nauzyatul's gharara didn't fit her well, and her jewellery hadn't arrived yet.

Mrs Vijayan repeatedly said, 'Keep quiet in the rehearsal room.'

Mrs Katju scurried from one task to another, struggling with her heavyset frame.

He went outside to check the lights. *These moving spotlights would soon shine on me*, he thought.

He went to see the dimmer box and was completely mesmerized. *This device would operate the lights.* He felt a wave of excitement rush through his body.

For the first time in his life, he had got a chance to wear such expensive and colourful clothes. Since the play was based in an Arab country, the clothes were rich and matched the historical setting. He was amazed at the mere thought that *he* would be donning these clothes.

The play was performed.

His mother and Jidda came to watch it.

The atmosphere in the hall was fragrant and electrifying. Every time he delivered a dialogue, waves of laughter rippled among the audience. Garrulous applause, loud cheers and guffaws …

After the play, he went home still wearing his fake beard and moustache. When his father opened the door, he burst into laughter at the sight of him.

'Excellent! Very good!'

'Today, he has outdone himself, Prabhash,' Jidda exclaimed as she entered the house.

'Wow, what a performance! And that girl with him … what was her name again? They made a perfect Ram and Sita pair.' (Later in life, this particular fantasy of Jidda's went on to wreak havoc.)

So it was that Hamlet had tasted the first blood of success.

'SIR' MEANS FATHER

In life, most people don't get what they need. Either they don't know what they need or they receive it so unexpectedly, that it takes them a long time to accept their good fortune. The same was happening with Hamlet.

It had been a year since he had starred in the play. Although he was now in the tenth standard, the memories of the performance remained vivid in his mind. Just thinking about those moments would ignite a spark within him, thrilling him to his core.

He felt that his confidence had increased at least a hundredfold after the play. He had gained a great deal of courage. Things were clearer and more organized in his mind.

But something like a noose tightened around him in other ways.

His affectionate father had begun to change. And the reason for this change was Anil Gupta.

Anil Gupta was the brightest student in his class. He was a master at mathematics and excelled in physics and chemistry, too. He had the answers to every question. The teachers were pleased with him, but the parents of other students were worried.

> IN LIFE, MOST PEOPLE DON'T GET WHAT THEY NEED. EITHER THEY DON'T KNOW WHAT THEY NEED OR THEY RECEIVE IT SO UNEXPECTEDLY, THAT IT TAKES THEM A LONG TIME TO ACCEPT THEIR GOOD FORTUNE.

His father stopped him just as he was about to leave for Pravesh's house one morning.

'How are your studies going?'

'Yes, it's going well.'

'Okay, but what about your grades? Sixty per cent isn't enough these days.'

'I am trying.'

'It doesn't seem like you're putting in the right amount of effort. Students who dedicate themselves to their studies tend to adopt a different approach. Just take a look at Anil Gupta!'

He took a deep breath.

The last time Gupta visited, he talked to Prabhash about everything, including his career.

'I want to pursue aeronautics in Bangalore, uncle. That's my goal,' Anil had said to his father.

'Have you even heard of aeronautics?'

'It's not entirely necessary that everyone knows about or has heard about every concept there is, sir. Right?' His tone was tinged with bitterness.

(He was unaware that calling his father 'sir' would become a permanent practice in the future.)

'How dare you speak to me like that?' His father's voice was brusque.

'I've said what I needed to say.'

'Have you forgotten how to respectfully talk to your father? And let me remind you, your board exams are next year. Do you realize that?'

(He was part of the first batch of the 10+2 system in India. The tenth board exams were a big deal. The number of textbooks had grown immensely ... they were heavier, too.)

'Yes.'

'What?'

'I realize it very well!'

Thwack! He felt the sting of his life's first slap from his father.

'Don't you have any manners when speaking to your father? Talking back so brazenly!' he roared.

Hamlet kept standing there. The slap was hard, but the effect of it was even harder.

FIRST SCULPTURE, FIRST VERSE

'I don't want to study,' he said, sitting in Pradeep Garg's house.
'So what do you want to do?' Pravesh asked.
'I don't know,' he replied, seething with anger.
'You have to do something, right?' Pradeep insisted.
He looked up.
'I know,' he said.

A stone from the drain nearby was placed in the centre of his house.
'What is this?' Jidda was startled to see it.
'A stone,' he responded in a flat voice.
'I can see that, you idiot! But what is it doing in front of the kitchen?'
'I brought it. I picked it up.'
'From where?'
'From the drain.'
'A stone from the dirty drain in front of the kitchen?' Jidda growled.
'I have kept it for washing.'
'What will you do with it?'
'I will sculpt it.'
'And from where have you inherited that skill? Not even your father can remotely dream of sculpting something. How daring!'
'Ask him that question!'
'So you're talking back?' Jidda picked up her sarauta and ran towards him fiercely.
'Hit me,' he stood there defiantly.

Jidda stopped. Everyone had noticed the recent changes in Hamlet's behaviour. He had become sturdier, both physically and mentally.

'Let Prabhash come. If he doesn't beat you up tonight, then my name isn't Tara Trivedi.' (That was indeed her real name.)

Prabhash came at night. And *thwack-thwack-thwack*. The slaps were harder this time. Their impact even more.

The next day, he carried the stone to the terrace in front of everyone. Jidda kept staring at him.

Prabhash returned home in the evening. He stood silently for a moment before going to his room and closing the door.

Within two months, the sculpture was complete. A clenched fist, symbolic of Hamlet's rage.

Now Hamlet had grown restless. He needed something, though he didn't know what it was.

He would wake up in the middle of the night, sit up and stare into the darkness. Then he would go outside. His father would wake up startled and sit up in bed, alert. Hamlet would open the latch and slip out.

'Keep him on a leash or he'll turn into a wild horse!' Jidda muttered.

Hamlet sat for hours on the terrace at night. Bhole chacha came up to him one day.

'Priyansh, why are you doing all this?'

'I should have done this a long time ago, chacha.'

'It will spoil everything, beta.'

'What's going right anyway?'

He often went alone to the hills of Mandre. Many a time Pravesh and Pradeep accompanied him.

'What's wrong?'

'Why doesn't anyone say anything?'

'Who?'

'Everyone. At home, outside.'

That day he returned. He latched the door. There was a writing pad in front of him and a pen in his hands.

His first-ever poem spilled onto the paper ...

ज़िन्दा हो हाँ तुम कोई शक नहीं
साँस लेते हुए देखा मैंने भी है
हाथ औ' पैरों और जिस्म को हरकतें
खूब देते हुए देखा मैंने भी है...
अब भले ही ये करते हुए होंठ तुम
दर्द सहते हुए सख़्त सी लेते हो
अब है इतना भी कम क्या तुम्हारे लिए
ख़ूब अपनी समझ में तो जी लेते हो...

You are alive, there's no doubt about that
I've seen you breathe
Your hands, your feet, your body
I've seen them sway to your rhythm ...
But now, even as you seal
your lips firmly, enduring suffering and pain
Now this life, too, is enough for you
You tell yourself ... you are still alive, at least ...

He continued writing, unaware that this poem would one day be worth millions.

THE ENTRY OF COMMUNISM

THE NEXT DAY WAS SUNDAY. THE PHONE RANG. (THEY HAD RECENTLY got a landline phone connection at home.)

'Tell him, there's a call for him,' his father said. Their interaction with each other was strained since the slap incident.

He picked up the receiver. Santosh Bhadbhade was at the other end.

'What have you decided?' Bhadbhade, who was a year younger than him, asked.

'I'm not in the mood,' he responded.

'Come on, let's go. Your life is going to change.'

'Where is it?'

'Nai Sadak, located behind Gwalior Talkies.'

The next day, Bhadbhade took him to the Communist Party office on Nai Sadak.

The place was bustling. In the front courtyard, a group worked on making flags bearing symbols of a hammer and sickle. Inside the room, countless books were stacked in big piles on the floor, with some books peeking out from the upper shelves as well. Comrade Baldev glanced upward.

'Come in, Priyansh! Santosh has told me about you.' He had a smile on his face. 'Welcome.' He stood up and shook Hamlet's hand.

'Why is life so difficult?' he inquired as he settled into his seat.

'Arre?' he chuckled. 'So eager? You won't get answers to all your questions immediately!'

'But I need them right away!'

'Please take a seat first. Arre listen, bring three cups of tea,' he said to someone outside the room as he sat down in his chair.

'Ask. What do you wish to know?'

'Why does all of this feel so strange?'

'Because we don't want change,' he said calmly. 'We accept things as they are. But do we not need change to progress? And who will bring it? We will! Without considering whether others are trying as well. Sitting idly is not the name of the game.'

'What kind of change?'

'Every kind. Change in our values, beliefs and way of life. Something is certainly wrong with what the country and society are giving us, right? Or will you continue living your life accepting it all as if it's the ultimate Truth? Communism points towards radical change ... Come on, let's have some tea.'

He sat with the communists late into the evening.

When he returned home, he was swaying with confidence. It felt as if someone had infused steel into his spine.

And the very next day, he caused a scandal.

Mahavir School was tucked in the lane behind his house. Its owner, P.C. Gupta nurtured the dream of marrying multiple women in this single lifetime. This one was his third wife, whom he had brought home after divorcing his first two wives. He appointed her as the principal of Mahavir School. She would sit all day doing principal-like activities, while Gupta ji watched her with deep admiration.

The couple had adopted a boy, Pandit ji's son. (Adoption was quite common in their neighbourhood.) Rameshwar was two or three years younger than Hamlet and referred to him as bhaiya. In fact, after Rameshwar had successfully completed a few chores for his 'bhaiya', Hamlet had bestowed upon him the title of 'Hanuman'.

Due to official irregularities at Mahavir School, the Madhya Pradesh Education Department had cancelled its registration. However, the influential Gupta ji refused to issue transfer certificates to any student. Rameshwar 'Hanuman' was among those who were affected. He lodged a complaint with Hamlet.

Fuelled by the courage from the play and inspired by Comrade Baldev's conversation, Hamlet went to Mahavir School and demanded Rameshwar's transfer certificate. He started softly, but his voice gradually grew louder. He directly confronted Mrs Gupta. Gupta ji initially tolerated it, but when he could no longer bear his wife being insulted, he grabbed Hamlet by the neck. Hamlet struggled to break free, and during the scuffle, he hit Gupta ji a few times. Gupta ji dragged him by the collar to Jidda's house.

'This is a family matter, Jidda. Otherwise, I would have killed him right there!'

Hamlet silently slipped into his room.

Jidda sat in a corner with fiery eyes. She didn't eat anything that day.

'Call Prabhash,' she said.

Even though her report against Hamlet could have been filed later in the evening, she insisted on calling him on the landline.

His father came back home urgently and listened to the full story with patience.

Jidda was in a dark mood and had isolated herself in her room.

'He has brought such shame to the family today, I cannot even begin to fathom it. That worthless, shameless man dragged him through the streets like a dog. Everyone saw it.'

His father stood silently. Then he picked up his walking stick.

'Listen ...' his mother's voice trembled.

And *crack-crack-crack*. He kept whacking him. He didn't care where the stick landed, how hard it hit Hamlet, or how many times.

'When will you learn ... when will you learn ... when!'

Finally, he tossed the stick aside and went to his room, panting.

Hamlet lay there quietly, tears streaming down his face, his body and his heart burning anew in the sweltering heat—not just from that moment alone.

The result for his board exams was expected any day.

And one day, the results were out. He had got compartments in two subjects and was expelled from the convent school. He got a transfer certificate alright. The reason? An illicit love affair with a young junior school teacher that tarnished the school's reputation.

His father was stunned. His mother was shocked. Jidda felt numb. And Bhole chacha remained quiet.

Hamlet cried alone. Not because of his results ... but because that was Miss Ginger Margaret's last day at school, as she was leaving forever to return home to Kerala.

FIRST KISS

ज़िन्दगी के सफ़र में गुज़र जाते हैं जो मुक़ाम
वो फिर नहीं आते ... वो फिर नहीं आते ...

In this journey called life, some milestones pass us by
Never to come back, never to come back

Hamlet experienced one such milestone in his life. Miss Ginger Margaret Philip.

It was the tenth grade. It was also his very first kiss ever.

A commotion broke out as soon as Miss Ginger stepped into the school.

While playing football, Jaju shouted, 'Abey, Zeenat Aman has come to our school! She'll knock the building down with her beauty!'

And Miss Ginger truly did create a stir.

It was a long-standing tradition in the convent to hire female teachers from Kerala. The Kerala Ladies' Hostel was also situated within the school campus. Miss Ginger Margaret Philip had arrived in Hamlet's life (and school) through this route.

Miss Ginger was fully aware of her stunning good looks and piquant nature.

During the morning assembly, when she came in, walking gracefully on the path that led to the hostel, sometimes in a crisply draped sari and sometimes in a fitted skirt—her body swaying gently, a soft smile playing on her lips—a sensational excitement rippled through the students.

Every student attempted to cross her path at least once a day. She acknowledged each greeting with a gentle smile and moved on, the students' gazes following her from a distance. Her presence brought smiles to the female staff and created a sense of restlessness among the male staff.

Mrs Vijayan couldn't help but smile. 'Good Lord, the way she dresses!'

Professor Raj stormed into the chemistry lab, aggressively mumbling, 'Is this a school or a fashion parade?'

While coaching the students in basketball after school, Rajput sir would remove his shirt and sit beneath the peepal tree in only his vest, right in front of class 2-B.

(Miss Ginger tutored the students in class 2-B.)

During the recess one day, she stopped Priyansh as he was hurrying down the stairs close to where the other students were seated.

'You did *Who Died First?*'

'Yes, Miss.'

'Miss' was a general address, regardless of the grade that the teacher taught in the school.

'I have a copy of a play titled *All My Sons* by Arthur Miller. Could you translate it into Hindi? I've heard your Hindi is very good?'

He had no choice but to agree.

'Meet me in class 2-B after the school.'

Students passing by eyed their conversation and glanced suggestively at Hamlet. He hastily moved away from there.

Then, they met in class 2-B (to-be or not 2-B) and kept meeting again and again. Hamlet gazed at Miss Ginger carefully. She was enchanting.

They started translating the play. She read while he listened. More than merely listening, he use to watch her intently. At one point, she looked up and caught him staring. He felt flustered.

'What are you looking at?' she smiled softly.

'Nothing, Miss.' He couldn't say anything else.

'Me?' She laughed heartily, brushing a strand of hair from her forehead. Hamlet lowered his head without saying anything.

She laughed even more loudly.

'Uff! Blushing like a girl?'

Hamlet finished translating the play in a few days, but their meetings continued.

'Please improve my Hindi.'

'How, Miss?'

'You're asking me?' As a habitual giggler, she let out another giggle.

Gradually, class 2-B started becoming a popular spot. All the Kerala staff teachers would meet there after school hours.

'He sings very well ...' Miss Juliet remarked one day.

'Arre wah! Could you sing a song for us?' Miss Ginger said playfully, in Hindi. Her Hindi was indeed improving.

'Which one?' His confidence was growing as well.

'That one... "O Sanam"...'

She'd heard him sing it on stage once. And he started singing.

'*Aa ja sanam madhur chandni mein hum ...*'

And almost everyone began to sway. After that, all the teachers quietly left class 2-B. Hamlet was feeling good.

Gradually, the Kerala staff began sending him goodies. Sometimes dosa, sometimes idli, sometimes chocolates, sometimes Chiclets. Hamlet noticed that

they deliberately used to leave just the two of them alone.

Conversations began to flow, covering all sorts of topics. In between, there were singing sessions, too. Ginger would ask him to sing a song for her often. She truly loved his singing voice, even though she did not understand the words because of her poor Hindi.

One day, she suddenly declared, 'From now on, I'll pay a fee for every song.'

'I don't understand, Miss.'

'Arre baba! You sing so well. Charge something!'

'I still do not understand.'

'Two kisses ... per song!' She giggled again.

He still didn't understand. When he realized what she meant, his ears turned red. She giggled again. 'Again! Blushing like a girl!'

He began singing.

'*Yeh raatein yeh mausam nadi ka kinara ... yeh chanchal hawa ...*'

The song ended.

'Now, the fee?' she asked mischievously.

He lowered his head. She gently turned his face toward her and kissed him on the cheek. To Hamlet, it felt very good.

One day, they were both sitting together. School had long been over, and the crowd of students had thinned. Class2-B was quiet, and Ginger was in an unusual mood that day.

'Sing something different today.'

'What do you mean?'

'Something different ... something sad ...'

'Why sad?' he laughed.

'Just like that. I feel like it.'

And he started to sing.

'Yeh nayan dare dare ... ye jaam bhare bhare ...
Zara peene do ...
Kal ki kisko khabar ...
Ik raat hoke nidar ...
Mujhe jeene do ...
Yeh nayan dare dare ...'

2-B was utterly silent, and his song made the air quieter still. She wiped her eyes with her hand and smiled.
'You sing really well.'
'Do you understand the meaning?'
'No. But I can feel it. It's sad.'
They were quiet for a while.
'Life is strange. Today, I'm here. Tomorrow, I'm gone.'
'Where do you live in Kerala?'
'As if you know the place.' She smiled at him.
'I'm just asking.'
'Marangattuppilly, Kottayam district.'
'Strange name.'
'Strange for you.'
They were both silent for a moment. Then, looking straight ahead, he said, 'Miss, I want to change my name.'
'What's wrong with your name?'
'It reminds me of my past.'
'What will be the new name?'
'Santap.'
'Means?'
'Sorrow ... unhappy ... disturbed.'
'Why such a depressing name?'
And suddenly, tears welled up in Hamlet's eyes.
'Priyansh ...' Ginger said with an alarmed concern, placing her hand on Hamlet's. Hamlet wiped his eyes.
'Why is life so strange?'
She turned his chin towards her.
'You know one thing? You should have been born at least ten years ago. I would have been very happy.'

Their eyes met, and they gazed at one another. Gradually, her lips moved and touched Hamlet's.

This was Hamlet's first kiss.

Gwalior was a small town, and the convent was even smaller. Rumours began to spread.

'Where can we find Priyansh?'

'Before school, in class 10-A. And after school, in class 2-B.' This statement inspired loud guffawing from everyone.

At home, his father asked him one day, 'You've been coming home very late from school?'

'I play basketball,' he said, bowing his head.

'Are you only going to play basketball or will you study as well? You have your board exams this year.'

The next day, Sister Repreta called him to her chamber.

'How are your studies going on?'

'Fine, Sister.'

'In class 2-B?'

Hamlet's throat went dry.

'What do you have to do with a junior-grade teacher? Sitting with her day and night?'

Priyansh hung his head.

'Call your parents tomorrow.'

The next day, his father came to school. He was in the Sister's chamber while Hamlet stood outside. At home, his father called for him.

'Who is this Ginger Margaret?'

'She is a junior teacher,' he said in a dry voice.

'Why do you spend so much time with her?' The conversation was taking place in front of the whole family.

'I was told that you were also seen in a compromising situation with her?'

Jidda slapped her forehead in exasperation.

'Oh God! I never thought I'd see this day.'

'You will head straight home from school. And until your exams, no more of singing and painting.'

The next day onwards, he completely stopped meeting Ginger.

He would avoid her if she stumbled on the way.

If she tried to talk to him, he would cut her off by saying, 'Excuse me.'

Once, he was looking at a book in the library. When he turned around, Ginger was standing behind him with a troubled expression on her face. He stepped back and attempted to get past her, but she grabbed his hand.

'What's happened?'

He pulled his hand away and walked out. When he reached the door, he glanced back. She stood there like a statue, tears in her eyes.

Often, while passing through the corridors, he felt like someone was watching him. He would look around and find Ginger sitting under a distant tree and staring at him. And many times, he felt that her gaze was following him everywhere.

After that day in the library, Ginger's behaviour changed. The always-cheerful Miss Ginger became very quiet, rarely smiling. The change was noticeable to everyone.

'The red fairy has become quiet these days,' Jaju said.

'Did you fight with her?'

Santap said nothing.

Exams were approaching. The students were engrossed in their studies and very few people were seen lingering around in the premises. It was everyone's first encounter with the board exams and the biting January cold did not help.

But Hamlet was miles away from his studies.

He found physics and chemistry torturous. He was afraid of mathematics. He enjoyed history and Hindi, but he didn't feel like studying. The memories of the play and the evenings spent with Ginger had shaken him to his core. Often, his eyes would fill with tears.

One day, he was pretending to study in his room.

Suddenly, Jidda burst into the room.

He swiftly covered his book. Even then, his newly made sketch concealed beneath it couldn't escape Jidda's sharp eyes.

She pulled off his blanket. Hundreds of sketches came flying off.

'Is this studying? Prabhash!' she screamed her lungs out.

A sudden smack to the face!

It was the hardest slap he had ever received. 'Get out of the house! Out!' his father yelled.

The next afternoon, he stood in front of class 2-B. Ginger was checking notebooks, but she paused and looked up. He stepped forward and buried himself in Ginger's arms, sobbing. Ginger held him tightly.

And then there was a knock at the door. They both looked up. Mary was standing there, staring at them.

The consequences were clear.

Hamlet had got compartments in two subjects in the board exams and was expelled from the convent school. The reason: an illicit affair with a young junior school teacher, a scandal that tarnished the school's reputation.

His father was stunned, his mother was shocked, Jidda felt numb, and Bhole chacha remained silent.

And Hamlet was crying alone because that day was Ginger Margaret's last day at school. She was leaving forever, going back home ... to Kerala!

At Gwalior station, the Kerala Express whistled. The station bustled with activity. Hamlet stood outside Ginger's window. Their hands were clasped, yet they remained silent.

'Say something...' Her eyes glistened with tears.

'What?'
'Anything! I'm going forever.'
Hamlet sighed deeply. 'Nothing to say!'
Then there was silence again.
Tears welled up in her eyes as she asked him, 'Will you remember me?'
'Yes,' he nodded silently.
'Will you come to Kerala?' she asked.
'No,' Hamlet responded quietly.
'Why?'
'Just like that,' Hamlet replied in a feeble voice.
'I mean it, you know? You should have been born ten years ago!'
The train whistled again and slowly started to move.
'Santap ...'
Hamlet realized in that moment that she was the first to call him by that name.
'I will never be able to forget you. You are my first love!'
All her anguish burst forth in her tears.
The train began to gather pace.
'Please come to Kerala. Promise me.'
She tried to look out of the window.
'I will try.'
But there was no point in going to Kerala; her wedding was scheduled for next month in Dhanbad. The train sped away.
Ginger was gone forever.

PIYUSH MISHRA

A QUIET LIFE

Hamlet was sitting atop Mandre Hill. Quietly. On a rock.

Behind him, the temple bells chimed, and before him lay the deafening silence of the valley. The evening was fading. A faint darkness had spread.

A car passed by on the winding road below. The glow of its lights spread on the road and then disappeared.

Hamlet was silent.

Suddenly, he realized he was weeping. He was surprised. There was no reason to cry.

No, of course, there was a reason.

He took a slow breath. After the Ginger episode, his father had burned all of his paintings and sketches. His sculpture had been shoved into a corner and his mouth organ and harmonium had been confiscated.

Birdsong swam in the evening air; the birds were returning to their homes at dusk.

His relationship with home was entirely severed. Jidda was always seething with anger, and his mother and Bhole chacha bore the brunt of it.

Sitting alone on the hill, Hamlet thought about how he had never seen his mother and father go out together.

His father would come home from the office and head straight to his room. Then, in the evening, he would come out to watch TV and eat. After that, the door of the room would be shut once more.

His mother was rarely seen outside the kitchen. When a guest arrived, she would emerge only to touch their feet before returning to the kitchen.

Bhole chacha chose to remain silent at home generally ... spending most of his time with little Reva.

Satveer chacha would sit aimlessly on the chabootra outside the house.

Hamlet rarely spoke to anyone.

He would leave home in the morning, sometimes after breakfast and sometimes without it. He returned only in the evening.

'Please come on time for dinner,' his mother would say in a beseeching tone.

Bhole chacha would stare at him with bleak eyes.

Hamlet's memories of the play were also becoming hazy. He didn't understand where his life was headed. He had started to feel very lonely and afraid of himself.

J.C. MILLS SCHOOL

Thwack! Pawan Sharma's heavy hand landed on Pravesh Sahni's face.

Pravesh staggered back. Tears welled up in his eyes from the slap and the shame.

'You think you are some big shot from the convent, bey?' asked Pawan Sharma, stepping forward.

All of this was happening at the main gate of J.C. Mills School, Birlanagar, in front of a large crowd witnessing it.

Gwalior exists in three parts: Lashkar (where Hamlet lived), Gwalior (where J.C. Mills School was located) and Murar (where he rarely went).

His father worked in Birlanagar. About fifteen kilometres from Lashkar, located in the main Gwalior city centre. He cycled to the office and back every day. Only after joining J.C. Mills School did Hamlet gain a firsthand experience of his father's struggles.

The Central Board had introduced the 10+2 scheme that year, with Hamlet's batch. Now, college admission was possible only after the twelfth grade. But the higher secondary or eleventh grade still existed in the Madhya Pradesh State Board.

All the Central Board students had applied to state schools to save a year. A large group from the convent was among them. His father used his contacts to get him a seat at J.C. Mills School. His work in Birlanagar had come in handy.

Birlanagar was an industrial area ... and by that association, it was also a hub of hooliganism.

'He has got a reputation for being a ladies' man,' Chikna said.

The entire goonda gang was sitting right there. All of them were students of J.C. Mills. Ragging was in full swing.

'Hit me, bhaisahab. You're older!' said Pravesh, stroking his cheek with teary eyes.

'Of course, we'll hit you, you convent pimps. This is J.C. Mills. You'll have to live by different rules here!'

Pawan Sharma was the boss of J.C. Mills. He was also the captain of the cricket team. They were all studying in higher secondary at this time.

'And who else is here?' Pawan turned to check.

All this was happening at the main gate. People coming and going didn't even bother to notice—it was a common sight there.

'This is Anil Gupta. The topper from the convent,' Kuldeep Randhawa said.

'Just focus on your studies here, bey! I'll gouge your eyes out if I see them wandering.' Pawan turned towards him again.

'What's your name?'

'Santap ... Santap Trivedi!'

'You are the one who got expelled, no? For trying to charm the teacher?'

Hamlet said nothing.

'Wah, bey. You had your eyes set straight on the madam?' He laughed.

Everyone was laughing. The level of cruelty of the ragging was getting worse.

'Had fun, did you?'

Hamlet didn't say a word.

'He does a lot of theatre, too. He did a few performances there,' Vineet said.

'That's nice! Come, show us here.'

'What?'

'Drama.'

'Here?' Hamlet's eyes welled up. His voice trembled. He felt helpless.

'So? What else? Will you go to Bombay and only then perform?'

'But here ... there's ... I mean ... I need a script ... I mean ...' His voice seemed stuck in his throat.

'What script?'

'Abey! You need a script to stage a play, bey. And an audience, too.' Chikna laughed.

'Well, he'll have to show us one without a script. And as for an audience, isn't there enough already? So many fucking idiots around!'

Hamlet stood there dumbfounded. His eyes welled up.

'Come on!' Pawan sat down on a square stone slab lying nearby.

'How can I?' Hamlet's voice was choked with emotion.

Suddenly, Anil Gupta stepped forward to help him.
'He sings very well, too!'
'Oh, that's great! Then sing a song. But if you stop, I'll break your jaw.'
Hamlet felt a little relieved. He wiped his tears.
'Yeah?' And he started singing.

> 'Raat ke humsafar ... Thak ke ghar ko chale ...
> Jhoomti aa rahi ... Subah pyaar ki ...'

Everyone was holding their breath. A couple of passersby even stopped and turned to watch.
The song ended. Everyone was silent.
After a brief silence, Pawan's voice broke through.
'One more.'
He started again.

> 'So jaa nindiya ki bela hai ...
> Aaja panchhi akela hai.'

A few girls sitting on the lawn turned to look at him. A few bystanders on the road came closer. The goonda gang fell silent.
From the back, Kuldeep spoke up—
'One last one.'

> 'Laakhon hain nigaah mein ... zindagi ki raah mein ...
> Sanam haseen jawan ...
> Aankhon mein sharab hai ... honthon pe gulaab hai ...
> Lekin wo baat kahan ...'

By then, the girls sitting in the lawn had moved closer to the group around Hamlet and positioned themselves amongst the crowd. The goonda gang remained silent. The passersby who had been compelled to stop in their tracks continued to stand still.
After a moment, Pawan Sharma got up. He came close and touched his shoulder lightly.
'Abey, wah bey! You sing very well.'
And he gave him a light hug. The goonda gang was clapping. Even the girls from the lawn joined in.

'If you have any problem, just let me know.'
'Yes, sir!'
'Just call me Pawan.'
'Yes, Pawan bhai.'
'Don't add "bhai".'

By the evening, the entire J.C. Mills School had heard that an artist had arrived at their school.

Later, Anil Gupta hugged him tightly.

'You saved me, bey. Thank you, yaar.'

'Why is life so strange?' Hamlet asked his friend Marathe one day.

Marathe was sitting right in front of him.

The goonda gang would go around beating people up. Many times, Hamlet also went with them.

'You should stay away! You are an artist.'

They were very kind people. Tough on the outside, soft on the inside. This goonda gang stood by with him always ... till the day he left Gwalior ...

MY FRIEND MARATHE

O<small>NCE</small>, <small>WHEN</small> H<small>AMLET WAS WITH THE GOONDA GANG ON ONE OF THEIR</small> missions, he met Marathe.

Goonda gang member Pappu Talli had been beaten up by a boy. The goonda gang members had arrived at Roxy Talkies to avenge Pappu Talli by beating up the other boy. When they reached their destination, a lanky boy stepped forward to calmly and respectfully explain that Pappu Talli was to blame. He had cat-called the boy's sister, and the boy had then beaten up Pappu. His explanation was so compelling that Santap found himself listening in rapt attention. That day, the goonda gang retreated quietly.

On a few occasions, Hamlet casually met the lanky boy, whose name was Marathe, while he was passing by on his motorcycle. He smiled, exchanged a 'Hello,' with Hamlet and went on his way. He was always warm and kind.

One day, he appeared at Hamlet's house.

'Will you teach me to play the mouth organ? I have heard you play very well.'

'How did you know?'

'It is just a rumour floating in the air.' And he burst out laughing.

That same Marathe was now sitting right in front of him in his room.

It was raining outside.

'Why is life so strange?' Marathe just stared at him. This question had taken over his mind, bothering him for so long. 'We are born, we live, and we die! There must be some purpose to life?'

'What do you think?'

'There is someone above who creates a purpose. Our job is just to fulfil that purpose.'

'What is your purpose in life?'

'I haven't figured it out yet. What about you?'

'I'm confused, too.' Hamlet said.

'It doesn't suit you to be confused. You do so many things!'

'I don't enjoy any of them.'

'That's not a good sign. You should have figured it out by now. Look for answers in art. You'll find them.'

This friendship was meant to be long-lived ... for a lifetime!

It was a Sunday morning. Everyone was going about their daily routines at home. Hamlet had just entered the bathroom with his toothbrush when he heard his father saying something to him.

'We're going to J.C. Mills today. Birlanagar.'

He thought maybe he was talking to someone else. They spoke to each other rarely these days.

'Vikram has called. It's his birthday today.'

No. His father was indeed talking to him.

'Yes?'

'I said Vikram has called us. It's his birthday today.'

He didn't understand.

'But why am I going?'

'You have been specially invited. We have to go at five in the evening.'

He didn't understand what was happening. He kept brushing silently.

At five o'clock in the evening, they were both sitting in a tempo.

Vikram Rathore was a colleague of Prabhash's. Prabhash liked him very much. The thirty-five-year-old Vikram also held a great deal of respect for Prabhash. However, Hamlet continued to be unsure about why he was 'specially invited'.

They reached Birlanagar. Vikram's house was located in the staff quarters.
There must have been around ten guests at the party.
After a little snack, everyone sat in the drawing room.
'I'm just waiting for the evening to fall.'
Vikram smiled. Everyone laughed.
As evening descended, a tray of whisky arrived and was passed around for the guests.
After that, a harmonium was brought in, and along with it came a tabla player.
Then Vikram began. He was very fond of music. Hamlet had heard Prabhash praise Vikram before.
He sang one song. Then another. Then a third.
The third round of whisky was underway when Vikram moved the harmonium toward Santap.
'And now, I introduce a young singer to you. Please listen and share your thoughts.'
Hamlet felt bewildered. He kept shifting his gaze between the harmonium and Vikram.
Prabhash was surprised, too, and said, 'How do you know he sings?'
'It's just a rumour floating in the air.' And he laughed.
Hamlet remembered Marathe's words.
Hamlet picked up the harmonium and began to sing. This was his first time singing with a tabla.

'Hum aapki aankhon mein
Iss dil ko basa dein toh ...'

The song continued, then ended, followed by applause. Hamlet noticed that he had no trouble singing with the tabla.
'One more,' a request came.

'Aankhon hee aankhon mein ishara ho gaya
Baithe baithe jeene ka sahara ho gaya ...'

When he looked around the room, everyone was swaying to the music.
'What a talent, beta. Such a blessing at this young age!'
His father sat there, completely stunned.
'What a talent, Prabhash ji. What a gift you have given your child.'
Prabhash was speechless.

Later, while the party was in full swing, Hamlet was sitting quietly, sipping his juice. Prabhash kept looking here and there restlessly for a long time. Then he surreptitiously sneaked up to Hamlet, away from everyone's gaze.

'You sing very well.'

Hamlet said nothing.

'If you don't mind, may I have one too?'

'Ji what?'

Prabhash silently gestured toward the whisky bottle.

'Ji, why would I mind?'

'No, your mother won't appreciate it.'

Hamlet shrugged.

After Prabhash had two pegs, the food arrived.

By the time they were returning in the tempo at night, it was dark. Hamlet felt his father's head resting on his shoulder. He looked at him carefully. He was getting old.

His father uttered, 'Sorry, yaar. Sorry for everything.'

Hamlet looked ahead at the houses passing by. He remained silent.

A deeper darkness seemed to be taking over outside.

BHAGAVADAJJUKAM

In January that year, J.C. Mills School was going to celebrate its Annual Day. Preparations were in full swing everywhere; with an array of performances featuring plays, music and dance dramas. J.C. Mills placed special emphasis on cultural activities and, in fact, allocated separate grace marks to be added to the students' marksheets at the end of the academic session on the basis of their participation.

This time, Verma ji had chosen the play *Bhagavadajjukam*. Written over two thousand years ago by Ashvaghosha, this Sanskrit comedy was part of the classical Indian plays canon. B.M. Shah, from the National School of Drama, had come to direct the Hindi adaptation of the play.

Verma ji was an economics teacher at the school and also served as the general secretary of the renowned drama institution in Gwalior: Kala Mandir.

Kala Mandir was soon set to stage Premchand Kashyap's play *Dilli Teri Baat*

Nirali. B.M. Shah was indeed in town for this. Due to his personal relationship with Verma ji, he had also agreed to direct the J.C. Mills school's play. Rehearsals were scheduled to take place during the day.

All the casting had been completed. Only one role remained. Small, but important. That of Yama, the God of Death.

The only problem was that Yama had to appear on stage naked, wearing only an underwear, and painted black all over. No one was willing to take on that role. No one wanted to become a laughing stock in front of the entire school—especially the girls—by emerging on the stage naked and painted black. A huge audience was expected to turn up for the play. It was in that dire moment that Verma ji caught hold of Hamlet.

'Why don't you take up this part?'

'I have to study.'

'Everyone has to study. Besides, grace marks for this will also be added to your final marksheet.'

He remained silent.

'A true artist does not worry about performing naked if the role demands it. And we're here to support you in any case, you know.'

And so it was that the news spread throughout the school that Santap was doing this role. Laughter echoed everywhere, especially among the girls.

Rehearsals commenced.

B.M. Shah had a commanding presence. He would personally enact the role and demonstrate to everyone how to perform.

Pravesh Sahni and Sanjay Apte were playing the main roles.

Hamlet sat and watched. Pravesh, who used to bully students in the convent otherwise, looked quite small on that stage. There were many transitions in his role. Multiple costume changes. He had to change from a boy to a girl and then from a girl to a boy. Hamlet sat there wondering why Pravesh wasn't portraying the role better.

He also had an issue with Sanjay Apte's physique. With such a slender, almost frail build, would he able to perform well? He wouldn't even be noticeable on the stage. (At that time, he didn't understand anything about stage presence.)

Leave it. Focus on your role. He told himself.

Yama had to enter the stage with a loud roar, magically and accidentally switch the bodies of a girl and a boy with each other and then come back again later to correct his so-called mistake before exiting the stage finally.

Hamlet started imagining the scene in his mind. From the movies, he had a good idea of what heaven might look like. King Indra with his apsaras, angels and dancers. Billowing smoke and clouds. This much he could envision. The rest of it, however, was his imagination.

He began taking orders from Indra. He even had affairs with a few of the apsaras. Then, he also tried to observe the earth from above. Gradually, the idea of his naked body painted black also began to make sense to him. When he roared, his voice echoed. He also observed that Shah ji was giving him fewer instructions in time. He would simply sit and watch Hamlet's performance carefully.

On the day of the performance, the play started and a huge crowd had gathered. Everyone eagerly awaited Santap's entry: naked and painted black. A large group of girls seemed especially enthusiastic about the idea.

And then he entered. As expected, bursts of laughter immediately filled the room.

Hamlet was fully aware that he was on stage. Indeed, he had stopped noticing the audience. His eyes were either fixated on the actor in front of him or on the spotlights surrounding him. He couldn't see anything else on or around the stage. He was growling and roaring. He had forgotten that he was only in his underwear.

And slowly, the laughter ceased. Now, his entry on the stage left the audience awestruck. Hundreds of eyes were fixed on him and he could feel their piercing gazes over his whole body.

As soon as the play ended, a storm of thunderous applause erupted. His appearance at the curtain call received the loudest cheer. The crowd was ecstatic. He was bowing and greeting them, but the clapping continued unabated.

B.M. Shah, who was sitting in a dark corner of the side entry, said to Verma ji, 'What do you say, Verma ji?'

'I'll talk to him today. He will be the youngest member to join Kala Mandir.'

And after the play, every member of the goonda gang came to congratulate him.

'Did you smoke weed, bey? You were on fire!' Chikna said.

CONFUSION

HIS HIGH SCHOOL WAS OVER. HE HAD PASSED. (VERMA JI WAS RIGHT. HIS marksheet included grace marks for the play.)

Now the search for a good college began.

Hamlet had no desire of becoming a professional artist. So, the possibility of joining a performing arts college had ended even before it could begin.

He wanted to pursue an honours degree in Hindi and expressed his desire to join the Maharani Laxmi Bai College in Gwalior.

'What will you do with a degree in Hindi?' Prabhash asked.

'I like the language.'

'You have to become a doctor. Your career will be secure.'

'I don't like medical science.'

'You will start liking it. Everyone in our community is a doctor. Apply for admission to a science college.'

Prabhash walked away without saying anything else, or waiting for a response. Hamlet felt helpless.

There was no one at home that day. Bhole chacha and Satveer chacha were at their workplaces. (They both worked for Indian Roadways.) Jidda had gone to a relative's place with Reva. It was a quiet afternoon at home when his mother entered his room.

He was lying on the bed. He sat up straight.

His mother stood silently.

'Yes?' Santap broke the silence.

'Why can't you obey your father?'

'Because I don't want to become a doctor.'

She was silent. Then after a while, she said, 'He is getting old, Santap.'

'Everyone has to age.'

'He is getting weak.'

'Is that my fault?' he said in a harsh tone.

'He won't give up his stubbornness.'

'And I won't give up mine.'

She was silent. Then she said, 'Have you noticed that he doesn't talk much with anyone? He is always locked in his room?'

'Why?'

She paused for a moment. Then her voice trembled.

'He takes afeem, Santap!'

Santap was stunned.

'The burden of the family fell on his shoulders at a young age. When he could have become a doctor, he got into the trucking business instead. When he could no longer manage it, he took up a job. He doesn't have many years left. This O.P.M. is a devastating thing.'

The word O.P.M. sounded strange coming from his mother's mouth.

'Now it's all up to you. You can fulfil his wish. Why do you have to be so difficult? Give up your stubbornness. We will remain stuck like this always otherwise.'

She wiped her tears, turned around, and walked out slowly. The door closed behind her.

(Hamlet understood the meaning of addiction years later when he became a victim to it himself. However, at that time, immense hatred for his father took root within his being. He was infuriated. He wishes now that he had understood the complexity of the situation beyond his fury at the time.)

His first year at the Gwalior Science College was ongoing, as was his first year at Kala Mandir.

'I will keep doing theatre. It is my passion.'

'What do you gain from being on the stage?' Prabhash asked in a harsh tone.

'It's difficult to explain.'

'It shouldn't interfere with your studies.' Then the door opened and closed again.

He bagged a small part in *Dilli Teri Baat Nirali*, playing the role of Haklu. He had to enter from the left wing, get thrashed, and then fall from the right wing while being whipped by the city's police officer, before exiting the stage.

'An actor needs one line in his life to show that he is an actor!' Many years later, Dr Anuradha Kapoor said this to him at the National School of Drama.

'Will he be able to do it?' Premchand Kashyap, the playwright, had asked B.M. Shah.

Eventually, the play was staged.

'You're brilliant, yaar. It was just a two-minute role.' Ramakant Vishnoi came and shook his hands after the play.

'Thank you, sir. You are an incredible actor.'

'Will you come with me? I want to introduce you to someone.'

And the very next day, he was sitting in front of Prabhat Ganguly of the Jhansi Road-based Rangasri Little Ballet Troupe.

L.B.T. was a renowned institution in the country with a dedicated wing for drama. He had watched Vishnoi perform in *Kambalon ki Paratein* there. The L.B.T. campus was distinct, teeming with greenery. It offered accommodations for the artists. Two large halls served as venues for rehearsals; and the ground for endless discussions about art all day long. It was impossible to not be entranced by the magical atmosphere.

'Kala Mandir is a good institution. But there is too much politics.'

Prabhat Ganguly commented while sitting in his room. He was the principal choreographer there. And he had travelled the world. He was a renowned name in the national theatre circuits. He had also received the Sangeet Natak Akademi Award.

'Art should exist for art's sake,' he said, pronouncing his r's with a rough 'd' trailing behind them. 'If any other ulterior agendas are attached to it, it becomes tainted. This is a professional ballet troupe, and making money is essential to us. It supports our families. However, we pursue drama as a hobby and only classics are performed under the banner of L.B.T.'

Santap liked what he heard.

'I really enjoyed your performance in *Dilli Teri Baat Nirali*,' Ganguly said in his Bangla-mixed Hindi. 'That's why I asked Ramakant to introduce you. Come, let's go outside. It's evening now.'

Everyone stepped out of the room. To their right, in a rehearsal room, at least sixty types of musical instruments were on display. Hamlet's gaze was fixed on the sitar.

'Namaste, dada!' a voice called, and Hamlet turned. He continued to gaze at the person standing before him with wide eyes. It was a girl not more than twenty years old.

'Come, come. Santap, she is the proprietor of our troupe, Sangini Dwivedi,' he said with his arms outstretched.

Hamlet had forgotten how to blink. At that moment, only one thought crossed his mind: this girl's innocent beauty would leave anyone mesmerized for life.

Hamlet's life had changed. He had officially left Kala Mandir. Verma ji was very angry. But Shah ji was very happy.

'You won't find a better institution than L.B.T. Art lives here. You will get to learn a lot from Prabhat Ganguly. There is really a lot of politics at Kala Mandir. Never regret your decision.'

Now he would go to the Science College in the morning. And after crossing a sea of stars, he would reach L.B.T. (L.B.T. was right next to the Science College.) Then he would sit there and play the sitar. (It was his new hobby.) Then he would leave and go straight home to eat. Exactly at two o'clock in the afternoon, he would be found standing outside at the gate of Chirantan Dharma Mandir Kanya Vidyalaya. And then he would wait …

SANGINI

'SHE'S TWENTY-EIGHT, BUT SHE LOOKS TWENTY,' RAMAKANT VISHNOI said as he gathered some material for the havan at his home.

'Eight years ago, there was a car accident on the Muraina highway that claimed the lives of her father, brother and sister-in-law. At a young age, she began working at Chirantan Dharma Mandir Kanya Vidyalaya. She lives in Daulatganj with her mother and a six-year-old niece …'

'So simple? As clear as glass?'

Vishnoi laughed. 'She is completely transparent. Whatever is inside is outside. It is very difficult to resist her charm.' Indeed, Hamlet couldn't escape her charm.

'I love sweeping the rehearsal hall,' she said one day. 'And I'm dying to work backstage. Just don't send me on stage. I get terribly nervous there.'

Sangini giggled, putting down the broom. She loved to giggle.

'You've got very close to me in such a short time. I can sit with you for hours. You're a great listener and talking is my favourite hobby.' She sat on a stone outside and chuckled again.

She sat behind him on the carrier of Hamlet's bicycle—he was going to drop her home.

'When my father and brother were around, there was so much joy in the house. Then one day, everything suddenly became silent.' Her voice sounded hushed. 'That day, I decided to always keep my spirits high in this life. God forbid ... but you never know when someone might leave.' And then she started giggling again.

One day, Hamlet arrived at the gate of her school during the break. Then they went home together, where he met her mother and little Chandni, too.

'After finishing school and tuition, I go to L.B.T. in the evenings. I feel good there. I feel very light and refreshed. All the tiredness of the day fades away,' she said, picking up a cup of tea.

Hamlet was getting more and more immersed in her.

हाँ प्रिये तुम हो निकट नि:शब्द मेरे पास में
श्वास में हो तुम उपस्थित तुम अटल विश्वास में...

Yes, my love, you are near me, wordless, so close to me.
You live in my breath, you are present in my steadfast belief.

He stopped. Vishnoi sat on the stone in front of him and now asked him lovingly, 'And then?'

क्यों प्रणय का हो निवेदन
या निमंत्रण दृष्टि भेदन
क्यों रहे आवेग देह में
क्यों रहे ये देह नेह में
मूक बैठें दो ही प्राणी
ना हो स्मरण क्या है वाणी
प्रेम ही बस हो निरन्तर
काल ना बन पाए अन्तर

स्वर्ग ही तो है छिपा
इस अनकहे आभास में ...
हाँ प्रिये तुम हो नकिट नि:शब्द मेरे पास में ...

Why should I plead for love anew
Or invite you to pierce the view
Why should passion move this frame
Why should love speak your name
Two silent souls sit side by side
What use of words when hearts confide
Only love alone should stay
Which even death can't steal away
Only heaven lies hidden
In this rush, serene and unseen
Yes, my love,
You are near me, wordless, so close to me ...

Inside the building, rehearsals were in progress. The play was Jaywant Dalvi's *Arre Sharif Log*! This was Hamlet's first significant role.

His scene was yet to come. The two of them were sitting on a stone outside. The L.B.T. garden seemed to be swaying, its colours in full bloom.

'Very beautiful. Where did you get the inspiration from?' Vishnoi asked him mischievously.

'That is irrelevant. Tell me how you liked it?'

He paused. Then he said, 'Such heavy words at such a young age. What have you thought about your life? What do you intend to pursue after college?'

'All of that is still blurry.'

'Have you heard of the National School of Drama?'

And suddenly, director D.K. Jain peeped from the rehearsal room.

'Santap! Your scene is next. Be more attentive about your entry at least, yaar.'

'Oh, sorry,' he got up.

'I have caught you staring at me many times. Why do you do that?' Sangini asked, waving her scarf in the air.

Both of them were sitting on the rocks atop Mandre Hill. Sangini's family had gone to pay their obeisance at the temple nearby. Dusk had fallen. Cool winds swept the evening sky.

'Tell me,' Sangini nudged him. He was startled.

'I mean ... just like that.'

'You like me a lot, don't you?' she gave him a mischievous smile.

'Well ... yes, that's true.' He also laughed.

'He likes me too.'

'Who?'

'Vishwas.'

'Vishwas?' He still couldn't understand.

'Vishwas Upadhyay. My childhood friend, my lover.'

Hamlet felt a punch to his heart.

'The centre of my life. My everythingship.'

Hamlet was stumped.

'I don't know, but I want to share all this with you. Vishwas is my childhood friend. He is currently pursuing CA in Delhi. If this tragedy hadn't befallen my family, we would have been married by now.'

Hamlet felt the blows deep in his heart.

'He is willing to look after my mother and Chandni. Where do you find such people these days? To me, he is truly like a god.'

Hamlet was watching her. She was looking somewhere else.

Then she took a breath and turned towards him.

'I can talk to you about anything and everything, isn't it?'

Hamlet was silent.

'You are so nice. Very nice!' She placed her hand on his.

'Bua, we are back,' little Chandni chirped from behind them.

'Arre, my banno,' she hugged her tightly.

The next day, he couldn't concentrate during rehearsals.

'I am not able to do this part, sir.'

'Arre, what is so difficult in this?'

'Please enact this once for me.'

Sangini stood at the door, watching him intently.

When he was back outside, he met Vishnoi, who asked him, 'Do you remember? I had asked you about the National School of Drama.'

'Yes, I do. But I am not keen on it, ji. I'm going to die right here,' he said in a defeated voice.

Sangini was still staring at him.

Prabhat da was heard asking, 'Who will drop Sangini home?'

'I'll go with Santap.'

'I have got some stuff to do. Please go with someone else.'

'Come on.' She grabbed his arm.

They were cycling down Mahal Wali Road, with her riding pillion. Both remained quiet. After a while, she said, 'If I'm not mistaken, you're still upset about what happened yesterday, right?'

He kept pedalling but didn't say a word.

'Isn't it?'

After a while, he muttered, 'Why would I be upset?'

She remained silent for a moment before saying, 'Santap, after Vishwas, you're the closest male friend I have. If you act like this, I'll just stop talking to you.'

'Don't talk to me then. What difference does it make to me?'

'It really doesn't matter?' she asked, her voice choked.

'Nope.' There was utter silence as they made their way home, only the sound of pedalling could be heard.

And some time later, they were standing outside Sangini's house.

She got off, and stood there. Hamlet waited as well.

She placed her hand in Santap's.

'You're eight years younger than me, Santap!' she said, her voice echoing in the dark.

'Is that my fault?' Hamlet asked, his tone scathing.

'Will you meet me outside the school tomorrow? At two o'clock. Promise me.'

'I will never meet you again,' he said, as he rode away on his cycle.

And the next day, there he was, standing right outside Sangini's school. She saw him and smiled.

'Let's go get some coffee at Subhash Market today.'

PIYUSH MISHRA
BETTER BAD THAN INFAMOUS

Gwalior was indeed a small town, but it brimmed with more than enough people always gawking at you, hunting for gossip.

'Look, Santap. This is Gwalior, people are always talking behind your back. And well, in your case, they really are at it. You are the talk of the town. Even my mother asked me about it yesterday.' (Marathe's mother was a headmistress at a school and news like this one spread like wildfire in the teachers' community.)

They were at his house in Kampoo. The fan was spinning overhead. Pramad Dubey was sitting nearby.

Pramad was his new friend. Stout, simple-hearted and obstinate to the point of foolishness.

'Arre, we are not in a relationship, yaar.'

'Arre, then why don't you tell everyone about the kind of relationship you share?' Pramad's voice was serious.

'Arre, what do I tell? Whom do I tell?'

'Tell your family? Tell the world?'

'Arre, I'd tell if there was something to tell. But first and foremost, do *you* get it?'

'It's more important that they understand, not just us. They're the ones who raised you, you know. Is this how you're paying them back for bringing you up?'

'Be careful with your words.' He was furious.

'People are gossiping behind your back, Santap. Put it out before this turns into a full-blown fire,' Marathe said. 'We get it … but at this moment, others must understand it, too.'

'What is it that you want to do in life? And what's holding you back?'

It was nine o'clock at night. Katora Tal, near the medical college road, was tranquil at this hour. Its clear water mirrored the neon lights around the pond.

'I just don't want to study,' Hamlet said.

'Graduation is a necessary qualification for any job.'

'I won't be able to finish that either.'

Ramakant Vishnoi had taken over the role of his mentor. Twelve years older, Vishnoi exuded a calm and serious energy. He valued knowledge and practised meditation. He was Hamlet's closest confidant.

'Before that, you'll have to do something else.'
'What?' He looked up.
'The fire from rumours about your so-called relationship with Sangini has assumed serious proportions in Gwalior. Are you even aware of this?'
He was stunned. He hadn't realized that it would escalate so much.
'You go to her house to pick her up every morning. Then you drop her off every afternoon. The whole town sees you returning from L.B.T. with her riding behind you on your cycle in the evening.'
He was silent. Then he asked, 'Do you also find something wrong with this?'
'What I feel or don't feel does not matter here. We live in a civilized society, and it is our duty to uphold its values. We wouldn't want this situation to escalate into something terrible, would we? These matters don't take long to turn into wild storms.'
But the hour was too late and the matter had become a city-wide scandal. So it was that it had stormed its way into his home as well.
'Who is this girl? So much older than him, too. Shouldn't she at least understand?' Jidda had asked.
'If I get my hands on that wretched woman, I'll scratch her face off,' his mother had said, seething with anger.
'Do you think she'll come to you? Go to her school and confront her. Ask her why are you hell bent on ruining my son's life?'
Santap's mother, that naïve, rustic woman actually fell for Jidda's words. She reached Chirantan Dharma Mandir School to give this other woman a piece of her mind.
She was standing there in front of the school, shouting at the building. 'Bring out that wretched woman. Did she only find my son to ensnare in all of Gwalior?'
Sangini was huddled inside, sobbing inconsolably. Her colleague, Vrinda, somehow managed to calm Santap's mother's frayed temper.
'Look, this is a girls' school. Surely, you have a daughter yourself?' The matter seemed to be somewhat contained that day due to the low attendance in school, but that was not to be. The talk of Santap's mother's fury spread widely despite the low attendance.
Later, Hamlet's brief meeting with Sangini left him burning with fury. Marathe was with him on the motorcycle.
'Listen to me. Don't do anything stupid in anger and haste.'
'Drop me home and go back.'
Hamlet entered his house. Everyone was sitting in the living room.
He headed straight to his room, closed the door and took out a new blade.

The door to his room swung open. He stepped out, soaked in blood and holding a stained blade in his hand.

'Arre,' Marathe stepped forward.

'That's it,' he said, raising his hand. 'Today onwards, the father-son relationship is over. I'll address you as "sir" from now on.'

His father sat stunned in his chair.

'And you, you whore! You're the one who instigated my mother, right? She wouldn't have dared otherwise.'

Jidda had begun howling, concealing her face in her saree.

'Arre, she was trying to trap my son! Should I have stayed silent? I exposed her in front of the entire school.'

And *khachak*! The blade in his hand sliced his skin.

A fresh fountain of blood spurted from his arm.

'Bhaiya!' Reva, who was sitting nearby, screamed and tied a cloth tightly around her head—which would remain tied for many days. Her face gave away her discomfort and alarm. 'How could you make such a foolish mistake, amma?' she said, and then rushed into her room, crying. Marathe and Bhole chacha stood there, speechless. Silent.

NATIONAL SCHOOL OF DRAMA

'There's discipline in every bit of indiscipline. You just need the right perspective to see it that way,' Vishnoi said. 'What we don't understand, we label as a miracle. If you open your eyes and truly see, you'll recognize that it's simply the reality.'

It was the same Katora Tal, the same quiet night, the same clear water and the same neon lights reflecting on the water's surface.

They sat there, freezing in the February chill. The entire city of Gwalior was shivering in the biting cold.

He had started to consider Vishnoi as his mentor. Under Vishnoi's guidance, he had read all of Vivekananda's works. He read extensively about Karmayoga, Rajyoga, Bhakti and Vedanta. Now, he was aiming to finish the Bhagavad Gita. This was his first brush with lessons in spirituality.

Three months had passed since that blade incident.

'So, what have you decided?' Vishnoi asked.

'I have to leave Gwalior.'
'Got a plan?'
He was quiet for a moment and then ...
'Not really.'
'What's wrong with the National School of Drama? You do plays, right? And it'll get you out of here.'
'I don't want to take up theatre professionally.'
'You don't want to study; you can't take exams because your attendance is five per cent. What do you want to do in life? Keep cutting yourself with a blade?'

He was fuming.

Everything around them was quiet.

'Just give the interview a shot. If you don't want to go, then don't.'

'Why didn't you go? You're a great actor, too.'

'Arre, my path has changed course, yaar. I'm moving in a different direction.'

At times, he failed to understand Vishnoi.

'I've got an NSD form at home. I got it for myself. Would you like to fill it out?'

He was quiet, then said, 'Should I tell everyone at home?'

'You'll have to. It's not like you can go without asking them, right? Why are you so scared?'

'I'm not scared.'

'You're filled to the brim with fear, Santap. I've noticed it from the beginning. Maybe it has to do with the things that happened when you were a child, or perhaps it's linked to your past life. Did you follow through with what I had asked?'

Vishnoi had taught Hamlet a yogic breathing exercise.

'That's how I've found peace. That's why I'm so calm now. Try to take it a step further.'

'What?'

> **'YOU'RE FILLED TO THE BRIM WITH FEAR, SANTAP. I'VE NOTICED IT FROM THE BEGINNING.'**

'You need to clear your mind of all thoughts. You don't smoke and you've avoided booze so far. And I assume you're still single?' He laughed. 'And stubborn too. All these qualities are favourable for practising yoga. Do it. God will take care of you.'

That night, Hamlet sat in his room, in sukhasana. He tried to focus. Initially, his mind raced with thoughts. However, he gradually started to gain some control over them, at least partially at first.

One night, Santap was sitting in his room when he suddenly realized that his breathing was slowing down. Then he realized that he wasn't breathing at all. Everything around him had come to a halt. (Years later, he learned this was Vipassana.) He started to vaguely remember the experience in front of the convent library. A wave of light washed over him. Gradually, that light seemed to envelop his entire being.

All the thoughts racing in his head were washed away. There seemed to be no pain, no trouble, no worries. He felt a jolt of electric energy rush through him. Suddenly then, he smiled. He wasn't scared anymore. And then his eyes snapped open.

His room was dark. He found the fan's gentle whirring to be soothing.

He quietly opened the door and came out.

Prabhash was asleep in the living room.

He opened the door that led to the terrace through a flight of stairs and climbed up.

The imli tree looked beautiful that night. Its ghosts and spirits had vanished. Moonlight was scattered everywhere. The stone statue glowed in the dark corner.

He touched his forehead. He was sweating even in the cold, but it wasn't because he was feeling hot.

He stayed in that trance-like state for about half an hour.

The next day, he called a family meeting. Everyone gathered in the living room.

He calmly informed them that he would no longer study science. He was going to NSD, the National School of Drama. While speaking with them, he realized that he didn't fear anything at all now, nor did he lose his cool.

His father asked in a quiet tone, 'Where's that?'

'Delhi. It's a national institute. They teach theatre as a science. Nadeem Shah and Som Puri are famous alumni of NSD.' (They were critically acclaimed names in the world of cinema.)

'How do you get into the institute?'

'Two interviews are conducted—one preliminary, one main. Then a scholarship. The government pays for three years.'

'Qualifications?'

'I've got them already.' Back then, NSD required applicants to have passed their higher secondary exams.

'How many seats?'

'Twenty. Two from Madhya Pradesh.'

His father's face fell. 'And you think you'll make it?'

'What's the harm in trying?' Hamlet's voice was calm. He was surprised to hear his own quick response.

'Go for it,' Prabhash said. Not like he had an option.

He went to Vishnoi's place in Didwana Oli, filled out the form and mailed it.

He got called in for the interviews and went to Delhi.

He didn't need the state scholarship. He got the central one. He'd topped the interview.

For the first time, he saw that his father looked flabbergasted. Indeed, he was overjoyed. (Due to its distinguished alumni such as Nadeem Shah and Som Puri, the National School of Drama's reputation had elevated to even greater heights in those days.)

He was leaving by train the next day.

'You're going to a good place. Keep doing yoga and meditation. Everything will be fine,' Vishnoi said.

He'd already sought Prabhat da's blessings earlier.

Sangini said, 'Congratulations. Gwalior will also get a break from spreading rumours finally. But I'll miss you dearly.' Her voice choked. 'The road to school will feel empty without you,' she concluded with a lump in her throat.

The Taj Express whistled at the station.

Many people came to see him off, including the young theatre folks from Gwalior. (Getting into NSD was a big deal back then—it still is.)

His father was beaming. If only Santap could have understood his happiness.

'We'll meet you on the silver screen only now, right?' Pramad said.

To Pramad, NSD meant only cinema.

'This is awesome, yaar. You've found your calling,' Marathe said.

'You've made us so proud,' Pradeep bhai said.

Pravesh Sahni just smiled and waved at him.

The Taj Express let out its final whistle. Hamlet boarded the train.

Finally, the train started to move. Everyone was waving at him.

Hamlet was smiling, excited to finally do what he had always wanted to do. He didn't know if his life was about to get better or fall apart, but he knew it was about to change.

He didn't realize back then that he'd made a terrible mistake.

> **HE DIDN'T KNOW IF HIS LIFE WAS ABOUT TO GET BETTER OR FALL APART, BUT HE KNEW IT WAS ABOUT TO CHANGE. HE DIDN'T REALIZE BACK THEN THAT HE'D MADE A TERRIBLE MISTAKE.**

TUMHARI AUQAAT KYA HAI, PIYUSH MISHRA

DELHI STRIKES

NSD WAS IN A STATE OF FRENZY BACK THEN.

The golden age of Alkazi sahab was over. B.V. Karanth had taken his place. And only that year, when Hamlet joined NSD, B.M. Shah had taken Karanth ji's place. Coincidentally, Shah ji was also Hamlet's first director in his theatre life.

This was in the year 1983.

Back then, a Kingfisher beer bottle cost twelve rupees, a pack of Gold Flake King Size was for six rupees and a Nirodh condom was thirty-five paise. (Hamlet didn't need any of these things yet. But later, he'd need way too many of them.)

As far as the state of the nation was concerned, the country was on fire, but the flames had not yet reached the kitchen. People were, however, waiting for them to get there, with the same patience and skill that they had mastered since 1947.

Punjab was burning. Kashmir was blazing. The rest of India was not faring any better either.

This is when the Bharatiya Janata Party was still in its embryonic stage. Congress was running the show. The Communist Party (Marxism) was agitated, as usual.

A new student union had debuted at NSD, encouraging students to partake in other activities than the purely academic—such as boycotting classes and participating in uncalled-for strikes.

The interest in acting, however, arguably remained strong and many conversations in the campus often centred around it. But when the acting teachers arrived, everyone fought over who would get which part to play. Those who were assigned small roles formed their own group and boycotted rehearsals, leading to countless strikes.

Students were often seen sitting under the trees in the parking area. Even though they intended their conversations to focus on acting, the discussions rarely extended beyond their admiration for the theatre legends Nadeem Shah and Som Puri.

Classes started early, but students mostly skipped the 6 a.m. yoga class to catch some sleep in their hostels. Even if they dropped by, they would wait for shavasana because that's when they could *officially* sleep.

Then they would go to the mess for breakfast, which was located near the girls' hostel. The boys' hostel was a short walk from NSD, in Vakil Lane.

Perhaps this would be the right time to say that the boys' hostel was quite magnificent. It featured tiled bathrooms that made the students feel like they were rich celebrities already—tiled bathrooms being a luxury few could afford back then. Bahawalpur House was within walking distance from the hostel.

First-year students shared dorms. The hostel had two dormitories. From the second year onwards, two students got a room to themselves.

Right next to the school, in Bahawalpur House, the girls' hostel of the Kathak Kendra was situated. It housed the famous dancer Birju Maharaj's female students. In fact, Birju Maharaj often taught Kathak at the Kathak Kendra. NSD boys eagerly awaited the end of the girls' Kathak classes. That is when a series of playful glances, flirtatious teasing and affectionate side-eyes would be initiated, culminating at Alka Tea Stall, near Omi's Fruit Chaat Centre on Bhagwan Das Road. If one were lucky, sometimes the banter would extend as far as Nathu Sweets in Bengali Market as young lovers strolled along. One thing, at least, was certain. Every year, two to three couples from the two institutions ended up getting hitched.

These few changes at NSD notwithstanding, the teachers were still good. In the makeup room, Kulkarni sahab would sing praises of Alkazi sahab's era instead of teaching the students about makeup, leading students to curse their parents for not having conceived them sooner. If only they had been born earlier, they would have had the chance to experience Alkazi sahab's glorious era.

General body meetings were often held in the yoga room. They discussed everything from no water in the toilets to too much chilli in the food. Then, they talked about the acting teachers. After all that was done, students would go out into the school courtyard to stage their protests.

Hamlet was watching, listening and observing all this happening around him but he never said anything about it.

But another thing was quite certain: Delhi was incredibly beautiful. And the National School of Drama was even more so.

Situated in Delhi's Bahawalpur House, the National School of Drama brimmed with colours.

There was a reception area at the main gate. Miss Anita Thomas had recently taken charge. Inside, to the right, a corridor stretched all the way to the end. The director's room was on the right, while his personal assistant's was on the left. Posters of all the plays performed at NSD in the past lined both sides of the corridor. Further down was the academic block. The classrooms were accessible via stairs.

A few more steps led down to the beautiful open-air corridor that connected the entire campus straight to the mess. The girls' hostel was situated right across from the mess.

There were three studios in the school.

Studio number one served as the yoga hall, studio number two functioned as the circulation unit and studio number three upstairs was designated for conducting various physical exercises. Plays were performed in the circulation unit. (Despite being a national institute, NSD didn't have an auditorium of its own.)

The mess, too, was run by the students themselves.

Greenery and plants were everywhere. (Which often reminded Santap of his L.B.T. days.)

Outside the main gate was the parking lot where a neem tree stood in a corner. (This space would later become famous as the Ank Ek theatre group's as well as Santap Trivedi's open-air office.)

As far as Delhi was concerned, Hamlet felt as though he had suddenly arrived straight from the Sahara Desert to a vibrant, pleasant and enjoyable oasis, a lush patch full of life.

Mandi House served as Delhi's cultural hub. Seven different roads converged here, including Bhagwan Das Road, on which also perched NSD. Mandi House was flanked by Janpath on one side and Connaught Place on the other. India Gate stood at one of its ends while Pragati Maidan was located at the opposite end. Which meant that this neighbourhood offered plenty of adventures for those who sought them.

In Hamlet's early days in Delhi, the city was abuzz with activity—not only cultural, but also political. He visited Jantar Mantar within the first few days of his arrival in Delhi—to pay homage to his relationship with Comrade Baldev—as political protests and sit-ins were most commonplace here.

Later, Hamlet realized that the truly alluring thing about Delhi is that it turns over a new leaf with each season. In summer, the heat in Delhi is blistering, but its winter is as lovely as a second spring. As for autumn, that

> **AS FAR AS DELHI WAS CONCERNED, HAMLET FELT AS THOUGH HE HAD SUDDENLY ARRIVED STRAIGHT FROM THE SAHARA DESERT TO A VIBRANT, PLEASANT AND ENJOYABLE OASIS, A LUSH PATCH FULL OF LIFE.**

is a different matter altogether. Jamuns raining from the branches of tall trees, the drizzle of dry leaves collecting in golden pools by the roads, or the fountains across the city aglow with neon lights—Delhi's aura was intoxicating.

But even back then, autorickshaw fares were ridiculously high. Santap discovered that girls had to rely on a man to accompany them if they wanted to go out after eight o'clock at night.

So Delhi was what it was, and to borrow the famous words of Shakespeare, something was rotten in the state of ... the National School of Drama! NSD was in a state of decay. And then something happened that added fuel to Hamlet's burning frustration.

Another general body meeting was to be conducted that day. The campus had been buzzing all morning. The yoga room was packed to its full capacity. The

> **JAMUNS RAINING FROM THE BRANCHES OF TALL TREES, THE DRIZZLE OF DRY LEAVES COLLECTING IN GOLDEN POOLS BY THE ROADS, OR THE FOUNTAINS ACROSS THE CITY AGLOW WITH NEON LIGHTS—DELHI'S AURA WAS INTOXICATING.**

Nathu Sweets chap had messed up again.

Usually, when the classes ended around six o'clock in the evening, students followed their customary ritual of heading to Nathu Sweets in Bengali Market in groups of three or four.

Their favourite hobby was discussing Shakespeare to death over a cup of tea. Damned Shakespeare had left behind many hundreds of holes in his stories that kept young and opinionated theatre students talking about them for hours on end. The owners used to get annoyed by the students engrossed in these discussions, occupying all the space for themselves. In retaliation, they used to stop serving tea to them. (By the way, a cup of tea was only fifty paise at the time.) There were other places in the neighbourhood that served tea, but it was as if the students had tasted blood; Nathu Sweets became a haunt where they could spend long hours every day. More often than not, after much pleading, the owner, with a heavy heart, used to give in and serve the students tea again. But this one time, the Nathu Sweets staff was hell bent on imposing restrictions.

The meeting started that day. After much discussion, they decided to do everything peacefully and in an organized manner. About seventy students would enter Nathu Sweets in groups of two or three and take over all the tables. Then they'd order only fifty grams of bhujia on each table. And then they would start pecking one piece at a time to while away time. After all, surely there was a provision in the Indian Constitution that an owner cannot kick a customer out while they are seated at a table. Anyway, as the NSD students would acquire the tables, eventually the crowd at the shop would grow. And they would continue their sit-in until the owners started serving them tea.

'Operation Tea' commenced. Gradually, Nathu Sweets was overrun by students. Since it was a Sunday, more people than usual were out. Customers were puzzled about why so many people at each table had ordered only fifty grams of bhujia, eating it slowly but not really finishing it. In the meantime, cars had started to line up outside the shop.

Customers waiting their turn were getting restless. Some of the boys who were waiting were from Old Delhi. Their frowns deepened. One of them grabbed Janardan (a first-year student at NSD) by the collar and lifted him up.

'Abey, why aren't you finishing this bhujia? Why are you taking so long?'

And then all hell broke loose. Hundreds of hands and feet rained down on that boy. A storm erupted in the shop. That boy ran out with his friends. The drama school students were waiting for this moment. They followed the boys. Some others attacked the sweet shop. Crash, bang, smash. Dishes were broken, shards of broken glasses flew everywhere, tables were overturned ...

Hamlet was watching, listening, observing—but he did not say a word. He was witnessing total chaos and anarchy; chairs were flying across the shop, tables were lying broken on the floor and clashing plates and glasses made a ruckus. And suddenly, Hamlet felt as if he had started laughing. He heard a twisted guffaw from within himself and found himself slamming his hand into a glass cabinet.

He pulled it out, it was bloody. And then he hit the cabinet again. Then another time and continued hitting it repeatedly.

'Saala nothing's happening! Something should fucking happen! Hit, kill, fucking destroy everything!' His mouth boiled with hysterics. And *thump, thump, thump*, he continued hitting the cabinet.

It was eleven o'clock at night. The police had arrived at the Vakil Lane hostel. Hamlet sat quietly in the second dormitory, staring into the abyss of darkness. His hand was bandaged.

Shirish Dobhal peeked in. He was the union president.

'The police are outside. Come give a statement.'

'About what?'

'That it wasn't our fault. Their party started the fight.'

'I'm not coming.'

'You will need to respond to the union tomorrow. It's a question of student unity.'

'I will.'

Shirish stared at him, then the door closed behind him as he left.

Coincidentally, a photographer from *The Times of India* was at Nathu Sweets that day. The next day, a picture of Hamlet causing a ruckus was featured on page three of the daily.

Sangini sent a letter from Gwalior.

'I felt sad to see it. You were not sent there to do this.'

Hamlet clenched the letter in his fist. His eyes were burning.

Decisions occupy a place of great significance in life. They can either make you or break you.

He had decided he would never leave Gwalior. But then he had changed his decision.

He had decided he would be an actor. That's why he had come to Delhi. But when that decision got into his head and solidified, a darkness fell over his life.

Marathe was happy. He hadn't made any big decisions about his life yet, but he was still glowing.

Pramad was a straightforward, practical man. He had his life thoroughly planned out—studying for several years, getting married at a certain age, having kids by a certain age, and then retiring at a certain age. Everything in his life was organized.

Pradeep bhai's father had many businesses, so he didn't have to bother to do anything on his own.

Pravesh joined Maharani Laxmi Bai Arts and Commerce College. He was also thinking about getting into business.

All his other friends had either chosen medicine or joined the armed forces.

Among them, there was only Ramakant Vishnoi, whose decisions he still couldn't figure out.

'I've found my path. You'll understand when the time comes. Or maybe you won't ever understand it,' Vishnoi said, totally absorbed in his thoughts. And then continued, 'This world is no illusion. Everything matters. The path is right here. But what you perceive as the path may not be the true one. You, too, will one day arrive at the same destination that I'm heading to. It's just that we are taking different routes.'

'Don't you think all this is pointless?'

'All what?'

'You know, relationships, connections, work, profession, alcohol and girls?'

'Look, there are two types of people in this world: "iti-iti" and "neti-neti". "Neti-neti" individuals possess extraordinary will power. They can relinquish anything in an instant, whether it is fame, fortune, or relationships. In contrast, "iti-iti" people follow a different path. They are meant to immerse themselves in this world, savouring all its pleasures, and then only gradually

> 'THIS WORLD IS NO ILLUSION. EVERYTHING MATTERS. THE PATH IS RIGHT HERE. BUT WHAT YOU PERCEIVE AS THE PATH MAY NOT BE THE TRUE ONE.'

distancing themselves from it.'

'But what is the need to distance oneself?'

'How long can you enjoy it? You'll leave everything and die one day. Then what's the point of life?'

'That means that happiness lies somewhere else?'

'Happiness and sadness are two sides of the same coin. Bliss is something else. You'll recognize it when you find it. *Sat, Chit, Anand*—Truth, Consciousness and Bliss!'

Santap reminisced about his experience at the convent.

'Is that why you quit theatre? Because you were afraid of becoming too attached?'

He laughed. 'You'll figure it out in time. Just concentrate on your work for now.'

'In that case, what if we take the example of a girl like Sangini? Her whole life is about laughter.'

'Those who laugh the most, cry the most. You need detachment even for that. Laugh as a witness. Watch yourself laughing. Do everything as a witness. You'll find bliss.'

And before Hamlet could find that bliss, there was a strike at the National School of Drama. It was against the irregularities prevalent at the institute, the chaotic management and lack of acting faculty there.

> 'THOSE WHO LAUGH THE MOST, CRY THE MOST. YOU NEED DETACHMENT EVEN FOR THAT. LAUGH AS A WITNESS. WATCH YOURSELF LAUGHING. DO EVERYTHING AS A WITNESS. YOU'LL FIND BLISS.'

'I'm Vishwas. Vishwas Upadhyay.'

The strike was in full swing at NSD. Students took turns sitting under the neem tree in front of the parking area. Theatre songs echoed all day long. The drums thumped. Everyone sang passionately. Flags were made. Posters were put up. The student union office buzzed with activity.

Students took turns going on strike. Santap had just finished his turn when the receptionist, Miss Thomas, handed him a note.

'Someone came to see you. They'll be back in the afternoon.'

Santap looked at the note. He didn't know anyone named Vishwas.

Suddenly, Sangini's face flashed in his mind.

In the afternoon, Vishwas stood before him. Next to him was a dusky complexioned girl.

'I'm Vishwas Upadhyay. I'm Sangini's friend.'

Hamlet was sitting with Vishwas Upadhyay in Bengali Market.

'This is my colleague, Prabha Sanyal,' he introduced the sharp-eyed girl sitting beside him. Hamlet shook her hand too.

'What'll you have?' Bengali Market was bustling, as usual.

'Only tea.'

'Arre, come on, have something else. We're meeting for the first time.'

Hamlet didn't like this uncalled-for familiarity.

'Masala dosa.'

Vishwas placed the order.

'I wanted to meet you. Sangini has told me a lot about you.'

'You went to Gwalior?'

'I didn't get the chance, yaar. I've been quite caught up with work. But we talk on the phone. And well, long live the gift that is letter writing,' he laughed.

Hamlet was quiet. He couldn't really put a pin on it, but he felt that all these conversations were in vain. Prabha was constantly staring at him.

'Ji, do you want to say something specific to me?'

'Nothing specific. Just wanted to meet you. Generally, people take a liking to Sangini quite easily, but it's rare for *her* to like someone to this extent.'

Hamlet was quiet.

'I've known Sangini from the time that we we were just kids. I was in Gwalior when the accident happened. It was terrible. They were a lovely family.'

Hamlet was still quiet.

'I can't talk about Sangini with anyone here. No one knows her. So when I learned about you and that you knew Sangini, I came to meet you. At least now I can remember her by talking about her with someone.'

His dosa and tea arrived.

'Can I come see you again? I mean, if I miss her. I mean, if you don't mind?'

'I still don't get what you're saying.'

'I mean, if I want to talk about her or seek advice?'

'Why would you ask me for advice? You two share an intimate relationship. You shouldn't need anyone else's opinion.'

Hamlet didn't like Vishwas. It was jealousy, or maybe it was something else.

'Sometimes, even in intimate relationships one needs another's opinion. I'll come again.'

Prabha kept looking at Hamlet constantly.

The meeting was over. Hamlet couldn't make sense of it.

MEETING ROBERT DE NIRO

'What is this, yaar! You're just sitting in the dorm all day. Come, I'll take you to Pragati Maidan. They're doing a Robert De Niro retrospective there.' One day, Dinesh Khanna caught hold of him.

Life was passing by, and he didn't know why, but he felt disenchanted with Delhi. But then he had felt the same way about Gwalior as well …

'Let it be.' He shook his head.

He'd stopped stepping outside the dorm altogether.

Sure, his classmates were a riot. They had all come with a hell lot of theatre experience. It seemed that his batch had been exceptionally handpicked.

Dinesh Khanna hailed from Lucknow. He knew all the speeches from *Macbeth* and *Julius Caesar* by heart. He was a skinny guy with a wrinkled face, who went on to become a brilliant actor and also the executive director of the National School of Drama later in his life.

Vijay Deepak Chibber was from Haryana. Handsome Deepak got a French name from Santap upon his arrival at the National School of Drama. Vous des Chèvres.

Bapi Bose was from Calcutta. He used to describe himself as fierce and violent, but deep down, Bapi was a softie. (At that time, every Bengali called himself a Naxalite. A relative of Charu Majumdar.)

Vibha Sahota was from Delhi. Super funny and carefree. Later, as Vibha Chibber, she made a name for herself on television.

Alka Srivastava was from Darbhanga, Bihar. Her Russian name was also Santap's doing: Olohkya Seera Vastanoff.

Tall and broad-shouldered, Hargurjeet Singh hailed from Punjab. A fun-loving person, he was an incredibly realistic actor. Unfortunately, he never received the recognition he deserved until the very end.

Ajay Malkani was from Ranchi. Every morning, he'd announce his arrival with 'Jai Baba Vishwanath'.

There were others too. Matured, educated and experienced. Finally, giving into Dinesh Khanna's demands, he reached Shakuntalam Theatre with him for the De Niro retrospective.

Santap had learned about Robert De Niro only after arriving in Delhi. He recognized him and realized that he had seen him in *The Godfather II* at Yadav Talkies, unaware that this actor would have a significant impact on his life.

The ticket was for three rupees. (His scholarship was only three hundred and fifty rupees.)

They watched *New York, New York*. Santap found Robert De Niro just okay.

'He learned to play the saxophone for a year for this role,' Khanna said.

'Arre yaar! Famous people always seem to be doing such great things. Who knows if it's true? Tomorrow, when you become famous, people will say that Dinesh Khanna sold peanuts in the lanes of Lucknow for a year.'

'What do you think? He'll become famous by playing the role of a peanut seller?' said Sudarshan Juyal, laughing heartily.

Juyal was from Nainital and after Bapi Bose, he was the best mimic in the batch. He was damn good at it, especially when imitating Bapi.

The next day, they watched *Raging Bull*. Twenty minutes into the movie, he asked Ishaan Trivedi where Robert De Niro was.

Ishaan smiled. (He was also from Nainital, born in Moradabad.)

Dinesh smiled too, 'That's the answer to your question from yesterday.'

Santap was dumbfounded. Robert De Niro was right in front of him, on the screen, and he couldn't recognize him. The movie was based on the life of the famous boxer Jake LaMotta, and Robert De Niro played the lead role. The slender-looking Robert De Niro from *New York, New York* had transformed into the boxer from the 1940s with such perfection that Santap was dizzy with shock.

And then on the third day, his mind was completely blown.

'No yaar. Acting can't be done like this. This is impossible.'

He was watching *The King of Comedy*.

The world's best actor was playing the role of the world's trashiest actor. Directed by Martin Scorsese, the movie was about a struggling, pathetic actor desperate for work. Robert De Niro, especially when compared to Jerry Lewis on the screen, *appeared* to be the worst actor ever.

They went back to the hostel. Hamlet was quiet.

'What do you have to say?' Dinesh Khanna nudged him.

'What can I say, yaar? This is unbelievable.'

'He's got other movies too. *The Godfather II*, *Awakenings*. We'll watch those too.'

And the next day, they watched *The Godfather*.

'What's so special about him?' He meant what was special about Marlon Brando.

'You didn't like him?' Dinesh Khanna seemed surprised.

'He's an old guy, so he's simply old. What's surprising about that?'

'How old do you think Brando was when he played this role?'

'He must have been sixty at least.'

'Forty-four!'

Hamlet realized that he was living in his dreams. Indeed, he had accidentally stepped into the world's greatest profession.

A seed within him had begun to grow. He became increasingly quiet.

'I want to understand the word "acting" down to the micro level.'

Only his temperament worked in his favour. All the other conditions, however, were against him.

> **HAMLET REALIZED THAT HE WAS LIVING IN HIS DREAMS. INDEED, HE HAD ACCIDENTALLY STEPPED INTO THE WORLD'S GREATEST PROFESSION.**

THE FIRST PEG

THAT NIGHT, A PARTY WAS ORGANIZED FOR THE FIRST-YEAR STUDENTS IN the dormitory, to celebrate the allocation of dormitory spaces in the hostel. Santap was in dormitory number two.

'Cheers!'

Glasses clinked. 'Here's to our first year and first semester at the National School of Drama, and to Robert De Niro, whom we all have to pledge to be like!'

'No, yaar, I don't drink,' Santap refused, when someone offered him one.

'Arre, come on, just have a bit of beer, at least. This is not liquor,' Hargurjeet urged.

'Then why do you drink it?'

'It's just barley water. Gives you a little buzz. Only five per cent alcohol.'

Santap took it.

'The first peg is poison for an alcoholic. The rest of the bottle does the job,'

Raj bhai had been telling him this for years.

Hamlet had tasted that poison.

The party was raging. It was two o'clock in the morning.

'You haven't read Shakespeare? You haven't read Tennessee Williams? Why did you even come to drama school?' Dinesh Khanna said.

'To read all this stuff,' Santap slurred. He had two whiskies after the beer.

'I want to know everything about acting.'

'Abey, that everyone here wants to know. Or do you think the rest of us came here to get fucked?' Deepak laughed. He was wasted.

> 'THE FIRST PEG IS POISON FOR AN ALCOHOLIC. THE REST OF THE BOTTLE DOES THE JOB ...'

'I want it more than any of you. That Robert De Niro has messed with my head.'

'You haven't seen other actors. Robert Duvall, Marlon Brando, Anthony Quinn, Dustin Hoffman. You'll go crazy when you see Al Pacino!' Juyal exclaimed. He was a huge fan of Al Pacino.

'Yaar, how does one even act? There must be a modus operandi? Or a method, right?'

'First, study. Memorize your speeches. The more you read, the more your world will open up. Then imagine. Imagination includes everything, even what isn't in the script,' said Dinesh Khanna, who had established himself as the guru of the gang.

'O, Dineshlavski. You need visualization along with imagination,' Bapi said. 'Look at Shambhu da.'

(Dinesh's extensive knowledge had earned him the nickname Dineshlavski, after Konstantin Stanislavski.)

Like every Bengali, Bapi was also extremely proud of being a Bengali.

'O Bapi, you Bengalis are always stuck on Shambhu da. Acting and life go beyond him,' Juyal chirped.

'Oye, he's renowned for his acting prowess not only in Bengal but throughout India. Even the big shots worship him.'

'He's old now, yaar. This is the era of Nadeem Shah and Som Puri.'

And then suddenly, the room fell utterly silent. Those two names were heavyweights in the acting world.

'Yeah, man. I saw *Aakrosh*! I was blown away.'

'Believe in today. Yesterday is behind us. Acting has travelled many miles forward and reached new heights. If you remain stuck in the past, you'll be considered outdated,' Juyal said.

'Why isn't everything running smoothly at NSD?'

'People who believe that acting is debauchery are at the helm of affairs, that's why. There is no discipline. When Alkazi sahab was here, everyone took everything seriously,' Dinesh Khanna said, rather glumly.

'Was everything truly as good as they say it was during Alkazi sahab's time?' Santap was deep in thought.

'Look at his students. Nadeem and Som are from his time. They reflect his values so well.'

'What about the other teachers? Anuradha ma'am, Kirti ma'am, Robin Das, H.V. Sharma?'

'They're from his time, too. They were appointed by him,' Dinesh added.

'We just need to be cautious. These strikes are futile. They're simply a waste of time. They should demolish the union office and convert it into a public toilet. The union office is where all the toxicity originates.'

Santap took a deep breath.

'I wish things would return to how they used to be!'

'Oye!' Someone was knocking on the door. It was Alka's voice. 'Is everyone dressed?'

'Where'd she come from?' Deepak scrambled for his lungi.

'Come in!'

Alka entered. 'The strike has been called off. The management has agreed to almost everything. We'll have Alaknanda Samarth next semester.'

'What?'

'They've also made promises to the second and third years. Those students have no objections either.'

'Superb! Do you want some booze?' Juyal raised his glass.

'I need to hurry. I have to share the news in dormitory number one as well.' She turned to leave.

And so it was that Santap's first semester of the first year came to an end. Dry, desolate and sad.

PIYUSH MISHRA

EVENING, SNOW AND SILENCE

Winter had arrived. December had started.
Hamlet did not go home to Gwalior for the holidays.
The entire hostel was vacant. All of his friends had left for home; the dorms were deserted. Hamlet didn't understand why he found this desolation so appealing.
He would wake up early. Take a cold bath despite the December chill in Delhi—which sometimes made him think otherwise. Then, he would head to the Refugee Market for breakfast. (The mess was closed for the holidays.) After that, he'd stroll around the quiet NSD campus, sometimes sitting under the neem tree in the parking.
He had received two letters from Gwalior.
The first one was from Reva.

> Dear Bhaiya,
> I heard you're not coming home for the winter? Please come home. It's so quiet without you. There's silence everywhere. Maa and Pita ji look older. Jidda doesn't have anything to say anymore. Let the past go. You've found your path. Why hold on to anger? Forgive everyone, including yourself.
>   Your sister,
>   Reva

Santap took a deep breath.
He opened the second letter. It was from Sangini. Her cheerfulness was jumping off the page.

> I heard you met Vishwas? What did you think? I'm dying to know. I met your dad in a tempo yesterday. He wouldn't let me pay the fare. When I insisted, he scolded me, saying, 'I am much older, so you do not have to pay when you are with me—consider it your right, no questions asked. I'll pay.' He's a good man, Santap. He's not to be blamed. Forgive him. He's getting old and who else does he have but you? I once saw Reva on the street. We made eye contact and she smiled. She's a nice girl. She's growing up and maturing. Come back soon. The road to Chirantan Dharma Mandir feels empty without you. A new chaat shop has opened in Victoria Market. I'll go there with you first. And I swear, after Vishwas, you're the

second man in my life. I'm asking you again ... what do you think of Vishwas? Share new stories from your plays.

Waiting ...

Sangini

Santap stared at the letter for a while, then put it in his pocket.

Dinesh Khanna had invited him to Lucknow for the holidays. 'We will rehearse *Macbeth*,' he had said.

After thinking for a while, he packed his stuff. He had his scholarship money to spare, after all. And so it was that he found himself standing at the Interstate Bus Terminal.

The bus to Lucknow was ready to depart. He didn't move.

His feet turned towards the Himachal Roadways bus.

'Where's it going?'

'Chamba,' the conductor said.

'How long will it take?'

'Eighteen hours.' This time, the conductor looked at him closely.

'One ticket!' And he got on the bus.

And eighteen hours later, he arrived at the Chamba bus station. The cold was biting. He didn't understand why he was enjoying this torture.

'Doesn't it go further? Up there?'

'There's nothing up there. Just mountains and wilderness. What'll you do up there?' The conductor sounded surprised.

'What's the other way to go up?' His voice was steady.

'Private cars. But there'll be tons of snow up there. And a chill that will leave you numb.'

'That's what I want.'

He bought a ticket for a private car.

'Bamkot, Surai and Lagga are up there.'

'Lagga,' he said quietly.

The car stopped at Lagga. He got off. A profound silence enveloped the area. It was evening, yet it felt like night. Snow-covered peaks were visible in every direction.

He took shelter in a tent. He'd bought warm clothes at Chamba station.

It was quiet everywhere. Desolate. Empty.

He discovered that he truly enjoyed this emptiness. Even while shivering in the tent, he experienced an indescribable joy. It felt as if all of nature belonged to him. *Maybe I've been here before, in a past life,* he thought to himself.

THE SAME EXPERIENCE, AGAIN

When he returned, the second semester of his first year had begun.

Alaknanda Samarth's classes lived up to the meaning of her surname—she was indeed brilliant.

'Today, we'll take a walk. During this walk, you should change three different expressions. It's simply an exercise in feeling from within. Let's see how much you can transform yourself without makeup or a script.'

'Cover your hands and body with a sheet and lie back on a chair. Now express yourself using only your feet. Create three different expressions. Acting involves the entire body.'

'Grab a rope. Two people pull it from opposite sides. Now place the rope down. Now there's no rope. Just visualize it. Pull the imagined rope. The rope's weight and length, and the force in your body should match that of the real rope. This is called an action-reaction exercise.'

The classes were awesome. Santap was having a blast. But they ended in only fifteen days. Alaknanda Samarth used to observe Santap closely during those classes.

After one of her final classes, she said something to Santap.

'You're brimming with talent, Santap. Don't get lost in the wrong direction. People like you often suffer from an "extreme syndrome". And never give up acting. That's where you'll find respite. Good luck.'

Then came Shri Ram Gopal Bajaj. He often handled the school's responsibilities in Shah sahab's absence. (Shah ji was often away on sick leaves. Actually he was scared of union strikes and protests.)

Bajaj sahab had a remarkable teacher hidden within him. Santap's batch performed Mohan Rakesh's short play *Bahut Bada Sawaal* under his tutelage.

'Don't get too close to the other actor. You risk losing your aura and they lose theirs, without even realizing it.'

'The voice must resonate enough to reach the audience in the last row. Never speak softly on stage. Use a low pitch and high volume!'

'Act with control. Not with the flow.'

Amidst all this, Hamlet had started enjoying his time in Delhi—and the city itself. The fear within him had almost vanished. *There are still two and a half years remaining at NSD*, he told himself repeatedly. *Surely there's more to learn*

> 'YOU'RE BRIMMING WITH TALENT, SANTAP. DON'T GET LOST IN THE WRONG DIRECTION. PEOPLE LIKE YOU OFTEN SUFFER FROM AN "EXTREME SYNDROME". AND NEVER GIVE UP ACTING. THAT'S WHERE YOU'LL FIND RESPITE. GOOD LUCK.'

from here.

At the end of Bhagwan Das Road stood the Working Women's Hostel, then the Supreme Court and then Mathura Road.

Santap's favourite thing to do during those days was to walk all the way to Mathura Road. He would be sitting in a gathering of people, and suddenly get up and go for a stroll. All sorts of thoughts would come to his mind. He would repeatedly shake his head, trying to enter his own world. His world. Just him. Yes, Robert De Niro was hanging out with him a lot these days. Occasionally, Vishnoi's seriousness and Sangini's laughter would lift his spirits.

Where was life heading? This question had entered his mind a long time ago. Now it was starting to spread its roots wider. *What's the meaning of life? Live, live, and live! And then die one day? Then why were humans even born? Maybe to work and work a lot. Then, am I working? What's my work or calling? Acting, or to put it another way, creating, so am I creating? What's the point of NSD?*

Many such unanswered questions swirled in his mind. He'd certainly get answers, right? Someday! And then one day ...

That day, he was walking from the Supreme Court to the Working Women's Hostel. He had just crossed Tilak Road when suddenly his feet froze. He tried to move his hand, but it wouldn't budge. Despite that, he didn't *feel* strange. There was no pain. He couldn't imagine a more natural state than this one. His body was still. His breath was steady, or rather, it was oddly balanced. Sweat dripped from his forehead.

Everything around him paused. No pain, no sorrow, no noise. It was completely quiet. He could hear the buses and cars passing on Tilak Road. Everyone appeared happy. He stood in one place, perfectly balanced.

'Excuse me?'

Someone was touching him. He was startled.

'Are you alright?' It was a girl, maybe from the Fine Arts College.

'I ... I ... Oh!' And slowly he came to his senses.

Two girls stood near him. They had a surprised look on their faces.

'You've been standing like this for two minutes. Are you okay?'

'Yes ... I ... Uh ... nothing. I'm fine. Thanks.'

The two girls gave him an amused look and walked away.

He stood there for a moment. Then he suddenly caught a bus and went towards Curzon Road. There was an STD booth in Eastern Court.

'I had that experience again today. The one from the convent.' He was on the phone.

'What do you feel?' Vishnoi's calm voice echoed.

Santap explained everything in detail.

'Hmm!' Then there was silence on the phone for a while. And then ...

'Keep moving. There are many more milestones to cross still.'

'But what is it? It's happened to me twice now.'

'I don't understand it either. But if it brings you peace, it's not wrong. Some experiences aren't immediately understood.'

That night, Santap slept soundly. No trouble, no stress. He could visualize everything with his eyes closed. The burnt-out tube light, the chatter of students sitting outside, and the occasional sound of cars passing on Vakil Lane. Yet, there was no anger within him. Everything felt peaceful. Everything was quiet.

THE FIRST SONG

The following day, the school was buzzing with activity. B.M. Shah ji had resigned.

'I'll pursue theatre in peace now. I can't manage the school anymore!'

Simple at heart, Shah ji may not have excelled as an administrator, but he had a distinct fan base among the students. Everyone was shocked and concerned. Who would be called in as the next director? That was the big question.

'Before the end of my term, I will ensure one final play is performed here.'

He selected *Mashriq ki Hoor*, a renowned Parsi play by Radheshyam Kathavachak. Shah ji was a master of Parsi theatre.

Santap felt both surprised and frustrated. He still had two years left at NSD. In the aftermath of Shah ji's resignation, it seemed as though no one was prepared to assume the role of director. Everyone's future hung in the balance.

'I've had enough now, yaar. I don't want these responsibilities anymore. I still have a job at St. Columbus. Only active theatre is my life now. Mohan Upreti will be the music director for this play.'

Mohan Upreti was the head of the music department at NSD and an expert in Garhwali folk music.

Rehearsals for the play started. Santap bagged a major negative role. (Shah ji, having left all the stress behind, was incredibly happy and enjoying himself.) The play was progressing well.

And then suddenly everything exploded. Fifteen days into rehearsals, Mohan ji sent a message saying he wouldn't be able to direct the music. He had to rush to Nainital for some work.

'Arre, how can this be? What about my play? A Parsi play without music? Who will step in to provide the music on such a short notice?' Shah ji's face revealed the storm raging inside him.

A meeting was held in the circulation unit, studio number two.

'Look, I'm sorry. I wanted to do one last play with the freshers. But now this mishap has happened. What's the point of Parsi theatre without music? I'm dropping the production.'

A hand went up in the crowd of students. It was Hamlet's.

'Sir, may I do it?'

Shah ji was shocked.
'What?'
'The music,' Santap said.
'It's a Parsi play. Fourteen songs. You're only twenty-one. It will require a hell lot of work.'
'Sir, I'll try.'
There was no choice. Shah ji didn't want to leave NSD with a failed production behind him. He quietly uttered, 'Do it!'
And the next day, a song was ready.

... ई रक्शे महे खूबाँ
ई शीश बो पैमाना
ई इशरते बेपायां
ई रौनक़े मयखाना ...

... A dance of graceful beauties in the moonlight
A crystal cup holding the warmth of wine
A joy unbound; pure delight
The glow of the tavern, so fine ...

Hamlet was playing it on the harmonium. The entire class was seated there. Shah ji was listening.
'You have composed this yourself?'
'Yes, sir.'
'Hmm. Create another one.'
And the next day, Hamlet brought another song.

हैं हम कमाल हैं हम जमाल
दोनों दिलावर बड़े बहादुर
लासानी और बेमिसाल...

We are the wonders, we are the charms
Brave at heart, with fearless calm
Bold, unrivalled and beyond compare ...

Shah ji looked at him and said, 'Let's choreograph this.'
And within seven days, the music for *Mashriq Ki Hoor* was ready.
And Hamlet realized he could do this too.

The play happened, and it was a hit. A roaring success.

'This boy is amazing. He'll go far.'

The way his classmates addressed him had changed. Older students such as Sudarshan Juyal and Bapi Bose started calling him Santap bhai. And Hamlet felt satisfied that he had at least accomplished something this semester.

GWALIOR ONCE AGAIN

He was returning to Gwalior after a whole year.

His first year at the National School of Drama was over. The one accomplishment he had to show was the music he had produced for *Mashriq ki Hoor*, which, arguably, was a calling he had no intention of pursuing further.

Robert De Niro was stuck in his head. And a bunch of other actors whose movies he'd watched in his spare time. His mind was numb. What would happen next year? And the year after that? And after that? He shuddered at the thought.

When the autorickshaw turned from Jayendraganj into the right lane, he knew that he had reached Jinsi Nala.

The autorickshaw stopped. He paid the fare. His house was right there.

He rang the doorbell. Bhole chacha opened the door, his face brightening up as he saw him.

'Arre!'

Santap touched his feet. His father's chair was empty. Then Santap remembered, he was obviously at work.

Bhole chacha turned.

'Bhabhi … look who is here!'

His mother walked out from the kitchen, drying her hands with her sari.

'Arre! Didn't you miss home? You have come back after so many days!'

He touched her feet as well. He realized that the house was filled with the same familiar silence, which remained unbroken even with his arrival.

He didn't bother touching Jidda's feet or talking to her. He went straight to his room. His mother came in.

'Your father has been sleeping in the drawing room lately. We have made his bed there now. He said, "The boy has grown up now. He needs his own room."'

She placed the tea on the table.

Santap sipped his tea in silence.

There was a lull at home. He wanted someone to talk to or that someone would at least initiate some conversation, but then he couldn't think of anything to say. He just lay down on his bed quietly.

He had spent twenty years of his life in this house, enduring countless adversities along the way, including the beatings from his father. The sting of his blows and the stinging pain from those memories ... those memories still lingered in his mind.

After resting for a while, he went to Marathe's house. He had opened an office in a separate room under his house in Kampoo. He had started a business of distributing fax machines, which, by chance, was doing well. Which is to say Marathe was settled in his own life.

A while later, Pramad came too.

'So ... what's up, bey?'

'It's fine, yaar. Good school. I'm getting by.'

'You say that with no enthusiasm, almost as if you are dead. Your face also looks sad. Are you coming from a graveyard?' Pramad asked.

'What more can I say? It's stuff related to the school. You wouldn't understand!'

'Of course, we're just fucking idiots, right? We don't know anything at all.' Pramad said saltily. He always thought of himself as Mr Know-It-All.

'And listen, by the way, always remember, you didn't leave Gwalior to perform *nautanki*. We want to see you in movies.'

Hamlet looked straight ahead, then said, 'Hmm.'

'Hmm what?'

'No, nothing. I have to rejoin in two months. What do I do for two months? That's the question.'

'Stay home. Talk to your folks at home. What else?' Pramad said.

'Yeah,' he sighed. 'What's up with you?' he asked Marathe.

'It's going great, yaar. This business took off. I didn't expect it.'

'That means you are settled too.'

'Yes, kind of. But tell me, why are your spirits so withered?'

'Don't know, yaar. Did I make a mistake by going to the National School of Drama?'

'Why? It's a good place, just your kind of place. What good were you up to here

> 'TELL ME, WHY ARE YOUR SPIRITS SO WITHERED?' 'DON'T KNOW, YAAR. DID I MAKE A MISTAKE GOING TO THE NATIONAL SCHOOL OF DRAMA?'

anyway?' Marathe joked.

'True. Is your bank doing well?' he asked Pramad.

'It's going great. Just take care of yourself.'

A few minutes later, Pramad left. Then Santap, too, got up to leave.

When he got home, his father was back.

Santap bowed and touched Prabhash's feet and then went straight to his own room.

He locked the door from the inside. (Reva had gone on a college trip.)

When he came out for dinner, he saw his father sitting in the living room. He sat sunk in his beloved chair.

'Ah, come ... sit down ... what's up?'

Santap sat down reluctantly.

'How many years are left still?'

'You know that already, right?'

'Yeah, yeah! I was just asking. What do you plan to do after completing your course?'

'I will do theatre.'

'Okay, okay, but do you have any plans to pick up a job ... I mean, are there any other job prospects?'

'We don't have jobs.'

'Then what happens? How will you make a living?'

'Look, it's not like I asked you before filling out the form, did I, sir?' His voice was bitter. 'I'll do theatre; that is my work. What else will I do?'

'That's what I'm asking. What kind of work?'

'It's hard to explain.' He got up.

'Arre yaar, tell me. I'm your father.'

'I told you already.' And he got up, ready to leave.

'What does that mean, yaar? What do I tell people when they ask me?'

'Tell them I have taken to vagrancy.' And he walked out of the door.

The joy that his father's face had radiated when he had been accepted to NSD had vanished after this conversation. Prabhash was concerned about what Santap would do in the future.

Santap, on the other hand, felt his father had become a bit too eccentric with age.

The next morning, he was out of his home at six o'clock. Everyone knew where he was heading, but no one dared to stop him. Perhaps they knew that Santap had strayed too far from them by now.

Sangini saw him from afar in Patankar Bazaar and grinned. She pretended to threaten him with her clenched fist.

He, too, was was feeling a bit lighter by then. When he saw her fist, he laughed.

'How rude! I've written fifteen letters. You've only replied to two. Why?' she asked, stepping closer. 'And what was that photo in the newspaper all about? Did you go there to fight?'

'Arre baba. So many questions in one go? We need to rush to school,' he said, laughing.

'Let the school go to hell. Answer my questions first. I'm dying of anxiety here, and the little prince is having the time of his life there. Have you found a girl?'

'Arre baba, first you tell me. Which route are we taking today?'

'We'll go through Lohia Bazaar. But after school, all of your time is mine.'

And the duo turned towards Lohia Bazaar.

Sangini was a wave. Sangini was spring. Sangini was light. She greeted everyone she met on her way with laughter. She couldn't live without laughter. She bombarded him with questions on the way as well. He could only answer a few. The others he dodged. Her questions only stopped when they had reached her school.

'I'll meet you outside the school. Meet me at the gate, okay? We have to inaugurate that shop in Victoria Market. Then we'll go home,' she said quickly and then went inside.

Santap wandered around till two o'clock in the afternoon. From this street to that street. He even took a tempo in between to while away time. He took a round of Birlanagar and Murar, too. Needlessly.

Sharp at two, he stood right before the Chirantan Dharma Mandir School.

First, the crowd of students came out. Then Sangini with some other teachers.

'Bye!' She waved at the teachers and walked towards Santap.

'Now, tell me, where are we headed?'

'You told me that we would go to Victoria Market.'

'Let's go. We'll hitch a ride on a tempo from Ghoda Chowk. Or we could take an auto. Today is a special day.'

Later, they were sitting at Navyug Chaat Bhandar in Victoria Market. Sangini had ordered two samosa chaats and two cold drinks.

'Now tell me, how are you?'

'I'm fine. It's been a nice feeling. At least I'm not in Gwalior.'

'Why do you feel that way about Gwalior? You were born and brought up here.'

'Sure, I was brought up here. But you know well enough what that was like.' His voice turned dark.

'Forget all those things. Everything's new now. It's a new life. Everything will change now. Won't it?'

He was quiet. 'I'm stuck somewhere. I can't express myself.'

'What happened? Aren't you liking it there?'

'It's not that. I ...' He nearly blurted out Robert De Niro's name.

What would I say? How would I explain? Would I be able to explain anything? And would anyone understand?

'How do I explain? Here, I was a regional actor. Regional values. Regional standards. Everything's changed there. The level there is national. The values are bigger. The desires are growing, and the drive to fulfil them is stronger. But how? This is what I don't understand at all.'

'Are you scared? Is there a lot of competition?'

'There is. And I have to make my mark there.'

'It's okay. You'll figure it out. It's only been a year. Leave it to time. God will make everything right.'

Their chaats had arrived by then. They started eating.

Then Sangini looked up while eating. He was looking at her. She smiled softly. He smiled too.

'What?'

'What?'

'Why did you smile?'

'Why did *you* smile?'

'You tell me.'

'You want to ask me something.'

'Good. That means you understand me well.'

'He's fine. I mean, okay. He'll work, I guess.' And then he laughed out loud.

'I'll throw this plate of chaat at you! Now tell me more about him.'

'Arre, he had come to meet me with this feisty-looking girl. "My name is Vishwas. Vishwas Upadhyay." That's his name. Now what's the big deal about that name? Did he expect me to soak it in honey and suck it up like a lollipop?'

'How rude! But tell me what did you *think* of him?'

'What do *you* want to hear?'

'Good things,' she smiled, sipping her cold drink.

'He's alright. But he was saying some weird stuff. He asked me, "Can I meet you again?"'

'Yeah, so what's wrong with that?'

'What will he gain by meeting me? He should try to meet the person he wants to meet.'

'That's what he's trying to do. We're getting married next year. Then you'll see. I'll come to Delhi ... and make your life a living hell there.'

Santap became a little serious. He didn't know why, but he didn't like this update one bit.

'Have you two discussed more about your next steps?' he asked.

'Our relationship has evolved beyond mere conversation, Santap. Now, we don't just talk. We feel one another. Even in silence, much is communicated and understood,' she said seriously. 'He's my only support. And then you're the other one.' Her laughter returned. 'Make Gwalior and us famous soon, okay? And look, if you find a nice girl, try to win her over. Then introduce her to me. Tell her she needs my approval before your family's. And then ... that's it.'

And she burst out laughing. Santap just kept looking at her.

How can I betray her innocent cheerfulness by telling her that I didn't like Vishwas? He took a deep breath.

'Let's move. Let's go home now and meet my mother. Chandni's been asking about you.' She stood up.

They went to Sangini's house. He met everyone there. Sangini showed him Vishwas's letters. They were lengthy ones, as if he had written about entire months in each of them.

Later, he made his way back home alone.

NATYA SHASTRA

Vishnoi had become much calmer. He was alone in his house in Didwana Oli. The whole family was out.

'Don't you ever get angry?'

'Yeah, I do. That's my only vice, I think.'

'I've never seen it.'

'How often do you visit me? You don't know all of me yet. Tell me more, what's going on there?'

'Routine classes. Nothing special to take pride in as yet, except *Mashriq ki Hoor*. I'll tell you about that.'

'Hmm. Have you read the *Natya Shastra*?'

'Saw it in the library. Will read it now.'

'It will provide you with the true definition of theatre. You will learn about characters. Obviously, an actor must know how to perform a play, but also the reasons behind doing it, which this treatise will help you understand.'

'Why do we do it?'

'*Natya Shastra* has been called the fifth Veda. To imbibe different characters and then throw them out, to become clean again, that's acting too. You know what a *"patra"* is?'

'What?'

'*Patra* means a vessel. In theatre, a patra refers to a character. When you fill a vessel with poison, it becomes a vessel of poison. If you fill it with alcohol, it transforms into a vessel of alcohol, and with milk, it becomes a milk vessel. However, if you empty it, it becomes just an empty vessel. Neutral. Lacking any *character*. Clean, pure and detached. Yoga also describes a similar state. Where a yogi can reach through meditation, you can reach through acting. Acting needs a reason, not merely a method. An actor is sinless, spotless and detached, much like a yogi. Embrace this path.'

'How?'

'Continue your efforts. Work is essential to life. Once an action is taken, it does not vanish without yielding results.'

On his way back home, Hamlet thought deeply about Vishnoi's words.

> 'WHERE A YOGI CAN REACH THROUGH MEDITATION, YOU CAN REACH THROUGH ACTING. ACTING NEEDS A REASON, NOT MERELY A METHOD. AN ACTOR IS SINLESS, SPOTLESS AND DETACHED, MUCH LIKE A YOGI. EMBRACE THIS PATH.'

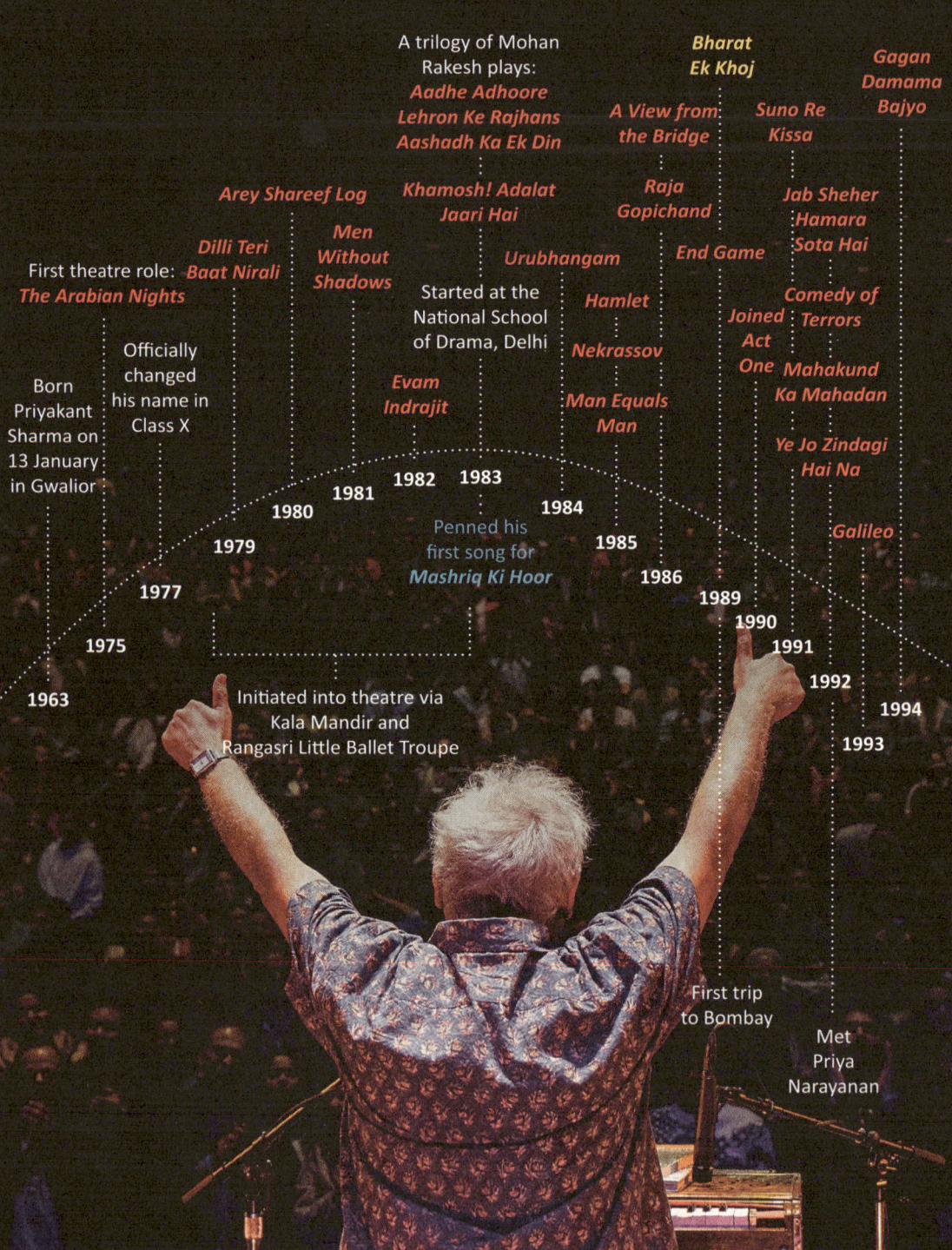

Legend
🎵 Music 🎭 Theatre 🎬 Film and TV

Timeline

Theatre works:
- *Einstein*
- *Accidental Death of an Anarchist*
- *An Evening with Piyush Mishra*
- *Hamlet Kabhi Bombay Nahi Gaya*
- *The Shaukeens*

Music:
- *Jheeni Jheeni Mehki Mehki Seeli Seeli*
- *Matrubhoomi*
- *The Playback Singer*
- *Salt City*

Film and TV:
- *Maqbool*
- *Tere Bin Laden*
- *Palki*
- *Dil Se* (Bollywood debut)
- *Gulaal*
- *Happy Bhaag Jayegi*
- *The White Elephant*
- *Revolver Rani*
- *Pink*
- *Matsya Kaand*
- *1971*
- *Kanjoos Makhichoos*
- *Jhoom Barabar Jhoom*
- *Gangs of Wasseypur*
- *Azaad*
- *The Legend of Bhagat Singh*
- *Tamasha*
- *JL50*
- *Illegal*
- *Rockstar*

Years and events:

- **1995** — Married Priya on 1 June
- **1996** — Death of his father and Fritz Bennewitz on the same day
- **1998** — Joined Asmita Theatre Group
- **1999** — Birth of Josh
- **2002** — Moved to Bombay with his family
- **2003** — Met Rahul Gandhi—who later managed his career
- **2005** — Collaborated with Indian Ocean for *Black Friday*
- **2007** — Birth of Jai
- **2009** — Suffered from a life-threatening brain stroke
- **2010**
- **2011**
- **2012** — Met Nishant—founded Ballimaaraan with him
- **2013**
- **2014**
- **2015**
- **2016** — Ballimaaraan's first performance
- **2020**
- **2021**
- **2022**
- **2023**
- **2024** — First USA Tour
- **2025**

KABIRA KHADA BAZAAR MEIN

The next day, he picked up a play, *Kabira Khada Bazaar Mein*. It was written by Bhisham Sahni. Reading it felt like the ideal way to spend those summer holidays.

His advertisement had been straightforward: 'Senior artists, please refrain from applying. I don't have the skill to direct you.' As for the seasoned actors ... they weren't even bothered.

'He has barely been to NSD for a year and now he wants to direct a production?' (There was a lot of party politics in Gwalior's local theatre landscape back then.)

L.B.T. had moved to Bhopal a year ago. The actors who had stayed started a new group called Kala Samuh, which was to stage the play under its banner.

It was to be a musical. Hamlet's spirits were soaring in anticipation. *I'll even do the music*! And thankfully, there was Ranu da from Kala Samuh to guide him. (Many moons ago, Santap used to learn the sitar from him.)

The idea had excited all the young folks and they had gathered to contribute to the performance. He had particularly liked Santosh Gupta and Arvind Bhadauria a lot. (They'd all end up being quite tight later on.)

Sangini would complete her schoolwork, go home and then head straight to the rehearsals. She took charge of everything backstage.

The whole Santap–Sangini affair had become stale news by then. Everyone in Gwalior had forgotten about that episode. Memories can be deceptive like that, they can ditch and fade away into oblivion in no time.

He called up Ishaan Trivedi, who came all the way from Moradabad to help him. During those days, Santap also realized that he was more suited to be a teacher than a director. Rehearsals for the play were on in full swing.

One day, he had been sitting on a rock with Sangini during a break. The old L.B.T. campus had now come under the aegis of the Kala Samuh. Shri Madhavarao Scindia had become its patron.

'I made a decision today.'

'Getting hitched?' Sangini had smirked while sipping tea.

MEMORIES CAN BE DECEPTIVE LIKE THAT, THEY CAN DITCH AND FADE AWAY INTO OBLIVION IN NO TIME.

'From now on, I'll call you Sangini. Calling someone by their name makes the bond strong.'

'What do you call me now?' she had asked him, still smiling.

'Nothing much. Or maybe Sangini ji, but it doesn't go well.'

'Vishwas won't like that. Only he is allowed to call me by my name, Sangini.' Her voice had been ripe with mischief.

'To hell with Vishwas. Don't even mention that fellow's name around me.'

'So stubborn, tch,' she had giggled. 'Fine, so be it from now on.'

The play was coming together finely. Music had been composed. Rehearsals were being done religiously. Then suddenly, Sangini had simply stopped showing up for the rehearsals.

Four days had passed and there was no sign of her. No one knew where she was. Santap had sent a messenger to her home, asking after her.

'I'll be there today.' The messenger had returned with her response.

Indeed, she had showed up that day. She had done all the work diligently but looked exhausted.

'What's the matter? Are you alright?' Santap had asked her and then touched her forehead gently.

'Not really. Just tired. I'll be fine,' she had said and walked off.

Santap had found her response and behaviour quite unusual.

From that day onwards, Sangini's behaviour had changed somewhat. Otherwise so bubbly, she appeared to have lost her spark in those days. She had grown uncharacteristically quiet and distant.

'What's up with you?'

'I'm fine. Just do your rehearsal.'

Finally, the day of the performance had arrived.

On the day, the grand rehearsal was on. Santap was occupied with overseeing it. Suddenly, Santosh came running to him.

'Sangini didi fell down!'

Everyone rushed behind Santosh to the spot. Sangini was sitting on a chair in the green room, and Arvind was fanning her. A boy stood next to her with a glass of water.

'What happened?' Santap thundered inside.

'You all are worrying unnecessarily. I just felt dizzy due to weakness. That's all.'

Santap remained quiet. Then said, 'You guys go. I'll be there soon.'

All of them left the green room. Only Santap and Sangini stayed.

'What's going on, Sangini?' He sat next to her.

'Look, you need to promise me. Do the show, and I'll tell you everything then.' Her eyes welled up.

'So, something is up?'

'Promise me,' she said, grabbing his hand. He looked at her and got up to leave.

The show was a hit. The play got rave reviews in the media. Particularly its music was critically acclaimed by everyone.

The next day, Santap was at Sangini's place.

'What's wrong?'

She was silent.

'Tell me, please.' He kept his hand on hers.

Tears started streaming from her eyes.

'Arre!' Santap clasped her hands in his.

'What's going on?'

'It's been a month and Vishwas hasn't written a single letter to me.'

'What the hell! Much ado about nothing! Is that it? I will go right away and grab him by the collar.'

'It's not a laughing matter, Santap. He used to write to me every week without fail. Now, whenever I call, I find out that he's on tour.'

'So he must be on a tour. He's got some work duties, right?'

'He could have called at least once, right?' She went quiet.

'Give me his number. I'll call him right now.' He regretted not taking down Vishwas's address and phone number when they had met in Delhi.

Sangini gave him his number.

'Now, wipe those tears and get back to your old form. We've got a cast party at the Kala Samuh tonight. Everyone's waiting.'

When he got home, a letter from the National School of Drama was waiting for him.

'You are hereby informed that the new school session will commence one month later this year, on 3 September.'

When he called people in Delhi to enquire about the notice, he was informed that a new director had finally been appointed at NSD, Mohan Maharishi. The commencement date of the new session had been pushed back by his order.

He hung up. Took a deep breath. He had also been told that the new director was from Chandigarh.

Vishwas didn't call or write for another month. All of Santap's attempts to reach him failed.

Sangini had completely shut down.

A month later, Santap reached Delhi.

NSD had undergone a makeover. Everything had been cleaned thoroughly. The surroundings looked spotless and shiny. All the teachers and staff were reporting to work on time. The common refrain was that the good old days of Alkazi sahab were back. Mohan Maharishi was a student of the legendary Ebraham Alkazi.

But Santap was lost elsewhere. Classes were starting the next day. Sangini had given him Vishwas's address. He hailed an autorickshaw outside the hostel and headed straight to D-40, New Friends Colony.

He pressed the doorbell. Vishwas opened the door.

'You didn't even call Sangini? Do you realize how worried she is!'

He was filled with rage. His voice was shaking with anger.

'Arre, come in, Santap. Look Prabha, who's here.'

Prabha Sanyal was sitting inside.

Santap stormed in. 'What was so important that you forgot to write to her? At least you could have called her once in all this time!' He couldn't hold his temper any longer.

'Arre baba, hold on a second,' Vishwas said, laughing lightly as he raised his hands in mock surrender. Santap wasn't pleased. He didn't like this behaviour one bit.

'Arre, I was on tour in the Northeast for two months. I just got back today. There were no phone lines there. I don't know why the letters didn't reach her, though. Prabha already gave me an earful. Here, I'll call her right now, in front of you.'

He picked up the receiver and dialled Sangini's number—the phone offered STD service.

'Hello?'

There was no answer from the other side.

'Hello, Sangini? It's me.'

Even without hearing anything, Santap could tell that she had begun to weep on the other end.

'Arre, hold on. Please listen to me. I was on tour for two months, which is why I couldn't call. I wrote to you, but you never replied.'

She probably didn't say anything in response.

'Alright, spit out your anger now, please. From now on, I'll write to you every week. I promise. Please smile. Please. Here, talk to Santap. He came all the way from Mandi House to New Friends Colony for you.'

He handed the receiver to Santap.

'Hello, Santap here.'

There was a sob on the phone.

'It's been sorted now. He'll call you every day. Now stop crying. Here, talk to him!' He gave the receiver back to Vishwas.

'I'll call you tomorrow. STD time is up; I need to hang up now.' And he hung up.

'Sit down, yaar. I wanted to talk to you anyway,' Vishwas said.

'I don't have time, Vishwas sahab. My work here is done. I must take your leave.' He joined his palms together in a namaste.

'Arre, please take a seat and at least have a cup of tea.'

'I have to go, sir. By the way, you've been blessed with a goddess. Keep her safe and secure in your house.' And for some reason, he started tearing up. Prabha was constantly watching him.

He turned and walked out of the flat. In the autorickshaw, he wondered why he had cried while talking about Sangini.

FRITZ BENNEWITZ

Mohan Maharishi had taken over as director, causing a sensation throughout the school. Everyone was on their toes. Firstly, Maharishi had such a robust figure, tall and imposing, that nobody dared to even speak in his presence. Secondly, his work ethics were so effective that everyone in the school began pulling their weight upon his takeover.

A new rule was issued for the students. 'You must have at least two books checked out from the library each week.'

'If you skip the morning yoga class, you'll lose your scholarship.' Everyone began rushing to attend the yoga class.

'If I see anyone with red eyes in class, I will straightaway push them out.' Students began finishing their drinks by nine o'clock in the night and hitting the sack early.

'If your clothes are unwashed and untidy, don't bother coming to class. I'll conduct the inspections myself.' In the dorms, the washerman became extremely important.

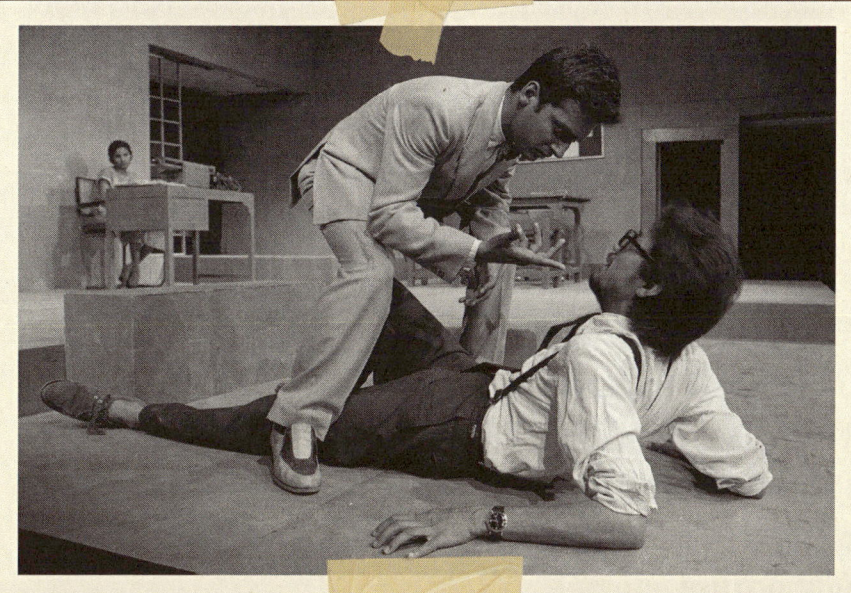

Another sensational notice was issued. This year, third-year and second-year students were assigned Fritz Bennewitz. And he was going to pick which play they would perform that year.

And Fritz Bennewitz arrived with a bang. He came straight from the G.D.R. That's what East Germany was called back then. The German Democratic Republic.

Fritz Bennewitz lived up to his reputation for being merciless.

Every time he walked into a room, the entire acting crowd would turn white. He was an expert in Shakespeare, Goethe and Brecht and he had directed plays in almost every Indian language, including Urdu, Kannada, Hindi, Chhattisgarhi and Bundelkhandi. Remarkably, even though he didn't understand a word of Hindi, he understood the universal language of theatre so well that one couldn't bluff in front of him.

He had been a Nazi soldier in Hitler's army during World War II and had participated enthusiastically in the invasion of Paris. After the war was over, he got hooked to theatre and joined Bertolt Brecht, the famous German playwright and director, and his wife Helene Weigel. In those days, when he had arrived at NSD, he was the associate director at the Berliner Ensemble, their national repertoire company, and was totally smitten with Asian actors. He was crazy about Habib Tanvir's Chhattisgarhi actors and believed that Pandwani was the best performing art form in the world. Seventy-year-old Fritz Bennewitz had the energy of a twenty-year-old. He strode around the campus and the ground seemed to shake beneath him. Despite losing an eye in a car accident, he could still spot a poor performance from a mile away. No actor could make any mistake and get away with it.

'Asian actors are the real deal, especially the ones in India. The variety of folk art forms found here is second to none.'

In the aftermath of losing an eye, when an interviewer had asked him if he felt sad about losing an eye, he said something that became quotable.

'No. I feel happy to save my one eye.'

The way he ran his rehearsals was incredibly intense. He used to commit to memory every single word of the

plays he was directing.

He didn't particularly enjoy performing plays in English. At NSD, he decided to take up Brecht's *Life and Times of Galileo* with the third-year students and Shakespeare's *Hamlet* with the second-year students.

The very air in NSD was tense with anticipation. Students were eagerly waiting for him to arrive.

And finally, Fritz arrived.

The first meeting happened in the academic classroom on the upper level. Mohan Maharishi was there too.

He stared at each actor one by one. That was his casting process. To examine the faces and then cast them as per the characters of the play.

And by the next day, the casting was already done. (Without any readings, mind you. Though, he did consider the opinions of other teachers.)

In studio number three, he pointed his fingers at the selected cast and informed them about their respective roles. 'You,'—Dinesh Khanna was in the line of his finger—'Polonius.' 'You,' he pointed at Alka Srivastava—'Gertrude.' 'You,'—he pointed at Vibha—'Ophelia.' 'You,'—he pointed at Malkani—'Gravedigger.' 'You,'—he told Chibber—'Claudius.' 'And you,'—he turned his finger towards Santap—'Hamlet'.

Some people were thrilled, others were disappointed. (In NSD, casting was a matter as serious as life and death.)

'Rehearsals from tomorrow. Read the play properly,' he said before walking out.

The next day, rehearsals started. On the very first day, Santap realized what he was in for.

Santap had walked into the most brutal torture chamber of his life.

'Hamlet is not a koota. You speak like a dog,' Fritz said in his German-English mixed with Hindi.

From day one, Fritz focused intensely on Hamlet's body language, speech, gestures, posture and voice; grilling him so hard that Santap felt as if he were in a Nazi concentration camp.

'Why do you speak like a machine gun? No sense of posture at all. Who told you you're an actor? Join some bank service job.'

And Santap almost lost his mind.

He wandered all day through the NSD campus, aimlessly. Everything seemed out of his control. He felt completely helpless. His thoughts, home, friends, Vishnoi and Sangini—everything felt so distant.

At night, he would cry his eyes out, holed up in his room. (He had his own room by the second year.) Then, he would wake up in a daze. He'd wander around again, through the empty hallways and corridors and then go to studio number three where he was to be ripped apart again and again. He'd stand at Alka's tea stall for hours, holding a cup of tea and staring at the passers-by with a lost gaze.

And then, in the midst of all this, another mishap happened that completely shattered Santap.

Third-year student Kiran Kulkarni had bagged the lead role in *Galileo*. Overwhelmed by his inability to do justice to the role, however, he attempted to electrocute himself. (Getting a lead in a classic play at NSD and being unable to pull it off was the equivalent of hellish torture.)

Santap felt shaken to his core. It was September 1984, two months after the rehearsals for *Hamlet* had begun.

Vishnoi called from Gwalior—'Meditate. Maybe it'll help.'

Sangini said, 'Just you wait, *Hamlet*

> **HE WANDERED ALL DAY THROUGH THE NSD CAMPUS, AIMLESSLY. EVERYTHING SEEMED OUT OF HIS CONTROL. HE FELT COMPLETELY HELPLESS.**

will be amazing.'

On 25 December 1984, Santap sensed that something bad was about to happen. He felt fine physically, but something was certainly amiss.

That day, rehearsal was expected to start a bit later than usual.

Fritz Bennewitz had to go to the German embassy for some official work.

Santap finished his meal early that day. Then he headed back to the dorm to rest. He lay there, staring at the walls of room number sixteen, when he felt something was happening.

He was numb. He was quiet. Suddenly, a bright light appeared before his eyes. He shook his head but didn't feel any pain or discomfort. There was absolute silence in the room. He shook his head again to snap out of it, but the silence only deepened. It dawned on him that he was experiencing this strange phenomenon for the third time. (Not knowing it would be the last time.)

He held his breath. And after a bit, he was completely calm.

Later on, the rehearsal was ongoing. Devendra Raj Ankur served as the local coordinator for the play. Fritz had still not showed up.

Santap delivered his speech:

'Rehna hai yaa nahi rehna hai, yahi sawaal hai ...'

And then he kept going. Everything around him had disappeared. The walls

of the rehearsal room melted away. (They were rehearsing in studio number two, where the final performance would take place.) Santap was in a state of mania. Words flew out of his mouth. No, his whole body was talking. He was under the character's spell. He completed his speech.

The studio was utterly silent. All his classmates stood still.

Suddenly, someone began clapping, shattering the silence.

Everyone turned around to see Fritz Bennewitz in the doorway, applauding. He walked over and gently cupped Santap's face in his hands.

'This is like a Christmas gift to me. Thank you for tolerating me for so long.'

Santap was speechless.

And on 1 January 1985, *Hamlet* premiered.

The buzz in Delhi reached all the way to Mumbai. Ketan Mehta, Saeed Akhtar Mirza and Basu Bhattacharya came to Delhi to watch it. *Hamlet* was a tremendous hit. Due to its immense success, they added nine more shows. Manohar Singh (the legendary stage actor) and Kavita Nagpal (Delhi's famous theatre critic) had their mouths gaping in awe during the performance. And there was someone else in the audience as well ... Ranjit Kapoor.

Ankur ji asked Santap, 'What did you do? Ranjit was crying the whole time while watching the play.'

Santap kept staring at him in silence, completely dazed. Ranjit Kapoor was a big-time director in India.

For some reason, Santap called his father in Gwalior. His father also came to watch the show.

After the show, he held Santap's hand for a long time, managing to only say this much in his trembling voice, 'Fantastic, yaar. Just fantastic.'

Santap introduced him to

> 'REHNA HAI YAA NAHI REHNA HAI, YAHI SAWAAL HAI ...' AND THEN HE KEPT GOING. EVERYTHING AROUND HIM HAD DISAPPEARED. THE WALLS OF THE REHEARSAL ROOM MELTED AWAY. SANTAP WAS IN A STATE OF MANIA ... WORDS FLEW OUT OF HIS MOUTH. NO, HIS WHOLE BODY WAS TALKING. HE WAS UNDER THE CHARACTER'S SPELL.

Mohan Maharishi. He was struggling to speak clearly. 'Sir, this is my father, Prabhash Sharma.'

Mohan ji shook Prabhash's hand and said, 'I'm not exaggerating, Prabhash ji. He'll reach the sky if he keeps his feet on the ground.'

Santap felt a chill course through his body.

Later that night, his father was sleeping in room sixteen of the boys' hostel on Vakil Lane. Santap was sitting nearby. The room was wrapped in a deathly silence. The ceiling fan was making a mechanical noise. The room was quiet, Vakil Lane was quiet, Delhi was quiet. Suddenly, Santap felt a jolt of fear. He was terrified. This success had come so suddenly, out of nowhere.

'Would you like to have coffee with me?'

'Would you like to have sex with me?' Harjot asked in turn, unbuttoning her kurti.

His life had flipped upside down. Everywhere he went, hundreds of eyes followed him. The girls at the Kathak Kendra wore a lovey-dovey look in their eyes. Teachers flocked to him. The air buzzed with cries of 'Hamlet, Hamlet' and 'A star is born!' Sudhir Kulkarni, the makeup teacher, was heard commenting in his quintessential style—'Johnny, Santap is done for! To portray a classical character with such finesse, and at just twenty-two ... It means for the rest of his life, Santap will walk like Hamlet, talk like Hamlet, poop like Hamlet and even pee like Hamlet! Look at Manohar bhai. He still goes around behaving like Tughlaq.' (This wasn't entirely true. After seeing *Sandhya Chhaya*, Hamlet's opinion of Manohar Singh had changed completely.)

Hamlet became quieter than ever before—more morose, even. He had access to Fritz. And while Fritz was there, he felt like he could act—really *act*. But when Fritz was gone? Could he still pull it off? He didn't *enact* Hamlet; Fritz *made* him perform it. But at least one thing was clear—he realized he had done nothing wrong in pursuing a Robert De Niro dream.

He'd spend hours at Nathu's Sweets with his classmates. They would often talk about acting and theatre. After *Hamlet*, everyone took his opinions seriously. He'd have long debates with Dinesh Khanna. Dinesh and Chibber were his contemporaries and competitors in acting.

One day, around seven o'clock in the evening, Dinesh Khanna and Hamlet were sitting on a bench beneath the tree in the parking lot. Students occasionally walked by towards the school.

'You know what? I get scared sometimes,' Hamlet said honestly.

'What are you scared of? Your career is established. People will pounce at the chance to work with you. You'll easily secure a seat at the Repertory.' (The Repertory is NSD's professional company, which hires the truly extraordinary graduates of the institution on an annual salary, and also helps them find work in the industry. Selection for the Repertory continues to be a significant achievement to be proud of.)

'No, it's not about that. I've had this fear since I was a child. I'm just telling you. I don't really know what it is that I fear. I'm even scared of success. I don't know if I can handle this fame. And Fritz is gone now, too. Can I even act without him?'

'Fritz won't be handholding you forever, right? And there's a world beyond Fritz. Did you come to this school just because of him? You've got your own life. Believe in yourself. Everything will be fine.'

The next production was to be directed by Ranjit Kapoor. It was titled *Nekrassov*. Jean-Paul Sartre's only farce. A comedy.

THE FIRST TIME

HARJOT KAUR STORMED INTO HIS LIFE LIKE A HURRICANE AND LEFT JUST as quickly.

'You did *Hamlet*, right?'

She peered over his book. Hamlet was in the library.

'Yeah,' he replied, looking up.

'Come outside. I need to talk to you.'

And then they both were outside.

'I won't beat around the bush. My name is Harjot Kaur. People call me a Sexy Sardarni, too. And I am! I'm currently going through a divorce. My husband is a jerk. He doesn't understand me at all. I live in Greater Kailash. I have everything at home. From a swimming pool to a squash court, everything.'

Hamlet was a bit lost. He was finding it hard to process this barrage of information all at once.

'I don't really get it,' he said.

'You don't need to try too hard to understand. I'm smitten with you. Is that a bad thing?' she said bluntly.

He slowly got the drift. He smiled.

'Would you like to have coffee with me?'

'Would you like to have sex with me?' Harjot asked in turn, unbuttoning her kurti.

'Arre, hold on!' Hamlet stopped her hand. She seemed so wildly passionate, he feared that she might strip right there. Later that night, he went with her to her place in Greater Kailash. It was a well-furnished house.

'My husband lives in Dubai. He visits every three months. He's too busy making money and spending it on his debauchery. Men are such dogs, right?'

'You're quite straightforward,' he said, walking toward the window. The sun was setting, casting a warm glow on the swimming pool.

'I'm a lot of other things too.' Harjot said, standing behind him.

He turned around. She had already taken off her clothes. She stood there, her body taut, wearing nothing but her undergarments.

'I'm amazing in two places, especially. Firstly, in the kitchen, and secondly, the bedroom.'

And that night, she rocked Hamlet's world. It was his first time.

RANJIT KAPOOR

Ranjit Kapoor had arrived. Preparations for Nekrassov were in full swing. He wrote a letter to Vishnoi. 'This is the second big step in my acting career. It's completely different from—and really the opposite of—Hamlet: a classic comedy, a farce. Ranjit sahab has magic in his pen. He's translated the script wonderfully. Let's see what happens.' He had also received a letter from Sangini.

'What did you say to Vishwas? He writes a letter every week. He even calls quite often. Best wishes for your next play.'

He had received a letter from Reva as well.

> Congratulations on Hamlet's success, bhaiya. Pita ji returned in such a frenzy of pride, 'My son's

'LOOK, BOB DE NIRO. I'M FOLLOWING IN YOUR FOOTSTEPS. AM I ON THE RIGHT PATH? IF I WERE TO BECOME AN ACTOR, I WOULD WANT TO BE LIKE YOU. OTHERWISE, IT'S NOT WORTH IT.'

always surrounded by girls.' He was beaming with joy as he told all about his time in Delhi. This time, I'll also come to watch your play with pita ji. I'm waiting for you.

Yours,
Reva

Hamlet set everything aside and devoted himself to rehearsals.

The action in the play was so hectic that there was no time to even catch a breath. Every entrance and exit had to be like a burst of fire. The timing had to be spot-on. Hamlet started running every morning to enhance his breathwork. To his credit, he already had good stamina. Alcohol and cigarettes had not entered his life as yet, after all. There was just one problem: Ranjit Kapoor was extremely laid-back about rehearsals and the script.

'Sir, we need the next scene. We're repeating the same ones every day.'

'It will come. I'll share by tomorrow. Arre, Malkani, go get me ten paans from outside. Tell him they are for Kapoor sahab.'

When Malkani went to the paan vendor, he said, 'Tell Kapoor sahab he owes me four thousand bucks. I'm not giving him any more paans until he pays up.'

The next day, Ranjit sahab went to speak with the paan vendor. No one knew what he said, but the vendor started giving him paan again, despite his previous dues remaining unpaid. Ranjit sahab truly had the gift of the gab.

During rehearsals, Ranjit sahab would sit and solve crossword puzzles.

'Sir, this scene is not working. I can't find the motivation.'

'Arre, you're studying at the National School of Drama, yaar, in your second year. And you want motivation from me?' he responded, smoking a cigarette.

'Sir, the costumes haven't arrived yet.'

'Arre, I'm writing the next scene. Don't bother me right now. Deal with it yourself,' he'd say, and return to his writing.

The day of the premiere arrived and the last sixteen pages of the script were still missing.

'Abey, we'll start the play, but where will we end it? There's no climax,' Chibber said.

The hall was packed on the opening night. Ranjit Kapoor was in the yoga hall, writing the final scenes.

Janardan was the production manager. He was tasked with taking the scenes from the yoga hall, one page at a time and pasting them on the board. The actors were instructed to read the final pages while moving between the entrances and exits, and then go on stage and perform the closing scene on the spot.

That was Ranjit sahab's modus operandi for every play. But it was said that he was a director with the Midas touch. He had an incredible knack for selecting plays, casting and understanding what the pulse of the audience's desires.

Nekrassov was performed. And it was a stupendous success.

Hamlet's career was set.

Ranjit Kapoor was a renowned name. The auditorium was packed, with not an inch of space to spare. People eagerly awaited Hamlet's entry on stage.

But Hamlet felt as if he were in another world altogether.

AND PANDIT ARRIVED

S<small>OME PEOPLE BARGE INTO YOUR LIFE WITHOUT KNOCKING, AND THEN</small> they refuse to leave, no matter what happens. That's how Pandit arrived in Hamlet's life.

After the play, Hamlet was standing outside the Circulation Unit, accepting everyone's compliments and congratulations. He noticed a skinny guy staring at him.

The guy walked over and stopped right in front of Hamlet. 'My name is Sharma, but I am more commonly known as Pandit.'

Hamlet looked at him closely.

'You had come to watch *Hamlet* as well, right?'

'I've watched all your plays and your scene work too. Long way to go, man, long way to go. Good luck.'

And then he turned around and walked off, taking long strides.

Hamlet sensed an incredible confidence in the guy's voice and walk.

Little did he know, their friendship and work would become legendary one day.

At this moment, Hamlet pauses to take a deep breath.

DILEMMA

Life was chugging along well. Indeed, it was the golden period of his life. He had a formidable reputation and immense fame at a young age. His performances were critically acclaimed. People flocked to his shows from distant cities, spending their hard-earned money on train tickets to see his plays. (He had to wait twenty-seven years to make his own money.)

He felt an inexplicable fury and a manic energy raging within him. The creative spark burned brightly inside. Robert De Niro came closer and closer to him in his dreams.

'Look, Bob De Niro. I'm following in your footsteps. Am I on the right path? If I were to become an actor, I would want to be like you. Otherwise, it's not worth it.'

But still, there was something that wouldn't let him be at peace.

He was restless day and night. He couldn't stay still. He always wanted a life in motion. He'd suddenly get up and head towards Mathura Road, thinking about who-knows-what while walking.

He felt unsettled deep down. In other words, he was scared in a strange way. What was there to fear now? He was no longer just a regional actor. His name and photo appeared in the national newspapers.

'Santap is the hope of theatre and cinema in the future.'

This was during the 1980s. Amitabh Bachchan's presence on screen was equated with the secret to box-office success. Whether a film had a good script or not was irrelevant, as long as Bachchan was there. Even a brief comedy scene with him was enough for a movie to become a hit.

Protests were always being organized in Delhi. At one point, he had himself done many rounds of Jantar Mantar to support artists' demands. Comrade Baldev would visit his dreams at night.

In the late seventies and early eighties, the country had returned to some form of normalcy for a while. However, Rajiv Gandhi, the pilot-turned-prime minister, probably didn't know as much about Indian politics as his head-of-state position demanded. The government was on shaky grounds once more.

Hamlet kept himself busy, not realizing he was growing lonelier by the day. Even when he talked to others, he felt lonely. At night, he'd lie on the hostel's terrace, gazing at the starry sky and wondering who created it all. These questions swirled in his mind. Then he'd fall asleep, exhausted. He tried to understand the reason for his restlessness but couldn't. In these moments, he missed Vishnoi and would write to him.

'How do you remain so calm always? I've never seen you flustered. Don't things affect you? Don't situations put you in trouble? You're always balanced. How?' He wrote to Vishnoi once.

Hamlet would greet Vishnoi's letters with laughter upon their arrival.

> You're in the golden period of your life. Be cautious. That's when people can go astray. You have an extremist nature, meaning you tend to go all in. Your sense of balance is fragile. Meditate. That is the essence of life. That's also where you'll discover all your answers.

He tried to meditate, but a girl had entered his life—and before he knew it, had left it too.

('*My husband came back. He says he messed up and won't go anywhere to wander now. Even though men are dogs, I'll give him one last chance. Let's see where life takes us.*' Harjot didn't want to leave her Greater Kailash house—equipped with the swimming pool, squash court and whatnot.)

He'd tasted the pleasure of sex.

His mind was restless. The world's pleasures were calling to him. He couldn't focus on meditation. In fact, he couldn't concentrate on anything.

Time was passing, and then one day when he was in the hostel Sangini called on the landline.

'Hello?'

'Listen, I'm feeling down. Something's off.'

'What do you mean?'

'I want to come to Delhi. Meet you and Vishwas.'

'Then come. The Taj Express leaves at five o'clock in the evening.'

Hamlet was in a strange mood that day.

'Please don't talk like that,' she said in a low voice.

'Then how should I talk, yaar? You're not happy there. If you want to come here, then come,' he snapped.

'Look, if you talk like this, I'll hang up.'

'Arre then hang up, yaar. Don't bother me.'

And she hung up.

ACTING

A NEW BATCH ARRIVED AT THE NATIONAL SCHOOL OF DRAMA. IRRFAN Khan, Alok Chatterjee, Idris Malik, Meeta Vashisht, and others. A new buzz was in the air.

'Abey, we arrived one year too early. If we had come a year later, we would have had a batch full of babes,' Hargurjeet said.

It was nine o'clock at night. The drama school boys were sitting at Sardar ji's parantha stall at I.T.O.

'I'm telling you again, sir. An actor's process starts from within. External gestures and postures come later,' Chibber emphasized.

Mohan Maharishi's acting class was in session. The topic was Stanislavski and his acting process.

'That's not true. Sometimes external gestures also assist an actor in going inwards,' Dinesh stated.

'I began with gestures in *Nekrassov*. I reached the inner part much later,' Santap remarked.

'That was a special character. What gestures can you use in a Mohan Rakesh play?'

'Gestures aren't just about waving your hands. They can be subtle, too. But I don't see the impact or relevance of Stanislavski's theories on new actors. Act for at least ten years. Stanislavski will make sense on his own. You can't learn acting just by reading him.'

'He only talks about exercises, Santap. He never said you would learn acting from them,' Maharishi ji said.

'But my question is, can acting be learned?' Santap asked.

'What do you mean?'

'An actor has an innate talent. He can develop his skills, but a workshop or drama school can't transform a non-actor into an actor. Every batch here includes individuals who struggle with acting. Can the school truly make them actors?'

'Nadeem Shah famously stated that while acting cannot be taught, it can certainly be learned,' Maharishi ji said.

'No, sir. An actor can gain depth, but he cannot be created. No school in the world can transform a non-actor into an actor.'

'So that means there isn't any acting method?' Bapi asked.

'Every actor probably has their own method. That's probably what method acting is all about. These terms can be so confusing, sir. Sometimes, they may even get you killed. It's better to trust your instincts. That's the only truth.'

'Abey, why do you drag the conversation all over the place, Santap? We're so done with this!' Hargurjeet said as soon as they came out of the class.

'That's why we come to drama school, you fool.'

'I was fine in Punjab, acting happily. Here it's this method and that method. And on top of that, I get to play a ghost.'

'Abey, it wasn't a ghost's role, you fucking idiot. You played Hamlet's father in *Hamlet*. Renowned actors would kill for that role.'

'If I had my way, I'd make Shakespeare stand at the intersection and hit him with my shoes. Let us live in peace, yaar. If there's peace, there'll be acting too. Abey, do you want to drink?'

And that night, they drank. Then they all went to I.T.O. to eat paranthas. Irrfan's batch joined them too.

Sardar ji's stall used to be super crowded at night. NSD, Maulana Azad

Medical College, School of Planning and Architecture—it was everyone's favourite spot.

'Abey, we arrived one year too early. If we had come a year later, we would have had a batch full of babes,' Hargurjeet said.

Irrfan's batch had four breathtaking girls.

'We only had two, and they were unavailable almost immediately.' Vibha was in love with Chibber and Alka with Ishaan.

'Abey, then whine about your luck. No need to be so jealous,' Ishaan said, laughing.

'Say whatever you will, the atmosphere at NSD is adventurous for sure,' Juyal said.

'You'll miss all this even more when you leave the campus. So enjoy it while it lasts,' Dinesh said, as if it were the gospel truth.

'What's going on with you?' Santap turned to Irrfan.

'Prasanna's coming to do *Fujiyama*. I heard that it's a really exciting play.'

'We're getting Fritz Bennewitz again.

> 'IT SEEMS LIKE A FAMINE HAS TAKEN OVER THE WORLD OF CINEMA THESE DAYS,' IRRFAN SAID.

He's doing Brecht with us this time. *Man Equals Man*.

'You're lucky, Santap bhai. You are getting Fritz twice,' Alok Chatterjee said.

'No doubt, we got some excellent directors to work with. We also have Karanth ji later. Our third-year tour is also going to Bhopal to perform plays in the Maach and Pandwani styles.'

'Yaar, we need to do something about the film club here. It's in a desperate state,' Irrfan said, deep in thought. He often seemed preoccupied.

'Ever since I saw *The Mission*, Jeremy Irons has practically been living in my mind. I haven't been able to drive him out,' Alok said.

'Honestly, Santap bhai, actors are beginning to seem unappealing to me. I don't know if it's the NSD education that's to blame or if it's something else,' Irrfan said.

'Try searching for them in India, no? You will find plenty of good ones here,' Dinesh said.

'It seems like a famine has taken over the world of cinema these days,' Irrfan said.

'Why? Motilal, Balraj Sahni, Jayant, Rehman, Yaqoob. All of them were great. The problem is we only obsess over foreign actors,' Dinesh said.

'One can count the good ones on five fingers, Dinesh bhai. Indeed, there's a famine. Luckily Nadeem and Som showed up, or this tradition would have never been broken.'

'That's so true, yaar. These two came like a breath of fresh air,' Ishaan said.

'And we must carry this tradition forward. How much is the bill?' Dinesh called out.

'Excuse me. You did *Hamlet*?' a girl stepped forward, coyly.

'Yes, ma'am!'

'It was wonderful. I'm a regular audience member at NSD ...'

'Very good. You're from?'

'SPA. The School of Planning and Architecture.'

For some reason, Hamlet felt a shiver when he heard that name. Perhaps his sixth sense was kicking in, as that place would become the equivalent of his in-laws' house soon.

MISHAP

Both *Fujiyama* and *Man Equals Man* were smashing hits. By this time, Fritz was crazy about Hamlet.

'What an actor! At ease in any role!'

Before the premiere, Hamlet was thanking his lucky stars that Nadeem Shah had missed his flight to Jodhpur.

Just as Hamlet was about to make his first entrance in *Man Equals Man*, Ishaan grabbed his shoulder and pulled him aside.

'Abey, Nadeem has come here to watch our play.'

Hamlet freaked out.

'Abey, did you have to tell me this right before my entrance?'

After the play, Hamlet seized the opportunity to meet Nadeem.

'That was awesome, yaar. Excellent!' Nadeem was beaming with joy in the green room.

Hamlet was levitating in his own joy. After all, Nadeem was his idol. He felt like he was on cloud nine. The next moment, he was at the Eastern Court dialling a number.

Vishnoi picked up the phone.

'Arre, guess who came to see the play today?'

'Did you call Sangini?' Vishnoi asked quietly.

'Listen to me. Today's the best day of my life!'

'Call Sangini. She needs you.' And the phone was disconnected.

Santap stared at the receiver for a moment, then called Sangini. A voice answered, 'Hello? What's going on? I called Ramakant, and he said I—'

'You must have received my letter by now. Don't try to call me again.' And she hung up. Hamlet was utterly confused. He ran straight to the letter room. Sangini's letter was lying right there. He opened it.

'By the time you get this, I'll be gone, Santap. Don't ever try to find me.' Hamlet read on, wide-eyed.

'Vishwas is marrying his colleague, Prabha Sanyal. He called. At least he sounded ashamed.' He could picture her teary eyes.

'Every street corner in Gwalior reminds me of him. If I stay here, I will never be able to forget him. I had applied for a job in Bhilai, and I got it today. I'm leaving with my mother and Chandni. Only Vrinda knows my address and she won't give it to you. She's been strictly instructed not to.'

Some of the words were smudged, perhaps by her tears.

Maybe I'll reach out to you someday, if the time is right. I'm burying my past life completely. I don't think I need to tell you that you will be dearly missed. You're the second man in my life after Vishwas.

Best wishes,
Sangini

Hamlet stood there. Speechless, stunned, oblivious to his surroundings.

He'd read Sangini's words. And he knew her well enough. Her stubbornness and determination were clear in the letter. There was no point trying to contact her again.

He walked out slowly.

He kept sitting under the neem tree that evening. Then it got dark.

Dinesh Khanna came out of the school into the hazy night.

'What are you doing sitting there? Come, let's go back to the hostel.'

'Go away, leave me alone,' he said harshly.

'Arre?'

'I said go!' His voice was even harsher this time.

Dinesh stared at him for a moment, then turned and left.

He sat there until midnight, then got up and left Bahawalpur House.

He began walking toward the women's hostel, crossed the Supreme Court and found himself in front of Pragati Maidan.

The streets were deserted. It was October, and it was getting chilly.

He kept walking, eventually reaching the Old Fort.

A police van pulled up next to him.

'Where are you headed, bhai?'

'Nowhere.'

'Arre, you must be going somewhere. Where do you work?'

'I'm a student at the drama school.'

'Then what kind of drama are you pulling here? Go back.' And the van drove off.

He returned, quietly slipped into his room, turned off the light and closed his eyes. A tear rolled down his cheek. He lay on his bed, gazing at the ceiling fan rattling above.

TUMHARI AUQAAT KYA HAI, PIYUSH MISHRA

LIFE WITH ITS MOUTH WIDE OPEN

And he was out of drama school.

His three years were up.

Life was staring him right in the face. A brutal, dangerous and ferocious life. Drooling at the jowls, ready to devour him.

Now he realized the importance of drama school. He was in heaven within those walls.

There was only one saving grace. He'd been selected for the NSD Repertory.

The news had reached home. His family's delight knew no bounds. Four thousand rupees were a big deal back then.

He was sitting with Pandit by the fountain in front of Omi's shop. His eyes were burning. 'Have you thought this through?' Pandit asked. He was Hamlet's constant companion, drinking whatever he drank and eating whatever he ate, always hanging out with him.

'Yes, I'm sure,' Hamlet said quietly.

'Four thousand is a lot of cash. And you get to pick the roles you like.'

'I am getting the roles I enjoy. I already performed in *Mashriq ki Hoor* in my first year at NSD.'

The Repertory was kicking off the season with that play, *Mashriq ki Hoor*.

'You'll be the first to have left the Repertory this quickly.'

'Someone has to be the first, sooner or later.'

And just like that, he quit the Repertory in eight days.

> **LIFE WAS STARING HIM RIGHT IN THE FACE. A BRUTAL, DANGEROUS AND FEROCIOUS LIFE. DROOLING AT THE JOWLS, READY TO DEVOUR HIM.**

Everyone in the Delhi theatre scene was stunned by his decision. No one could wrap their heads around him ditching the safety of a permanent job, especially with the Repertory.

'Why are you taking your anger out on everyone because of that girl?'

'She wasn't just some girl. And the world's pretty fucked up anyway.'

'What do you plan to do now?'

'I will loaf around the city with you.'

And so they began to wander.

Pandit would arrive bright and early. They would meet up and then *loaf around*.

Sometimes they went to Bengali Market, sometimes to India Gate, sometimes to Connaught Place. They'd talk a lot about everything—politics, religion, society, theatre and cinema.

In the end, they'd be found sitting under a tree in the parking lot.

'There's an issue everywhere in this country. This country needs something else, something new,' Pandit would say, getting all worked up.

He was a Communist with deep ties to the Communist Party of India (Marxist). It was through him that Hamlet had got the rundown on the party's central committee and Politburo.

'Look at Russia. What a government it had before Perestroika and Glasnost. Under the communists, everything was strict. Vladimir Lenin and then Joseph Stalin built up Russia. Books used to be piled up in the streets. There was such uncompromising discipline in the country and its citizens—even birds could not flutter their wings wantonly; everything had a purpose. That's when Russia became a world power. This motherfucker Gorbachev fucked it all up.'

Hamlet would listen intently.

'How many atrocities has America committed against the world? Arre why should your seventh fleet remain in the Bay of Bengal? Is it your father's land?'

They were having this conversation while sitting on the ledge outside Alka's tea stall. Surrounded by the mad, everyday bustle of the place.

'This damn America should be bombed and blown up. A bunch of bastards live there. If there is casteism here, there is racism there.'

Hamlet just listened. He had even made rounds of the CPM head office at 14, Ashoka Road with Pandit.

'Let's watch a film today. They're playing a Costa-Gavras retrospective at Pragati Maidan.'

So they headed over to Pragati Maidan.

'One must watch those early Russian movies. They are terrific. Eisenstein, Bondarchuk. You must've seen them all at NSD?'

'Yaar, Habib Tanvir knows theatre very well,' Pandit would confidently say at other times. 'There's a certain gravitas about him. *Jis Lahore Nahi Dekhya* and *Charandas Chor* are classics.'

And just like that, days passed with these discussions.

HE WAS SEEKING REVENGE. FOR WHOM, FROM WHOM, NO ONE KNEW. AND HE WAS BECOMING INCREASINGLY UNBEARABLE, ESPECIALLY TO HIMSELF.

He didn't have a place to stay at night. Sometimes, he would sleep at the hostel (they used to allow ex-students to stay), at other times, he would stay at a friend's place. Occasionally, he would go to his aunt, who lived in Sector 5 in R.K. Puram.

By that time, he had developed a taste for alcohol and there were many people to indulge him.

> **'HOW LONG WILL YOU KEEP BASKING IN THE GLORY OF THE PAST, WHY AREN'T YOU FOCUSING ON WHAT'S NEXT?'**

Every evening, drunkards would gather behind Alka Bhagwan's shop. They referred to it as the Mandi House open-air bar. Architects, painters, actors, journalists—everyone was there. And after a few drinks, he had observed, that he used to become quiet.

He was running out of cash. Pandit was his main support, along with his other friends. For work, it was mostly Ranjit Kapoor. He was Ranjit's favourite actor, but there was no money there either.

'Rehearsal tomorrow. *Arsenic and Old Lace*. Come to IIT.'

His shoes were worn out and skewed at the bottom. Lately, he'd caught hold of his cousin's racing bike. It helped him zoom off to IIT for rehearsals. He returned late at night, to hit the sack and doze off in no time, completely exhausted.

Girls would often ask him, 'Why do you suddenly become so absent-minded in bed? Completely disinterested? Don't you enjoy sex?'

'Maybe,' he'd growl.

He was seeking revenge. For whom, from whom, no one knew. And he was becoming increasingly unbearable, especially to himself.

Time was passing him by. It had been three years since he had left the National School of Drama.

It was a hot summer day and there was shade under the neem tree. It was around eleven o'clock in the morning; Pandit and Hamlet were sitting in the shade.

'Listen to me. And listen carefully. Something is wrong with you, bhai,' Pandit said.

'How?'

'Look, your golden days at NSD are long gone. Newcomers will soon take your place. Irrfan and Alok are excelling. It's only a matter of time before people start celebrating them over everyone else—and you.'

'So what?'

'How long will you keep basking in the glory of the past, with *Hamlet*,

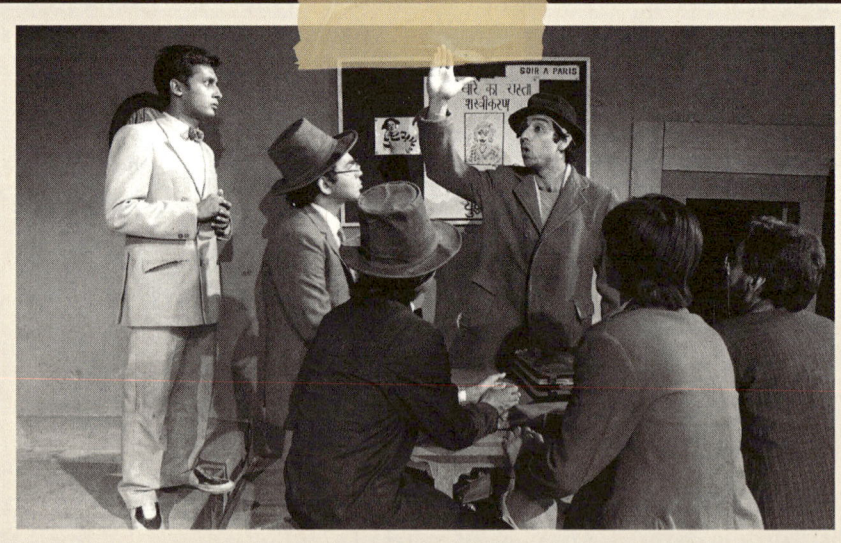

Nekrassov and *Man Equals Man*? They are all outdated. Why aren't you focusing on what's next?'

'I'm doing theatre still, right?'

'You consider these random four-five plays with Ranjit theatre? Nobody even knows about them.'

'Then what should I do?'

'Why don't you go to Bombay? Nadeem asked you to, didn't he?'

And Santap sighed. He had already turned down one opportunity to go to Bombay, and he hadn't even mentioned it to Pandit.

WOULD LIFE HAVE CHANGED?

He had two months left before graduating from NSD. The Sangini episode had just happened.

He received a message during a class. Mr Maharishi had called him to his office.

When he entered Mr Maharishi's cabin, he realized it was a serious matter. Another middle-aged gentleman was sitting in a chair.

Mr Maharishi introduced them to each other.

'He is a renowned producer from Bombay. He is launching his son as a director. What did you say is the name of the film?'

'*Maine Pyaar Kiya*,' the gentleman said.

'He has zeroed in on the female lead. He has come here to NSD to look for the male lead. I was talking about him.' He gestured towards Hamlet.

Hamlet shook hands with the gentleman.

He looked at Hamlet carefully. Then he took a purse out of his pocket. There were some cards inside it.

He pulled out a card, signed it, and handed it to Hamlet.

'This is my visiting card. My office is in Prabhadevi. Rajkamal Kala Mandir. When do you finish school?'

'Two months,' he said quietly.

'After two months, take the first train to Bombay. Do you have a photo of yourself?'

'I will give it to you,' Mr Maharishi chipped in.

'I will wait. Thank you!'

'Ji, thank you.'

And Hamlet turned and stepped out of the room. He heard the gentleman tell Mr Maharishi, 'What features!'

Ten days later, Mr Maharishi met him again in the corridor.

'I have received a call from Bombay. You have to leave right away.'

'Yes, sir,' he said half-heartedly.

(He arrived in Bombay exactly three years later. By that time, the film had been completed and released. It had also successfully launched an actor who would become a mega star in Hindi cinema in the years to come.)

He did not regret it, not one bit.

Sangini had left his life forever.

FIRST TRIP TO BOMBAY

The year was 1989.

Days had been passing rapidly. The money had run out.

Ranjit sahab's plays were often comedies. He enjoyed them but not all that much. He was longing to really *act*. Meanwhile, he did a TV serial. *Kile ka Rahasya*. Although he received praise for his performance, he was not at peace. He believed he was wasting his potential—that he was getting more while doing less.

Hamlet's fame was dimming. Critics had nearly forgotten him. He was gradually slipping away from people's minds.

He had stopped visiting Gwalior. In fact, he had begun to hate Gwalior.

Robert De Niro had begun to fade as well. Occasionally, he would return if Hamlet watched one of his films—his hopes were rekindled, but only momentarily.

It seemed like the arrangements for his visit to Bombay were organized by some divine intervention.

During a thorny period in his life, he had gone to 14, Ashoka Road after learning that Saeed Akhtar Mirza was also there.

The moment he stepped inside, he started talking.

'I am an actor. You have seen me before in *Hamlet*. I need work.' His tone was terse.

He was in a miserable condition. His inner turmoil was visible. His clothes were a mess. There was a stern look on his face.

Saeed Akhtar Mirza probably liked his dishevelled style. What this liking led to was a phone call that he made at Bajju bhai's house. (Shri Ramgopal Bajaj was famously known as Bajju bhai.)

'I am making a serial titled *Intezaar*. I need that boy for the last episode.'

They were having a conversation under the neem tree.

'Go,' Pandit had said.

'Money?'

'It will be managed.'

> **'I AM AN ACTOR. YOU HAVE SEEN ME BEFORE IN *HAMLET*. I NEED WORK.' HIS TONE WAS TERSE. HE WAS IN A MISERABLE CONDITION. HIS INNER TURMOIL WAS VISIBLE. HIS CLOTHES WERE A MESS.**

'How long will I continue to take money from you?'

'As long as I have it. Where is the shooting?'

'There is some place called Kasara. I will have to take a train from Dadar.'

And he had reached Kasara for the shooting of *Intezaar*.

The shoot was completed. His work was appreciated. His own judgement was that he had given an average performance, at best.

On his way back, he made a stop in Bombay. He met Nadeem, who was delighted to see him.

'Shift here. We will do plays together.' He was quite active in the theatre circuit, performing plays regularly. The name of their group was—Motley.

And so he moved to Bombay, completely unaware that many other terrible events awaited him there.

In Bombay, Nadeem introduced him to Gulzar sahab. At that time, the shooting of *Mirza Ghalib* was underway.

'You are the first actor Nadeem has introduced to me ...'

'... and also to Shyam Benegal,' Nadeem said, laughing.

'I have to give you work.'

The play happened. *End Game*. It was a famous absurdist play written by Samuel Beckett.

His performance was pathetic. He had lost his voice. His confidence was nearly gone. Only two people were on stage for the play. Nadeem and Hamlet. A voice came from the auditorium.

'Please speak loudly.'

During his year-long stay there, he did three episodes of *Bharat Ek Khoj* with Shyam Benegal and a documentary with Nandu Dhadekar.

Shabana Azmi was his co-star in *Bharat Ek Khoj*, and Mohan Gokhale featured with him in the documentary.

He felt that he could not belong to anyone, not even Nadeem. Indeed, he was aware that some problem within him had shifted the winds for him. It was his alcoholism.

He was a paying guest in the fifth flat of building number twelve in Manish Nagar Char Bangla. One of the three beds in the room belonged to him. The rent was five hundred rupees. He was not allowed to lock his cupboard. He had to leave home at nine in the morning and return by nine in the evening. His landlord was C.D. Dalal.

The landlord was free to use all his belongings in his absence. That license was pushed to its limit when he discovered his toothbrush was wet and soft one day.

'Ho ho ho. My toothbrush was actually broken!' the landlord neighed.

That day, Hamlet was carrying in his pocket the money he had received for *Bharat Ek Khoj*.

He decided to have a beer and headed straight to the restaurant House of Food in Apna Bazaar in Andheri. He realized that he was no longer having just one beer. He had downed six beers and two pegs of whisky as well.

> **HIS MIND WAS SLOWLY SLIPPING AWAY. HE WOULD VISIT EVERY PLACE WHERE HE EXPECTED TO FIND ALCOHOL.**

'If you start drinking once, you will continue drinking endlessly. This is both a mental and physical disease. Twenty out of every hundred people are alcoholics. Alcohol does not break down in an alcoholic's body. It keeps accumulating. The result can be either premature death or a slow descent into insanity,' Raj bhai told Hamlet, but many years later.

That night, he slept on the road.

His mind was slowly slipping away. He would visit every place he expected to find alcohol. Eventually, people began to object to his behaviour when he was drunk.

If he sat down for a drink with someone, he would remain seated. He was afraid to stand up. What would that person think if he could not get up? But if he remained seated, what would the person think in that situation?

His mind and heart began to feel hazy. He often sat with his head in his hands. The broker would come and ask him, 'Bhai, it's nine o'clock. When will you go out?'

In time, the money started running out as well. It became difficult for him to arrange even five hundred rupees to pay for his bed in the apartment. The storm in his mind had grown more intense. He had left Nadeem's group as well.

Then something happened that forced him to leave Bombay.

He was sitting in the House of Food. He had the last of his money left in his pocket. In fact, he had no money left to pay for food the next day.

He ordered a quarter of vodka. Then a second and a third. By the third quarter, he had lost his appetite. He promised the bar owner that he would pay the bill the next day. After that, he stumbled on his way through to his house in Manish Nagar; miserably sloshed. He had indulged so much that day that he felt his knees were wobbly, his legs unable to carry his weight.

The landlord's wife opened the door. She screamed upon seeing him.

Immediately, the landlord came running.

'How dare you come home in this condition? Vivek! Kumar!' She called out. His other roommates quickly landed on the scene.

'No, this is wrong. You should not do this, Santap bhai.'

He pushed everyone aside and entered the house. He found a cricket bat lying in front of him. He picked it up and—*Smash*—

The priceless painting in the drawing room crumbled to pieces on the floor.

He picked up the bat again and went on a rampage—*Smash, smash, smash* ...

Shards of glass were strewn across the floor in the living room.

'I will leave this house tomorrow morning. Until then, let me be,' he growled. And then went and sprawled on the bed.

It was against the rules to keep paying guests in the landlord's building. That was the policy of the housing society. The landlord could not cause much of a ruckus.

'Let it be, uncle. He says he will leave the house tomorrow, so let him stay until then.' Vivek's voice was filled with pity.

And the next day, Hamlet left Manish Nagar.

He borrowed two hundred rupees from Vivek in the morning.

'I am a man of my word. I will return it someday for sure.'

And then he was at the Dadar station.

In those days, Dadar West had amazing living arrangements. Countless people slept on the tracks by the roads in neat lines, next to each other. But the luxury room was situated one foot above the tracks on the footpath.

The fare for sleeping on the tracks was five rupees per night, while for the footpaths, it was ten rupees. This price difference was strategic. Drunk drivers' vehicles could not run over those who were paying ten rupees for the footpaths.

The second chapter of his time in Bombay had begun—but this too was destined to end in tragedy.

Many people slept on the footpath. One of them was Seenkiya.

Seenkiya was a slave to smack—heroin. Santap had forged a deep bond with him. Mostly because he used Seenkiya's tattered mattress and sheet almost every day.

'I can live without food, Santap bhai. But not without smack. I am addicted to it.' Seenkiya would say this to Santap every night before sleeping, crying bitterly.

Though he had been given a name at birth, people preferred to call him Seenkiya, after his thin, skeletal build.

Sleeping on that footpath was impossible until midnight because the local gangster, Bhedu, would kick them awake if they attempted to sleep before the

permitted time.

Santap would have to pay up ten rupees to Bhedu every night. Then he had to plead for sleep to take over him. The terrible lullaby of an empty stomach ensures that one does not sleep too easily.

And then on the twentieth day, something happened.

He felt that his soul was missing. His senses had abandoned him.

That night, Seenkiya returned to their spot stumbling. It was already midnight. It was November. In those days, the nights in Dadar West turned chilly. Hamlet was resting. Sleep felt miles away, partly due to the cold and partly due to hunger. He had not eaten anything for three days.

'Santap bhai ... Santap bhai.'

Seenkiya shook him vigorously. Hamlet was awake. The local gangster had seized the last tenner for the night and left.

'Go to sleep. And give me that sheet.'

Seenkiya sprawled next to Santap. He had returned after consuming a strong dose of smack. His mouth and body were stinking.

Hamlet turned towards him and closed his eyes.

Soon, both were asleep.

Around six in the morning, Hamlet woke up. His gaze immediately turned to Seenkiya. His eyes narrowed.

He looked closely. Seenkiya lay still, eyes and mouth open. Unblinking, staring at the sky. Hamlet could not comprehend anything. He placed his hand on Seenkiya's nose. Then, on his mouth.

Seenkiya lay dead. Hamlet had spent the entire night next to a corpse.

Hamlet caught the Andheri-bound local train. His body felt numb and his breath came in heavy gasps. His throat kept drying out. He had travelled without a ticket.

He reached Hargurjeet's house.

'I will return every single penny when I am in Delhi. Please just book my ticket.' He was pleading.

'Abey, such a small thing! Have you lost it? How much do you want?'

Hamlet was on the next Punjab Mail bound for Delhi. He left with a vow to never return to Bombay.

But this time, life failed to inform him that at last, his golden times awaited him.

TUMHARI AUQAAT KYA HAI, PIYUSH MISHRA

ANK EK/ACT ONE

Ank Ek Samuh as in Act One Theatre Group had taken the centre stage in Delhi. Pandit had already done wonders in the first play.

Hamlet unpacked his luggage in his 12-by-10 foot room at 1/6 Pant Nagar, Bhogal, and heaved a sigh of relief as he lay on the bed.

(Jayant had called him while he was at C.D. Dalal's place in Bombay—'A room is available in Pant Nagar. Should I take it?' Jayant was Marathe's younger brother and his new friend, but this new friend was about to land him in deep trouble soon.

'Take it. How much is the rent?'

'Five hundred. We will divide it in half.' And the room was taken.)

Hamlet attempted to stretch his limbs. His bones creaked in protest. That day, he enjoyed a full meal for the first time in about six months.

He called Reva in Gwalior to share his new address.

'Now I am in Delhi. I will stay in Delhi only.'

Two days later, Reva's letter arrived.

> Bhaiya, please come home. You haven't been home for three years now. The situation here is not good. Jidda has become even more unrestrained since you left. Pita ji is getting older and his eccentricities have increased. Mother has lost control over everything. I can no longer bear to see Bhole chacha's condition. My marriage is being discussed here, but no one in the house seems sensible enough to take the charge to move things forward. Please return. You also have responsibilities.
>
> Waiting for you ...
> Your sister,
> Reva

Hamlet saw the letter, then folded it and kept it in his pocket.

Everything was pleasant in Mandi House, just as before, with the same rush everywhere and the same crowd.

Hamlet felt reassured that while he was here, he wouldn't have to worry about food and drink. It was as though he had come back home.

Ank Ek performed *Netua*, a play adapted from a Bihar-based story by Ratan Verma. It was directed by Pandit with Samar Bajpayee in the lead role. The play was a huge hit.

Samar and Pandit had taken the theatre world of Delhi by a storm.

Now this was also the time when the Babri Masjid conflict was simmering. The likelihood of an attack on Ayodhya was high. Kalyan Singh was the chief minister of Uttar Pradesh during that period.

Meanwhile, in Delhi, Pandit had emerged as a stalwart—and he really was. He had a magnetic charm. A wide variety of actors from all over the country joined Ank Ek. The performance group had become remarkably good.

It was in those days that the era of Hamlet's roaring success in theatre finally began. As did the era of communism.

It had been a year since the murder of Safdar Hashmi in Delhi. SAHMAT—Safdar Hashmi Memorial Trust—decided to organize a twelve-hour cultural festival every year on 1 January in his memory, featuring various cultural activities, outside the Shri Ram Centre.

Hamlet arrived at Ranjit sahab's rehearsal quite unexpectedly. Ranjit sahab was preparing for Shri Swadesh Deepak's *Court Martial*, with the first performance scheduled to be staged on 1 January at the Shri Ram Centre. This was on 26 December 1990.

'Arre, where did you come from?' He was delighted to see Hamlet. 'Everyone meet Santap. Has anyone seen *Hamlet*?' His voice was chirpy. 'Now my play is sorted! Take this script.'

Santap did not understand anything.

'Oho, this is the script for *Court Martial*. It is being staged on 1 January. You will play Surat Singh, the main role. I had been wondering about who might be the perfect fit for the role for a while now.'

The play was to be staged four days later.

Hamlet went home and read the script. He developed cold feet. He went to Ranjit sahab's house.

'Sir, I will not be able to do this. Only four days are left. How will I prepare?'

'This is your special talent. Look, didn't I say that Santap would definitely come once and say that I will not be able to do this?' he asked his wife, who was sitting nearby. 'And then I had also said that Santap would do it and would do it well!'

And on 1 January, a programme of SAHMAT was held outside the Shri Ram Centre, while *Court Martial* was staged inside. The play was very successful. Hamlet kept praising Ranjit sahab's courage first and then his own.

A meeting of Ank Ek was taking place. The discussion focused on the prevailing religious atmosphere in the country.

'I have a harmonium. I will sit with it tomorrow onwards. I need to compose street songs—those sung in the real streets. Songs that have never been heard before. In the meantime, you focus on gathering people.'

And that's how *Hamare Daur Mein* began—with a loud bang.

Hamlet was putting the harmonium gifted to him by Santo chachi to good use. He knew he could compose music, but he didn't realize he could do it so well.

ये क्या हो रहा है, जो ना होना था हमारे दौर में,
जब रात गए मेरे गाँव की सड़क पर धड़-धड़ करती मोटरसाइकिलें तो...
मेरा बच्चा थर-थर करता है खौफ़नाक बारूद का देख अँधेरा,
ये जो सड़क पर खून बह रहा है उसे सूँघकर तो देखो...

What is this happening, when it was not supposed to happen in our times
When motorcycles roar down the roads of my village late at night ...
My child trembles looking at the dreadful darkness black like gunpowder,
Go on, smell the blood flowing on the road ...

Hamlet was drunk on words.

He experienced the warmth of family for the first time in his life in Ank Ek. And that, too, a family that was so passionate and full of life.

He would arrive at the CCRT—Centre for Cultural Resources and Training—a hut behind Bahawalpur House, at eight o'clock in the morning. Then, the very air of Mandi House would witness and bask in the music emerging from his fingers dancing on the harmonium and songs flowing from his soul.

Then, at ten o'clock, the entire Ank Ek group would gather around him. All the songs were rehearsed. After that, Ank Ek would go out to sing those songs on the streets, in schools and in colleges.

The songs, sung to the music of a harmonium and the beats of a naal—an Indian percussion instrument—had brought about a revolution in Delhi and its surrounding areas.

Schools and colleges demanded for the group to perform in their premises. And Ank Ek was fully committed to deliver.

Now, he remembered neither his family in Gwalior nor his time in Bombay. He had experienced the long-lasting pleasure of undivided attention to one's passion.

'You are doing good work. At least someone is focusing on his calling.' Vishnoi's

letter had come.

'What magic are you doing in Delhi, bey? So much praise you have been receiving in the newspapers.' Marathe had written in his letter.

'You have made us all so proud, Santap bhai. We keep hearing wonderful stories about your achievements.' He didn't know when Pradeep bhai had begun calling him 'bhai' in turn. His letter also included greetings from Pravesh.

> 'WHAT MAGIC ARE YOU DOING IN DELHI, BEY? SO MUCH PRAISE YOU HAVE BEEN RECEIVING IN THE NEWSPAPERS.'

Hamlet had become the darling of the Delhi University girls. Hundreds of admiring gazes stalked him.

This was the golden period of Santap's life—after the *Hamlet* era.

REVA'S WEDDING

He felt a strange surge of enthusiasm and excitement when he stepped off the Taj Express at the Gwalior station.

When the autorickshaw was about to turn right from Jayendraganj, he said, 'Keep going straight.' And only asked the driver to stop right in front of the Chirantan Dharma Mandir School.

'Do you want to get off here?' the driver asked.

'No, I want to smoke a cigarette.'

He got out of the autorickshaw. Scattered groups of girls were moving around on the premises. Perhaps it was lunchtime.

Some of his fondest memories of Gwalior were associated with this road.

He stared ahead for a moment before taking a deep breath and getting back into the autorickshaw.

'Take me to Jinsi Nala.'

'There's a marriage proposal for Reva. It is from a Thakur family. His name is Dilip Singh Pawar. He works at LIC. You should go and see.'

The conversation was taking place in the living room.

'I will go alone. None of you will accompany me.'

'Arre, how can we not go? The girl is ours too!' His father's resolve was unwavering.

'You go now. I'll go later,' he said as he got up.

'I know him. Dilip studied at Miss Hills School. He is a good boy. What is the problem?' Marathe said.

Santap was sitting in front of Marathe in his office.

'My house. It's fucking full of screwballs. Nobody knows how to talk properly.'

'You think you can talk properly?' Pramad's comment was laced with sarcasm.

'You keep your mouth shut. I know my family better.'

'Yeah, it's as if we don't ever know anything,' Pramad said, frustrated.

Pramad was the predictable type. If someone said in front of him, 'My uncle screwed me over today.' He'd always snap back, Don't tell me about getting screwed. Like no one's ever screwed me over?

'I don't see this marriage happening easily. There will be obstacles along the way,' Pramad said before leaving.

The marriage certainly did not happen easily. There were numerous quarrels. The primary reason was Jidda's stubbornness. She acted as if she belonged to the boy's side.

But despite the madness, the wedding ceremony was organized and Reva was sent away to her new home. After many days of festivities, the same familiar silence filled the house once again. In the morning, one day, his father caught hold of him. They were surrounded by all the other members of the family.

'What is your intention now, bhai?'

'I am doing theatre.'

'But we haven't seen you in a film yet. You went to Bombay. What happened to that?'

Hamlet took a deep breath. In India, or even internationally, an actor is considered an actor only when he appears in commercial movies. His father had similarly nurtured this desire to see Hamlet on the big screen since he had gone to drama school.

'There is no place for cinema in theatre. It is purely for entertainment purposes. For the country and society.'

'We are also a part of the country and society. We are getting old.' His voice was exhausted.

But Hamlet was drunk on the cocktail of success and communism in the aftermath of *Hamare Daur Mein*.

'I know that I will not come back to Gwalior at least.'

'We aren't even asking you to come to Gwalior. But at least try to find a job somewhere.'

'I know what I'm doing, sir. And whatever I am doing, I'm doing it of my own will. It's difficult to explain it to you.'

'But you are going to be responsible for our well-being soon.' There was a noticeable fatigue in his voice.

'What have you people ever given me by the way? The decision to go to NSD was my own, I did not ask you before going,' he said bitterly and got up.

'Arre, please sit down. Okay, what are your thoughts on marriage?' he said quickly.

'I'll do it whenever I want to.' He stepped out in a flash. In that moment, he found himself thinking about the Sangini episode. Jidda had chosen not to contribute anything during the entire conversation.

After much thought, he went to Vrinda's house that day. She lived right behind Chirantan Dharma Mandir.

'Please come in and take a seat.' She smiled at him. 'What would you like to have?'

'You know what I am searching for.'

'I cannot give you the address or phone number. Sangini has strictly instructed me not to do so.'

'Look, I will not trouble her. And why should I go to Bhilai to disturb her? I just want permission to write letters occasionally.'

'Sorry,' She said in a firm voice. 'You give me your phone number. If she wishes, she will call you.'

He gave her his address and phone number and left.

The classes had just ended. He watched the students leaving the school premises with a quiet sadness.

Then he returned home.

The next day, he found himself in Delhi, back with Ank Ek.

> **'WHAT HAVE YOU PEOPLE EVER GIVEN ME BY THE WAY? THE DECISION TO GO TO NSD WAS MY OWN, I DID NOT ASK YOU BEFORE GOING,' HE SAID BITTERLY AND GOT UP.**

PIYUSH MISHRA

CONTINUOUS EXPLOSIONS

Ank Ek had performed its next play as well, *Holy*.

Written by Mahesh Elkunchwar, *Holy* depicted the unruly behaviour of the student community. It highlighted how they become victims of the system and get entangled in criminal activity.

The play was a tremendous success. Santap acted in it and also composed its music.

Ank Ek had firmly established itself in Delhi's theatre circuit. As had Pandit. The skinny Pandit had amazing directorial skills. His visual sense was astounding. The play had transcended all boundaries. Kavita Nagpal had praised it, and generously too.

> 'Ank Ek has posed a challenge to the NSD Repertory. This group's style of working and unmatched enthusiasm are otherworldly. It holds great promise and potential for theatre in India.'

It was during these days that Shampa had come close to him. Shampa Choudhary was a Kathak dancer and a disciple of Shri Birju Maharaj. Her claim to fame was her growing emotional intimacy with Hamlet. However, the cruelty that stemmed from his all-consuming intoxication with theatre and complete devotion to Ank Ek led to the premature end of this relationship. She had left the city crying, boarding her train back to Calcutta from the Old Delhi Railway Station.

Hamlet regretted it. But much later.

He received an invitation from the Theatre Action Group. The play was Billy Russell's *Blood Brothers*, and the Hindi adaptation was titled *Suno Re Kissa*. The director of the play was Mr Barry John, while Hamlet was responsible for the script, lyrics and music. *Suno Re Kissa* proved to be a timeless classic in the Delhi theatre circle and in the history of TAG—Theatre Action Group. Hamlet was so proud to work for and with Ank Ek.

Ank Ek was a hurricane. It had created a huge stir. And the choice of the next play to be performed was also an indication of the effect it had had on the people.

Pandit was going to take them to watch a film today.

'Just watch it. And watch it carefully.'

The film was screened at E-64 in Railway Colony.

Directed by Robert Wise, written by Arthur Laurents, choreographed by

Jerome D. Robbins, with music composed by Leonard Bernstein and lyrics by Stephen Sondheim, the film *West Side Story* was not only famous for its ten Oscars but this Broadway musical inspired by William Shakespeare's *Romeo and Juliet* was considered a milestone in the modern history of world theatre in many other ways.

'We will perform this play. This will be the next Ank Ek production,' Pandit said.

'Are you crazy? We don't have the resources to do that much.'

'This is the issue with humans. They are constantly misled in comprehending their own potential.'

Inspiration was Pandit's second name. The word 'impossible' was not in his dictionary.

'Who will do the script?' said Santap.

'You!' was Pandit's order.

'I don't have the chops to write this script. Find someone else.'

'You will have to do it. And the lyrics and music, too. Edwin, start working on actors' bodies tomorrow. I need them fit and strong.'

And so, *Jab Sheher Hamara Sota Hai* was launched.

'You have given it a new name, bey?' Vinod Dua said excitedly. He was a friend of Ank Ek's.

'Santap has given it,' Pandit replied proudly.

Revolving around the doomed love story of a Muslim girl and a Hindu boy, this adaptation promised to be something truly unique. Santap had already completed the first song.

उजला ही उजला शहर होगा
जिसमें हम तुम बनाएँगे घर ।
दोनों रहेंगे कबूतर से
जिसमें होगा न बाज़ों का डर

It will be a city bathed in light,
In which you and I will build our abode of love,
Free from the fear of hawks to chase our peace,
Together we will soar like doves.

And the play continued to take shape ...

Ashutosh Upadhyay secured a sponsorship. Atul Kumar, Alok Mathur and Nikhil Verma handled production. Shefali Bhushan, Juhi Dogra and Rajeev

Gupta made their debut. 'Daddy' and Tribhuvan managed the lighting. Edwin G. Williams choreographed the dance routines. Uff, his gruelling, unforgettable dance classes ... his notorious migraines. For Hamlet, the smallest things became memories to return to and laugh at.

On top of all this, waves of Santap's songs resonated throughout Mandi House.

Omi's fruit chaat. Bale Bhai Mali's discreet supply of electricity to run the rehearsals. Babli's drums. Sher Singh ji and uff, Alka's tea! Samar Bajpayee, Ayush Vidyarthi, Arun Mota, Vijay chacha, Asad Khan, Gautam Chaddha, Prashant Narayan, Aseem Bajaj, Gajraj Rao, Ajay Chauhan, Aneesh, Arvind Babbal, Varsha Agnihotri, Neelam Mahajan, Anees Khan, Imtiaz Ali, Vijay bhai, Jaya Barnela, Sushil bhai, Vicky, Gandhi, Vikas, Mithu, Lokesh, Bhanu, Parul Kala, Akhilesh, Riya Mukherjee, Deepali Gupta, Sanjeev Vats, Vaman, Shubhendu, Sarvashish, Devashish, Bond, Poornima, Buggi, Santosh, Pushkar, Surendra Sagar and Anurag's commando squad. Dr Sushil's jokes. The sweet laughter of Soma Dutta Chaudhary. Nishi, Tabassum, Munmun, Parvati, Swati, Vijay Shri, Uma, Smriti Mishra and Shruti Mishra echoing from the Kathak Kendra. Dr Dinesh Sharma's sponsored cigarettes and the increasing ticket sales. The line of vehicles lengthening each day from the Shri Ram Centre to Bengali Market. The biting winters of December–January. The CCRT hut, the Ank Ek group performing dance movements in shorts at six in the morning. Sujit Sarwar's sound arrangement. John David's costumes. Odd props sourced from the junk market. A breathless Habib Tanvir rushing into the green room during the intermission to congratulate the team. The emotional audience. The stunned critics. The curtain calls growing longer daily.

Hamlet would never be able to make a list comprehensive enough.

Ank Ek had become immortal. So had the duo of Pandit and Santap.

Hamlet's enthusiasm was boundless. As was his consumption of alcohol and cigarettes.

His expenses were fully covered by Ank Ek, primarily by Atul Kumar.

'You only focus on theatre. Leave the rest of the worries to us.'

And Hamlet had truly forgotten to worry. Jayant turned out to be mighty helpful in his achieving that.

People had started flocking his home at 1/6 Pant Nagar.

All of them were Jayant's friends ... toxic and habitual drinkers. Hamlet was getting used to getting free alcohol daily. Surely there was Atul too, who, besides being his friend, also served as the President of Ank Ek—and a major financial supporter of his growing appetites.

Politburo comrade Khushhal Singh had said, 'There is something in your songs. They directly touch one's heart.'

Addressing a seething crowd of four lakh people at India Gate, Hamlet had picked up the microphone and roared, 'This system has been destroyed. It needs change.'

Pandit was preparing to perform *Pattar Anaaran De* at Lady Shri Ram College. And Hamlet was writing the songs.

लाहौर के उसे पहले ज़िले के दो परगना में पहुँचे

TENSION AND SARDAR BHAGAT SINGH SANDHU

RELIGIOUS FRENZY WAS AT ITS PEAK IN THOSE DAYS. THE BABRI MASJID had been demolished. And Santap observed that Pandit was changing as well.

The conversation took place in Calcutta. There was a festival featuring three plays of Ank Ek.

'We will repeat *Yeh Jo Zindagi Hai Na* in Delhi, right?'

Yeh Jo Zindagi Hai Na was an innovative and original play scripted by Hamlet that Ank Ek had come to perform in Calcutta.

'Cancel it, Atul. We will perform *Jab Sheher Hamara Sota Hai* in Delhi. The country needs it right now.'

Jab Sheher Hamara Sota Hai was about the religious anger brewing in the country.

'Okay.' No one dared to ignore Pandit's words.

'And Santap, what is that line that the boy from the Hindu gang says?'

'Which one?'

'That is how we got this life?'

The play was based on the gang war between the Funiyar (Hindu) and Khanjar (Muslim) gangs, which ends tragically.

'Yes. What should we do with it?'

'Cut it out. I don't want that line.'

Hamlet didn't understand. 'Why?'

'I just don't want it. Do I have to tell you why?' Pandit growled. He had started growling a lot during those days.

'But if that line is removed, then this play will become one-sided and completely in favour of the Muslims. That single line justifies the anger of the Hindu youth—that they are also victims of the system. The same poison is being injected into their hearts and minds as well.'

'I don't want to argue about this,' Pandit said and left. Any further discussion was futile.

That line was removed. The play was performed, but it did not prove to be as powerful as it had been previously.

'Yaar, I had written a neutral play. I don't want to side with one religion and even if I do, I want to take the side of both.'

But Pandit was changing. His behaviour was growing harsher and he was slowly becoming unbearable.

'The world needs us. We do not need the world. We will have to become arrogant. Intolerant too.'

Hamlet could not understand.

'Joseph Stalin was great. During his era, even his own children took a bus to school. That is the Russia I want to recreate here.'

He had started looking for his mini-Russia in Ank Ek.

'Hindus are fanatics. They will have to be stopped.'

Both of Hamlet's childhood friends, Qamar and Bhaiyye, were Muslims. He had never encountered such behaviour from them.

'If you cannot tolerate me, you are free to leave Ank Ek,' he declared. He also gave them a day to ponder upon their decision.

It was obvious that no one wanted to leave. Everyone had embraced Pandit wholeheartedly. Both as a director and as a friend.

For Hamlet, it was hard to imagine a life without Ank Ek.

'*I* am Ank Ek. Only *me*,' Pandit declared.

Santap remained silent.

Despite their love for the group, people were slowly leaving Ank Ek. Or were being thrown out. Santap stayed.

'I will stay with you till the end.'

'Let's do the next play about Bhagat Singh. These people have torn the country apart. Did people like Bhagat Singh die thinking that this is what their country would become?'

Jayant had moved to Indore. Santap now lived alone in his room. Occasionally,

Jiya would come over like a gentle rain shower.

He was performing a play at the School of Planning and Architecture. The rehearsal room was filled with people. Just then, someone walked by and her shadow fell on him. When he looked, he saw it was a girl.

As Hamlet gazed at the dusky, beautiful girl whose figure seemed to be sculpted from black ebony, a thought raced through his mind—*I will make her my life partner.*

As communists, we believe we have achieved neutrality. However, we are never truly neutral. We still take sides.

But Bhagat Singh has been one of those few people whose ideology cannot be questioned by anyone till date—neither Hindu, nor Muslim. Neither Jain, nor Buddhist, nor Sikh. He is as revered in India as he is in Pakistan.

'Who am I to write about this giant among intellectuals?' Hamlet muttered in surprise as he conducted his research on Bhagat Singh.

'He could not have been a human being, but neither was he a god. So, what was he? And to have such a rich legacy at the age of merely twenty-three years, five months and twenty-six days?'

He continued working on the play. And Hamlet became increasingly lost in Bhagat Singh.

Bhagat Singh who shared an incomprehensible friendship with Sukhdev. Bhagat Singh who was filled with affectionate respect for Pandit Azad. Bhagat Singh who maintained a special and unique view towards Mahatma Gandhi despite their disagreements. Bhagat Singh who had faith in Shrimad Bhagavad Gita and Vivekananda despite being an absolute atheist. Bhagat Singh who observed immense love for his father and family from a distance. Bhagat Singh who stood tall, straightforward and serious in the race amongst his comrades to sacrifice their lives first. Bhagat Singh who experienced a cycle of death and immortality with each passing day while enduring a unique 114-day hunger strike. The bookworm Bhagat Singh, the beautiful Bhagat Singh, the calm Bhagat Singh, the jovial Bhagat Singh, the intellectual Bhagat Singh, the visionary Bhagat Singh, the daring Bhagat Singh and the lover Bhagat Singh.

Bhagat Singh began to appear in his dreams. He started conversing with him. He began to embody him.

And the play happened.

Gagan Damama Bajyo.

Pandit had given this name.

The play was performed and it was wonderful.

'You are doing a good job, kids,' an elderly audience member said to them in his trembling voice.

'If this play ever gets published, we would like to gift it to our children,' another said.

'This is madness. Who could have guessed that creativity can take such magical forms?' the youth were heard saying.

Hamlet was deeply immersed …

In his mind, he had now begun shaking hands with Robert De Niro.

'Look, Bob De Niro. Am I meeting your standards? By now, I have also played Galileo. I have portrayed a ninety-year-old lady in *Woh Ab Bhi Pukarta Hai* and Tevye in *Fiddler on the Roof* as well. I am very satisfied. Are you, too?'

BHAGAT SINGH BEGAN TO APPEAR IN HIS DREAMS. HE STARTED CONVERSING WITH HIM. HE BEGAN TO EMBODY HIM.

But there was something in him that had cracked beyond repair. Pandit had now become truly unbearable.

JIYA, MY LIFE

The TV was on. Jiya Narayanan was sitting. The location was Chennai. The place was her home. Her parents were watching TV with her. Hailing from a respected Chettiyar family in Chennai, she was the daughter of a renowned man with a background in the armed forces.

Bharat Ek Khoj was playing on Doordarshan. These were its reruns. Directed by Shyam Benegal, with the lighting done by the legendary V.K. Murthy sahab. (The one who had done cinematography for most of Guru Dutt sahab's films.)

The Gandhi episode was on air. Santap appeared on the screen. Jiya's mother involuntarily remarked, 'What features.'

Jiya remained silent. Then she said, 'I want to marry him.'

An uproar erupted in that Chettiyar house.

This was the first inter-caste marriage in their family. Moreover, the boy was an aspiring theatre artist—jobless and penniless.

Things had worsened in Ank Ek. The first generation of artists had left. (Or had been thrown out.) The second generation mostly consisted of a group of Delhi University students. Hamlet struggled to find his place among them. He felt isolated there.

Pandit's transgressions had reached their limit. It was becoming difficult for Hamlet to even breathe around him.

'What do you want?'

The place was ITO's rehearsal hall. The conversation was happening right outside the hall.

'I want to stay in the group,' Santap said in a choked voice.

'You need to be loyal to the group,' Pandit had growled.

'I *am* loyal to the group.'

'No, you are not. You are nostalgic for the old Ank Ek.'

'I miss it a lot. Those were the good old days.'

'This is creating a problem in the group. You are not able to commit to the new people.'

'I am trying.'

'Well, your efforts are not impactful enough. The rest is for you to see now.'

'What?'

'Do you want to stay in Ank Ek or not?'

'What are you saying? I have also contributed to the success of Ank Ek, yaar.'

'Have you offered even one original idea in the last five years?'

Santap was dumbfounded. All the scripts of Ank Ek flashed in his mind.

'Answer me!' Pandit snarled.

Santap remained quiet for a moment. Then said—'No.'

'Then make your decision. I'm giving you a week.' Pandit turned and walked back inside the hall.

Hamlet felt as if he had just spoken to Joseph Stalin, not Pandit.

The letter had arrived from Chennai. Jiya's words were clear.

'Take me away from here. My folks will not agree.'

He had some money by now. He had shot a TV serial while being a part of Ank Ek. *Firdaus*. (All this while bearing Pandit's ferocity.)

He flew to Chennai.

The next day, he was back in Delhi with Jiya.

They reached Tis Hazari Court. Hundreds of couples were sitting in front of the matrimonial office. A young lawyer bumped into him.

'You worked in *Firdaus*, right?'

'Yes,' he said. Jiya was with him.

'What have you come here to do?'

'To get married.'

'Arre, I will get it done right away. Do you have a ration card?'

'No.'

'You must have a passport?'

'No.'

'Driving license?'

'No.'

'Birth certificate? Class tenth mark sheet?'

'I don't have anything.'

The eager helper thought for a moment. 'So, how will you get married? You need the documents, right?' Then he suddenly added, 'Do you have sixteen thousand rupees on you at least?'

Hamlet had that sum with him.

'Okay. Then I can get you married. But you will have to come with me to my house and have a cup of tea with my wife.'

And Hamlet had the tea. He got married on 1 June 1995.

Now, he was a married man.

The next day, he went to meet Pandit for the last time at a rehearsal of one of Ank Ek's productions. Pandit was busy.

He sat there for a long time. Pandit did not pay any attention to him.

After sitting for three hours through the rehearsal, he got up, left the room and walked out.

He heard Pandit's voice from behind. 'You think you can act without me, moron? Let's see you try.'

Hamlet had tears in his eyes. The first family of his life was lost. Ank Ek had completely succumbed to Stalin. Now, once again, he was alone.

No. Jiya was with him. But it took time for *him* to be with Jiya.

A lot of time.

'SIR' PASSED AWAY. FRITZ TOO.

13 S*eptember* 1995.

He received news from Gwalior. His father had passed away. He went to Gwalior.

In Gwalior, he received another news. This time from Delhi. Fritz Bennewitz had passed away. Both had died on 13 September.

He overheard Jidda saying, 'Killed her father-in-law as soon as she married into the family. We were better off without a daughter-in-law than someone like her.'

He returned to Delhi with Jiya, but now, four pairs of old eyes followed him daily.

Jiya had set up her household in a 12-by-10 foot room at 1/6 Pant Nagar, Bhogal. She was one of those girls who build their home by saving every bit by bit.

A MARRIED MAN'S ALCOHOL

E*very morning, he would leave his house and go to* M*andi* H*ouse.* There he would see Pandit sitting under a tree, along with the entire Ank Ek group.

He would go inside NSD. When he would come out, the group would no longer be there—they would have already left for rehearsal. He would stand there for a while, then go sit under the same tree, trying to immerse himself in old memories. Then, he would get up and head to Omi's shop for a cigarette and grab tea from Alka's. Afterwards, he would go to the fountain and sit there for hours. By then, evening would have fallen. Which meant that it was time for his drink. He would go to Connaught Place to buy half a bottle of rum. (He had recently bought a second-hand Vespa.) Then, he would buy Coca-Cola from Omi's shop and return to the fountain to mix his rum and Coke. There, he would sit and drink his fill. And then start the scooter, completely drunk. He would reach home, where Jiya would be waiting with dinner. He would force down some food, to fulfil an obligation, really, then collapse onto the bed, utterly wasted. Jiya would sit and watch him. Quietly.

Hamlet had earned considerable respect in the Mandi House circuit. He discovered this only after leaving Ank Ek. Truly, good work and talent speak for themselves.

Arvind Gaur was one of those who respected him.

Arvind had his own theatre group, Asmita. It was a big group. There were many people in it.

People would come and tell him, 'You should go to Bombay, yaar. You are needed there.'

Every time he would think of Bombay, a shiver would run down his body.

'I will not go to Bombay. I will do theatre here. And I will die here.'

Dying might have been easier. But to continue doing theatre without the affiliation or support of a group was certainly not.

His alcoholism was worsening every day.

That was the golden era of Mandi House. Delhi's cultural hub, Mandi House, was always bursting with liveliness and bustling with activity in those days. Omi's chaat stall served large crowds—almost eighty to ninety per cent of them flippant theatre folks. At Alka's tea stall, the vendor's fingers moved briskly—almost a blur of motion—as he brewed tea for droves of wannabe actors lined up on the pavement.

'I WILL NOT GO TO BOMBAY. I WILL DO THEATRE HERE. AND I WILL DIE HERE.'

With a ceaseless buzz of chatter, swirling cigarette smoke, more chatter, jokes, wisecracks, suggestive glances among the gatherers, but also sarcastic looks exchanged amidst the noise, the place was usually rife with chaos and madness.

Mrs Kirti Jain had recently taken over the reins at NSD, which helped the institute get back on track. (Mohan Maharishi had left by then. After his term ended, Ratan Thiyam took over. And after Thiyam, Kirti Jain was appointed.)

Around this time, the esteemed Alkazi sahab made a thunderous comeback to the theatre scene. He had established his school in the Little Theatre Group on

Copernicus Marg, which came to be known as Little Theatres.

Occasionally, the stormy plays of Habib Tanvir sahab and B.V. Karanth were staged, resulting in a frenzy for tickets at Shri Ram Centre and Kamani Auditorium. Energetic performances of Punjabi plays at Sapru House coexisted with small and large theatre groups rehearsing in every nook and corner of Mandi House. Countless theatre artists wrestled with lights and sets amidst hectic schedules. This era was utterly mesmerizing for the theatre enthusiasts in Delhi and they could have bet even the most enchanting moments of their lives to witness it all.

Hamlet wandered alone through all this. Unquestionably alone, clad in his black overcoat, he would wander. He drifted here and there, swayed, carefree, defiant, fearless, rugged and aimless.

'Why go to Bombay? What's so special about that city? I sow my own seeds and reap them too. I'll find my own success in my 12-by-10 foot room at 1/6 Pant Nagar, Bhogal. This is my territory, and these are my guns. From ITO to Feroz Shah Road, and from India Gate to Connaught Place ... I'm the king here. I fire my guns here, and the echoes reach Dibrugarh. Is Bombay the gold standard for judging one's talent? Samar Bajpayee went to Bombay. Let him go. He was a great actor. Ayush Vidyarthi also left. Not a bad actor himself. I wish him the best in Bombay. Sambal and Surekha Bhardwaj also left. They were a great couple. Good luck to them. Hundreds have left ... So, what does that mean? Should I leave as well? Bombay is like the dust on my shoes! I wash them daily, and it comes off quickly. Instead of running to Bombay, buggers, you should focus on honing your acting skills ... nothing else will save you when He asks what you were sent to do and what you ultimately accomplished. Drinking won't solve your problems. (He would pause, staring at the bottle of rum mixed with Coca-Cola in his hands, and then shake his head.) I mean, I drink too ... but you're just here in this world for endless fuckery, you bastards!'

Just a few days ago, he had narrowly escaped losing his left eye in a scooter accident around Nizamuddin. Presently, he caressed the left eye and moved along on his way. As he passed through, people bowed their heads and stepped aside. Some out of fear, some out of respect and most out of admiration.

He sat near the fountain and shouted, 'Abey, just act, you fools! Life is too short. You can't find salvation so easily!'

> **'WHY GO TO BOMBAY? WHAT'S SO SPECIAL ABOUT THAT CITY? I SOW MY OWN SEEDS AND REAP THEM TOO.'**

A boiling bout of laughter erupted from him, echoing across Mandi House. People turned in shock because talking to oneself was seen as a telling sign of madness even back in 1996.

He didn't know this madness was a manifestation of his growing fear. But things were way out of his control by then.

> 'BOMBAY IS LIKE THE DUST ON MY SHOES! I WASH THEM DAILY, AND IT COMES OFF QUICKLY. INSTEAD OF RUNNING TO BOMBAY, BUGGERS, YOU SHOULD FOCUS ON HONING YOUR ACTING SKILLS.'

'What should I do?'

It was the same Katora Tal in Gwalior. The same neon lights reflected brightly on the pond's clear water. It was nine o'clock at night.

Santap and Vishnoi were sitting.

He was in Gwalior because Jidda had passed away. Tobacco-related cancer often leads to unexpected deaths.

'What will you do?' Vishnoi's voice echoed.

A car passed by on Medical College Road.

'I have left Ank Ek. I neither have the courage nor the desire to form a group again. I am completely alone.'

'Jiya is with you.'

'It doesn't matter if she's there or not. If I'm okay with something, then she's also okay. And there seems to be very little chance of me being okay.'

'Do you still drink alcohol?'

'Alcohol has nothing to do with all this. I want to act. I have already experienced the joy of working relentlessly, without a break.'

'No plans to go to Bombay?'

A shiver ran through his body.

'I will not go to Bombay. That place is full of poison. I have decided to spend my life in Delhi.'

Vishnoi took a deep breath.

'You don't have the time to meditate or practice yoga now, I assume?'

'Everything feels so distant. When I attempt to concentrate, my thoughts slip away somewhere else.'

'What about your home and family here?'

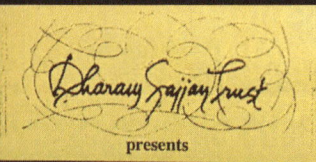

presents

AN EVENIING WITH PIYUSH MISHRA

Piyush Mishra

Piyush Mishra's one man performance is a truly electrifying phenomenon in the world of Hindi Theatre. In his performance you will find romance, comedy, emotion and a heart ache that reaches out. And in the plays, by his acting, narration and songs — Piyush creates visual images of not only incidents, multiple characters, trees and animals but even of abstracts — ghosts, trees, fragrance, climate, time smell and colours.

Piyush is one of the finest actor and termed as the wonder king of Delhi theatre. On screen he has worked with directors like Shyam Benegal, Mrinal Sen, M.S. Sathyu, Ketan Mehta and Kundan Shah.

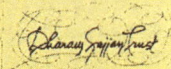

presents
ASMITA'S
"AN EVENING WITH PIYUSH MISHRA"
in
Vijay Dan Detha's
"Duvidha"
and
"Tara Pradhan Ko Gussa Kyon Ata Hai"
(An adaption of Arnold Wesker's –Whatever Happend to Betty Lemon)

At
**B.M. Birla Auditoruim
on 15th Aug. '96**
At
7.30 P.M.

To Commemorate
The Golden Jubilee Year
of
Indias' Independence
and
Founder's Day of the Trust.

Tickets
Rs. 100/-   75/-   50/-   25/-

Tickets available At:
Dharam Sajjan Trust
C-30, Lajpat Marg, C-Scheme Tel. : 374774
Readiprint
Hotel Imperial Building, M.I. Road Tel. : 373468

'I have to look after them too. It's my responsibility. Now everyone is alone.'

'Sell the house and move to Delhi. What is the point of leaving your family here if you have to work there?'

'I am also thinking the same.'

He returned home. More intense than ever before, a melancholic silence filled the house. It was unable to endure the sudden absence of two of its senior residents.

He had just sat down in his own room when his mother came and sat across him.

'Now take us away from here too, son. We are all alone.'

He kept looking at her quietly.

'We will place an advertisement in the newspapers to sell the house. Being near you in Delhi will be some comfort at least.'

Bhole chacha came and stood at the door. Time had etched deep lines into everyone's faces.

'Reva is visiting her in-laws. She will meet us tomorrow morning.' Her husband lived in Tikamgarh.

Hamlet shook his head. As he looked at Bhole chacha, it was impossible for him to imagine that chacha's days with them were numbered.

'I only want an empty performance space. You can keep all the money from the ticket sales.' Hamlet was speaking while sitting in Arvind Gaur's rehearsal room in Shankar Market.

'What is the harm in earning money from theatre?' Jiya asked in a muffled voice.

'I will not earn money from theatre. You can make me do anything else for money.' This was the influence of Comrade Khushhal Singh and Pandit on his mind.

'Theatre people also have families, Santap bhai. I also earn my living from theatre,' Arvind said humbly.

'YOU DON'T HAVE THE TIME TO MEDITATE OR PRACTICE YOGA NOW, I ASSUME?' 'EVERYTHING FEELS SO DISTANT. WHEN I ATTEMPT TO CONCENTRATE, MY THOUGHTS SLIP AWAY SOMEWHERE ELSE.'

'Sorry, I cannot. And anyway, I keep doing workshops here and there as well.'

'That barely covers the house rent, Santap,' Jiya said quietly.

They had recently shifted to Q-25 Jangpura. It was a big house.

'Then why did you marry a theatre artist?' His voice was bitter. Jiya fell silent.

'You keep all the ticket sales. Just give me the space to perform. Let's start from tomorrow.'

On their way back, Jiya sat quietly behind him on the scooter.

The scooter had just crossed Nizamuddin when Jiya said, 'I want to tell you something, Santap.'

'Tell me.'

'I am pregnant.'

The scooter screeched to a halt on the road. The vehicles following behind swerved to make their way through, the owners cursing the pair on the scooter.

'Why didn't you tell me sooner?'

'What difference would that have made?' Her voice trembled with emotion.

An Evening with Santap Trivedi marked Hamlet's life's third and most thrilling phase. The zenith of the (erratic) golden era.

Santap had chosen three pieces.

'Doosri Duniya' was a Nirmal Verma story, while *Whatever Happened to Betty Layman* was Arnold Wesker's play—in which he had to make a stage appearance as a disabled woman. 'Duvidha' was a famous Rajasthani folk tale written by Vijaydan Detha. Hamlet adapted all of these pieces into plays. The total time to stage all three was three hours, with a five-minute intermission scheduled after each performance. During these three hours, Santap was expected to stay alone on stage and portray at least twenty-five characters.

'Let's break the performance into three individual parts of one hour each, Santap bhai,' Arvind asked in a low voice.

'I'll perform for three hours straight,' Santap replied, swaying under the influence of alcohol.

Who can tell whether this conviction was due to extreme intoxication, an act of reckless courage or a means of getting even with Pandit.

Jiya had built her house by accumulating bit by bit. She used to leave for her office in the morning and return in the evening. By that time, Santap used to leave for his rehearsal. If she arrived at the rehearsal sometimes in the evening, Santap, already finished with his work, was to be found drinking. Nonetheless, he drove Jiya back home on these nights, in a drunken state. That they survived these rides without any accidents on the treacherous roads of Delhi was nothing short of a miracle.

Jiya was beautiful, self-respecting and quiet. She spoke only when it was necessary. That night, she found both the necessity and opportunity.

They were both in their bedroom in Q-25 Jangpura. It was eleven o'clock at night—pitch darkness enveloped the streets outside. The ceiling fan turned slowly above them as they lay flat on their backs, staring up at the ceiling. Quietly.

'Listen,' Jiya said.

'Hmm,' Hamlet replied.

'Today, you are more sober and clear-minded. Today, you will listen to me and perhaps understand as well,' Jiya said with silent eyes, gazing upward.

'Tell me.'

'Santap. Theatre and acting are your passions. I am an architect. And I do a regular job. Even if I want to, I cannot bring that passion to my job. A job like mine has own set of restrictions.'

'Okay,' Santap responded in a flat voice.

'Now Ank Ek is gone. Pandit is gone. All of your comrades are gone.'

'Keep speaking.'

'We will stay in Delhi for the rest of our lives. I understand you may not want to go to Bombay. But in a few days, our family will expand.'

'If it is a son, it will be Josh and if it is a daughter, it will be Joey.'

'Okay. But we will need something else as well.'

'What?'

'We will need to provide for the child's upbringing, nourishment; ensure that it has a happy childhood.'

'I will not make money from theatre.'

'What is the problem with turning your passion into a profession?' Jiya's eyes filled with tears.

'You knew about the hardships faced by a theatre artist. So why did you marry me?'

'Because I have married you, I will stand by that decision. I have promised not to seek a divorce, no matter what happens.' Even her tearful voice reflected determination. 'I say this not because I have left my parents but because my heart is attached to you. However, you can neither bring about a revolution nor support your family by staying hungry.'

Hamlet kept gazing at the ceiling. Suddenly, quite involuntarily, his eyes welled up with tears.

'Why do I drink so much?' His throat tightened.

Jiya turned toward him. She placed her hand on his cheek and turned his face to hers.

'Everything will be fine.' Jiya held him tightly in her arms. Hamlet burst into tears and so did Jiya.

'I will be with you, always. Will you come along tomorrow?'

'Where?'

'To the counsellor.'

> **'WHY DO I DRINK SO MUCH?' HIS THROAT TIGHTENED. JIYA TURNED TOWARD HIM. SHE PLACED HER HAND ON HIS CHEEK AND TURNED HIS FACE TO HERS. 'EVERYTHING WILL BE FINE.'**

'I will not leave theatre. Not even acting.'

'Who said that? You just need to take some time off.'

But the next day, Hamlet was off on his scooter to Mandi House for his rehearsal again. He was carrying a bottle in his pocket.

'I want to understand the craft of acting at a micro level. At any cost.'

But this time, the cost was too exorbitant.

Back in Chennai, Jiya's relatives and family had relented. Things were back to normal. Jiya had told everyone that her husband was a great artist. 'If you ever come to Delhi, I will take you to one of his performances.'

And that day also came.

An Evening with Santap Trivedi premiered.

And then suddenly and pretty much on its own, many titles were added to Santap's name. 'Wonder Boy of Delhi' and 'One Man Army' were prominent among them.

All the critics and newspapers were inundated with praise.

'This is impossible. And for the first time in the Indian theatre world.'

The audience was stunned. The entire gallery was filled to its capacity.

Housefull. This was the year 1997.

This was the most blazing phase of Hamlet's life. After a three-hour performance, he would collapse on stage due to exhaustion, but the audience's applause would not cease for a long time. Often, he would have to make curtain calls not just twice or thrice, but four times.

But life was becoming more complicated every day. So was his mental anguish.

'I am a nymphomaniac, sir. I cannot live without more than one man. But if you get even a single scratch, I will come running from the farthest corner of the world. I love you very much.'

Urvashi Thakur had said while crying. 'And Jiya di, too.'

This was Hamlet's first and last sin against Jiya.

THE ARRIVAL OF JOSH

'Mani Ratnam wants to cast you in his film.' Tigmanshu Dhulia had called from Bombay.

Three significant events occurred that year. The death of Bhole chacha, the sale of the Gwalior house and the arrival of little Josh in their home.

Santap had purchased his own house in Delhi: I-97, 2nd Floor, Lajpat Nagar, Part One.

It was only many years later that he truly felt the pain of Bhole chacha's death.

NYMPHOMANIAC

'I can't do theatre anymore. My body is broken. I am exhausted. I can't even walk anymore.'

He broke down in Urvashi's room.

Urvashi was a student of painting at the Fine Arts College on Tilak Road.

He ran into her at his shows. They began meeting, and gradually, it became a regular thing. And now he was sitting in her hostel room. It was six o'clock in the evening.

Urvashi stretched out her hands and placed Hamlet's head in her lap.

'Be careful, sir. You are a role model for the world. If you give up, then what will happen?'

'I can't provide for my own family. My elderly mother keeps staring at me. Satbir chacha keeps sitting. Jiya goes to work. Josh keeps sleeping. I was already a bad son and husband, but now I don't want to be a bad father too.'

Urvashi continued to caress his head in silence. After a while, Hamlet gathered himself, lifted his head from Urvashi's lap and prepared a drink for himself.

'Will you take one?'

'You know me. I don't drink.'

'Why don't you get yourself treated?'

'Why don't you quit drinking?'

'I can't quit, even if I want to.'

'This is my condition. I can't run away from myself. Sometimes, I feel like ending everything, but then I find my courage lacking.'

'Does your family know?'

'That's why I live in this hostel on Tilak Road, far from Paschim Vihar. I don't want to bring disgrace to my family. This is how my story will end.'

'Let's find a good psychiatrist. This disease can be cured through counselling.'

'I have tried everything. Now, I've made one final decision. Let's see how well it works. But you have found a goddess in the form of Jiya di. Don't wrong her in any way.'

'I wrong her every time I come here to see you.'

'It's impossible for me to resist your charm, sir.' Her voice trembled with emotion. 'But I will find a solution to this as well.'

And then he did the first film of his life: *Dil Se* with Mani Ratnam.

Shah Rukh Khan and Manisha Koirala played the lead roles. He thanked the gods that his shoots took place in Delhi and Jaipur and he did not have to go to Bombay. The year was 1998.

> 'BUT YOU HAVE FOUND A GODDESS IN THE FORM OF JIYA DI. DON'T WRONG HER IN ANY WAY.'
> 'I WRONG HER EVERY TIME I COME HERE TO SEE YOU.'

Dil Se failed at the box office. Hamlet also disapproved of his work.

An Evening with Santap Trivedi was finished too. Hamlet was now bored of it. But his lust was still alive.

'I will perform an extended improvisation without a script. I choose not to write one. Let's see how the show goes. Everything will be in my mind. If it works, great, and if it doesn't, it'll be even better.' *Hamlet Never Went to Bombay* continued for an hour and a quarter.

The day was 24 March 1999. The venue was Abhimanch and the occasion was the National School of Drama's convocation ceremony.

This was Hamlet's finest performance. The Delhi theatre circuit took great pride in his talent. Hamlet did too. But his fatigue had increased significantly by then.

Now, Hamlet followed a set routine. During the day, he conducted workshops at various colleges. And in the evening, he came to Mandi House to drink his fill and complain about his life.

Miranda House, Gargi, Ramjas, Daulat Ram, Shri Ram College of Commerce, Kamala Nehru, Dyal Singh, Maharaja Agrasen, Maitreyi, Lady Irwin ... There wasn't a single college where he hadn't conducted workshops. He was a regular acting instructor at School of Planning and Architecture and Lady Shri Ram College.

Exhausted from the day's rigours, he would return to Mandi House in the evening, only to face the emptiness of life. He would drain the bottle in his hand and flop onto the floor; sometimes falling unconscious.

On such evenings, he would often run into Urvashi. But she appeared disinterested and disconnected.

'I am fed up with my habits, sir. Now, this sick disease is becoming unbearable.' She cried in his lap. 'I will stab myself with a shard of glass between my thighs, sir,' she said, shaking her head. 'Today, my brother called me a whore. The word has travelled beyond college, everyone at home knows about it now.' She said, looking straight ahead with empty eyes.

And then one day, Nalini from the Fine Arts College came to visit Hamlet. Her eyes were brimming with tears.

'Urvashi has sent this for you.' She extended her hands to pass over a letter and immediately turned around to go back.

'My sir, by the time you receive this letter, I will have already left.' Santap was reminded of Sangini's last letter.

> My illness has crossed all limits, sir. Last night, two men were caught with me in the hostel. My parents have refused to accept me. They say that I am bringing a bad name to the family. And that I am discardable for them. I am leaving. I will attempt to seek peace wherever I can find it. This illness is a taboo in this society. It will be very difficult to explain to anyone.
> Go to Bombay, sir. Your entire career lies ahead of you. Goddess-like Jiya di is there for you. Little Josh is also there for you.
> If time brings us together again, we will surely meet. Until then, goodbye.
> Your student,
> Urvashi

'HOW LONG WILL YOU KEEP SACRIFICING EVERYTHING FOR YOUR OWN ECCENTRICITIES? REMOVE THIS GHOST OF REVOLUTION FROM YOUR MIND. COMMUNISM WILL NOT COME TO PUT FOOD ON YOUR TABLE.'

Hamlet immediately ran to the Fine Arts College, where hundreds of eyes stared at him with suspicion.

'We don't want to talk about her. She was a black spot on our college.'

He came back and hunted for her address, which she had never given him.

He called Vishnoi.

'She was such a strange girl.'

'Arre, *you* are the strange one, yaar! Your wife is at home, your mother is at home and you have a son now. How long will you keep sacrificing everything for your own eccentricities?

Remove this ghost of revolution from your mind. Communism will not come to put food on your table. Attend to your domestic duties. This will be for the best.' And Vishnoi slammed the phone down.

When he came home, Jiya was waiting for him.

'I received a call from Bombay. A film is in the works. It is a love story set in the pre-independence era. They have heard of your work, including the play, *Gagan Damama Bajyo*. Will you give them a call?' She handed him a slip of paper. Her hands were shaking.

And Hamlet stood there, stunned. This was the same Bombay where he had vowed to never go. That same Bombay had called him back. Respectfully ... with full honour, in fact. And a ticket to fly in with as well.

The year was 2001.

HAMLET IN BOMBAY

Hamlet was waiting at the Delhi airport, holding a ticket in his hand. Jet Airways—9W 420.

He read it carefully. 420. *Four hundred twenty ... this is fucking jinxed right from the beginning!*

No, yaar, forget it. There's nothing like bad omens. He was still carrying the remnants of communism within him.

The news was published in *The Indian Express*.

'The Last Loyalist of Indian Theatre Has Packed His Bags for Bombay.'

A grand farewell ceremony was held for him. Arvind pulled him aside and asked: 'Are you leaving, Santap bhai? You too?' And then he burst out laughing.

'Arre, I'm not going anywhere, yaar. I just need to write a script for a film. I'll return as soon as I finish it. Here. With you. I still have a lot of theatre left in me.'

'No one returns after going there, Santap bhai. It is a city of comfort and luxury. Anyway, you have also done a great deal of theatre already. Now, go live your life.'

Hamlet felt a sharp pang inside. A weird one.

'Santap bhai is leaving for Mumbai. He has received an offer to write the script for a big film. We wish him the best and hope for his happiness.'

The episode reminded Hamlet of his farewell ceremony at the Gwalior station many years ago, when he had left his home to attend NSD.

Jiya sent him off with a farewell hug. She was most pleased to see him head to Mumbai.

'Don't worry about things here. I will take care of everything. You write this film well, okay? Actually, there's no need for me to tell you this, I know you will write it most beautifully.' She kissed his lips. Hamlet continued to gaze at her. He was deceiving this innocent soul.

The news had reached Gwalior. Marathe called.

'Finally, the lion comes to his real turf. Tear them apart and only then come back. Sorry! Don't bother coming back at all.'

Pramad said, 'I had told you that now we will see you only on the silver screen, right?'

Vishnoi's voice was calm.

'You are heading to a new place with a fresh purpose. Be cautious. And about this alcohol, the less you drink, the better it will be for you.'

Suddenly, he remembered Sangini. Where could she be? How was she?

The flight took off. He was boarding a flight for the second time in his life. He was thrilled.

'The seat belt is tied like this. This end of the belt ...' Announcements were ongoing.

The flight landed in Mumbai. By that time, Bombay had become Mumbai. Hamlet wondered what else might have changed about the city.

A car arrived at the airport to pick him up. He got into the car, which dropped him outside the Laxmi International Hotel, Juhu.

It was a bright, sunny day in July. The weather was delightful. The Laxmi International Hotel was right next to Prithvi Theatre. He had a sea-facing room where a cool easterly breeze from Juhu Beach wafted in occasionally. He did not know why, but he felt that this time, his trip to Mumbai was going to be incredibly pleasant. Everything was going well so far.

After being allowed an hour to rest, he was taken to Seven Bungalows, where the director's office was located.

The director was somewhat overweight. No, he was quite overweight. (Hamlet referred to him as 'healthy' in an underhanded epithet.) Lunch was ordered and Hamlet had a little bit of it. Half of the chicken, mutton and fish that were ordered for lunch had been devoured by the 'healthy' director. The same treatment was given to the chips and bhujia offered before lunch as well.

They were supposed to meet officially and discuss the script after lunch.

'Actually, right now the dubbing of my upcoming film is being done. I will meet you later in the evening,' the director said and casually walked out.

Hamlet felt a bit strange. He had come all the way to work. He learned that the 'healthy' director preferred to work at night. The meeting finally happened according to the director's schedule.

'Come, sit. Let's talk now.' It was nine o'clock at night.

'What work have you done previously on pre-independence India?'

'Ji, I have read about it. I have researched about it. I even wrote a play about Bhagat Singh. And the songs used in the play.'

'Yes, yes, sing a song or two. Set up the mood a bit.' And he picked up chips from the plate on the table.

Hamlet started.

वतन की आबरू का पास देखें कौन करता है
सुना है आज मक़तल में हमारा इम्तिहाँ होगा ।

Let us see who protects the honour of the nation
We hear today we will be tested at the gallows

'Hang on! Wait a minute, what does this word *maqtal* mean?'

Hamlet continued to stare at him. By that time, the director had taken a handful of chips from the plate. Many other people were seated around them. Hamlet responded quietly, 'The gallows. It means the gallows.'

'Oh, ho, ho, that's good. Sing one more.'

इलाही आज गोरी की तबीयत फीकी फीकी है
इलाही आज उसकी भी ज़रुरत तीखी तीखी है।

O Lord, today the woman seems a little vanquished
O Lord, today her needs are even more desperate

And Hamlet continued to sing.

'The term "Ilahi" is used frequently in this. Sing something different.'

Hamlet sang 'Mera Rang De Basanti Chola'.

'Good, good, good. Who recommended him?' He turned. Complete silence in the room.

'Arre, someone must have recommended his name?'

No one said anything. Then the 'thin' writer of the 'healthy' director spoke, in a low voice.

'This play was quite famous in Delhi. What was its name?' He turned towards Hamlet.

'Yes, *Gagan Damama Bajyo*.'

'What does it mean?' asked the director.

'It symbolizes the war bugle's call, echoing through the sky.'

'Really, really, really? It is a difficult name and hard to pronounce in its entirety. Do you have another song you could sing?'

'Ji, right now I don't have anything else to sing. I can read the play for you though.'

'I will listen to the play as well. Arre, Deepak ji.' He picked up the phone and dialled the reception.

'Please connect me to Jiggy sahab,' he said, turning his revolving chair in the other direction to speak discreetly.

He continued talking on the phone while everyone sat in silence. Hamlet listened to the stillness of the room. The director put the phone down.

'Arre, bring another plate of this bhujia.' And then he turned towards Hamlet.

'Yes, bhai. You were talking about the play?'

By then, Hamlet's spirit had wilted. Dejected, he picked up the play and began reading the canteen scene.

Slowly, the 'healthy' director began to sit up straight. Now, he was sitting completely upright in his chair. He hadn't munched on the bhujia even once while listening to Hamlet's reading. Everyone around him was alert and listening to him intently.

The scene ended. The 'healthy' director was startled.

'Is it over?'

'Yes,' he said quietly.

'Arre, yaar. It felt like Bhagat Singh was speaking his own dialogues, Sukhdev's lines were delivered by Sukhdev, and Bhagwati Charan Vohra's lines by Bhagwati Charan himself. Excellent. It revived the essence of that time. The pre-independence era came alive. Excellent, excellent, excellent.' He had a peculiar habit of repeating words three times. 'You can leave now. Go rest. You must be tired. We will speak tomorrow. Okay?'

'Thanks, sir.' Hamlet got up quietly. *The meeting wasn't anything special*, he thought.

On his way back, Hamlet bought half a bottle of rum and returned to his hotel room. *Let's see what unfolds tomorrow morning.*

The next day, a car arrived at his hotel.

'The director wants to meet you alone.'

(Looking back, he really wished he'd never met that 'healthy' director alone.)

The car took him to Anand Studios in Pali Hill, where the 'healthy' director was waiting in his studio. He was delighted to see Hamlet and took his hand to lead him to his office, where a plate of snacks was kept on the table.

'It's wonderfulwonderfulwonderful. Verygoodverygoodverygood. You will write the dialogues for my film. Here, have some tea.'

'Thank you, sir. I have had it before coming here.'

'Arre, have a cup with me also. I was stuck trying to figure out what to do with the language of that time; I couldn't understand anything. Your dialogues have captured the essence so well—the language, the period and the expressions. I have discovered the tongue of my film.'

'I have some songs too.'

'We'll see about that too. We'll see about that. *Now* my film will be made. You are writing my film.'

Hamlet let out a sigh of satisfaction. As he walked back to the car, his steps wobbled with joy.

Today, I will drink to my heart's content.

He had sent the news to Delhi. Jiya was positively dancing with delight. His mother offered obeisance to the gods. And he felt proud that his first venture in Mumbai was successful.

The news of his arrival in Mumbai had spread like wildfire.

'Santap bhai is here. He is writing the script for a major film.' People were inviting him everywhere. His first project in Mumbai and the filmmaker had called him specially all the way from Delhi.

Swarms of people kept showing up at his hotel. Mumbai appeared very beautiful to him.

There was only one problem, though. There were more liquor bars than paan stalls.

PIYUSH MISHRA

MEETING FRIENDS

He had decided. He would work from the morning to the evening. At five in the evening, he would meet with the 'healthy' director. After that, he would return at nine. And then it would be time for alcohol and friends.

He had many friends. Eighty per cent of the people who came to Mumbai were from Delhi. All of them had either worked with him or seen his work. Moreover, his hedonistic nature worked in his favour. No one was denied entry to his room.

Sambal's call came first.

Sambal Bhardwaj was a music director, and his wife, Surekha Bhardwaj, was a singer. Both had made a name for themselves. Sambal, a graduate of Hindu College, had made his mark in the film industry with his first film. *Maachis* established him as one of the leading music directors. A friend and admirer of Santap, he had watched Santap set the stage on fire in *Jab Sheher Hamara Sota Hai* in Delhi and had been determined to bring him to Mumbai since then.

Surekha's voice had a most unique texture to it. Renowned for its distinctive *khanak*, it had become a treasured possession in the film industry.

Sambal said on the phone, 'My office is located in Oshiwara, on the sixth floor of building number thirteen. You can come there in the morning.'

Santap reached the address the next day.

The atmosphere was humid. The chances of rain high. A few clouds hovered in the sky. The weather was quite pleasant.

Sambal hugged him as soon as he saw him.

'Please meet Hitesh. He is my music programmer ... Hitesh Sonik.'

'Hi,' Hitesh shook Hamlet's hand, before moving away with a respectful smile.

'This is Salman.'

'Hi.'

'And this is Edwin ji. He looks after the management here.'

'Namaste.' Hamlet had folded his hands to greet them.

Both Santap and Sambal were sitting in his office. Tea arrived.

'What are you writing?' Sambal asked while sipping tea.

'It is a love story set in the pre-independence era. It is a big-budget film.'

'You have been asked to come in specially from Delhi. Do you understand its significance? This is a major break.'

'That is true. But why did these period films catch the fancy of filmmakers? All of a sudden?'

'*Gadar* and *Lagaan* were huge hits. The producers are focusing on the pre-independence era, believing that any film set in that time will be a blockbuster.'

'I don't understand.'

'This is Mumbai, my friend. It's a commercial city. Here, what you see is what sells. Does this subject have any substance?'

'Arre, it is full of substance. Take Bhagat Singh, for example. He was a historical hero. A fair-skinned Sardar, five-feet-ten inches tall, about whom his friend Rajguru once famously said that he had a tough time saving him from the admiring gaze of the girls. On top of that, he was a giant among the intellectuals. And he was a famous revolutionary who went to the gallows laughing. And he was only twenty-three and a half years old then. What more substance do you want?'

Sambal chuckled. 'You've got a killer way of talking. Your humour slays as well. Have you spoken to the director about money?'

'I will do it. If they called me here, I'm sure they would at least pay me some money.'

'Don't settle for the bare minimum, charge as much money as you can. They have called you especially from Delhi. We aren't smart in the matters of money. These people take advantage of our vulnerability. And remember, this is cinema, not your theatre. You must be brutal here to get your way.'

Hamlet continued to look at him. Then he exhaled.

'What is going on with you?' he asked Sambal.

'Same old, music. I compose songs. I record them. I need to do something big and successful soon. Life opens up after that moment.'

Hamlet continued to gaze at him, engulfed in a sorrowful stillness.

'I have a recording scheduled right now. If you'd like, you can join me there. Otherwise, we can meet in the evening at home. I'm hosting a party to celebrate your arrival.'

'Who all are coming?'

'Everyone you know. And those you don't, will know you now. Remember that you are a big name here. Everyone has heard about you. Everyone is curious about you.'

Hamlet exhaled deeply.

'Okay, I am leaving for now. Please send your address to my phone.' (He had recently bought an old mobile phone.)

'Let's go.' Sambal stood up and shook hands with Santap.

Hamlet moved towards the door. Sambal's voice called out from behind, 'And yes ...' Hamlet turned around.

'Be cautious of this director.'

Hamlet continued to look. 'What do you mean?'

'Time will reveal the meaning.'

Hamlet stood up, then opened the door and stepped outside.

That night, they held a party at Sambal Bhardwaj's home in Lokhandwala to celebrate Hamlet's arrival in Mumbai. Sambal was brimming with joy.

'I had told this fucker. Come here soon. But I guess better late than never.'

Many people were present there. He was meeting Surekha after such a long time.

'Do you remember that I had once recorded a song with you in Delhi?'

'Yes!' Surekha exclaimed.

'Oh, look. Santap has changed. He is speaking to us with due respect!' Sambal laughed. 'He will have to be baptized.'

Honey Trehan and Abhishek Chaubey looked at him with great admiration in their eyes.

'How are you, Santap bhai?'

'Fit, yaar,' he said, shaking hands. Both were his juniors from Mandi House.

'Isn't Samar coming?'

'He definitely will. The news has reached him. Look ... Ayush is also here.'

Ayush Vidyarthi was a veteran member of Ank Ek. He possessed a wicked sense of humour, sometimes even bordering on cruel. Everyone was rather intimidated by Pandit's beloved Ayush Vidyarthi. Recently, he had willingly embraced roles such as the one-eyed uncle, lame uncle and dangerous don in South Indian films. He was a star in that industry.

'Choose your work wisely. This isn't Delhi. No one will inquire about your theatre here,' he said carelessly. One couldn't expect anything else from him.

The party kicked off. Then the harmonium arrived. Sambal introduced Hamlet to the crowd and urged him to sing: 'Now you listen to these unique songs and compositions.'

'Ayush had made me listen to them while we were at Hindu College. I had gone berserk.'

And Hamlet started singing.

उजला ही उजला शहर होगा
जिसमें हम तुम बनाएँगे घर ।
दोनों रहेंगे कबूतर से
जिसमें होगा न बाज़ों का डर

It will be a city bathed in light,
In which you and I will build our abode of love,
Free from the fear of hawks who chase our peace,
Together we will soar like doves.

Everyone began to sway. Their eyes were filled with admiration.

'Sing that one. "Husna."'

And he sang 'Husna'. Everyone listened to him, stunned, in silence. He noticed Hitesh Sonik was watching him intently.

Finally, Samar took his hand and said, 'You are coming to my house tomorrow. Shastri Nagar.'

'This city is really good.' The next day, he was sitting at Samar Bajpayee's house.

'It will be even better when you find a job you enjoy. The first six months can be tough here. After that, this place takes care of you. But you are fortunate that the exact opposite has happened to you. You don't have to stress about food and accommodation for the first six months.'

Samar Bajpayee was also in Ank Ek once. He had become a sensation in the film industry in those days. After his roles in *Satya*, *Shool*, and recently *Aks* with Amitabh Bachchan, he had established himself firmly as a fine actor in Mumbai. Everyone was entranced by his brilliant acting skills. Hamlet was proud to have once worked with Samar.

'There is no obstacle in your life anymore. You have to simply work and enjoy your life. We have done enough theatre. We also deserve to enjoy some luxuries in life now.'

Hamlet sat there in silence.

'Now, write a great film. Buy a house here. Move Jiya, Josh and Amma to Mumbai. They have also endured so much. And remember, you don't need Mumbai, but it is Mumbai that needs you.' He placed his hand on Hamlet's.

BLOODTHIRSTY MUMBAI

AND SO HAMLET'S WRITING BEGAN.

This was his first job in Mumbai and that, too, of his own choice. He had the opportunity to write a film set in the pre-independence era.

He would sit down to write at seven in the morning and continue until one in the afternoon. Then, he would have lunch and resume writing until five in the evening. After that, he would walk from Lokhandwala to Seven Bungalows, where he would narrate to the 'healthy' director whatever he had written throughout the day. He would leave at ten in the night, buy liquor and then return to Lokhandwala.

Eventually, he was moved from the hotel to the producer's guest house in Lokhandwala.

One day, he wrote a letter to Jiya.

> Everything is going well here. I am writing confidently. My director appreciates my work and so do my other colleagues. My office colleagues

are fond of me. I am reconnecting with more old friends and visiting them. I will call you here soon. Also amma, Satbir chacha and Josh.

I am sending you some money. I have received the advance. My account was opened at the HDFC Bank's Juhu Versova branch. I will continue to send money in the future.

I have given you a lot of pain, my love. Now is the time for joy. I have great hopes for this film. The director is generous and the script is also turning out well. I have set this film in 1942, during the Quit India Movement. It is a love story featuring a boy who is Indian and a girl who is Christian. I have paid special attention to its commercial aspect. It will be a hit film.

P.S. ... The auto drivers here are amazing. They are honest and punctual, taking you to the right place on time, by the meter. There's no rush here like in Delhi. Anyway, I don't need an auto, as there is always a vehicle in service. Now it's up to me whether I choose to use it or not.

Your Santap

He wrote a letter to Vishnoi as well.

It is a strange city. No one knows when it sleeps at night or when it wakes up in the morning. As soon as it awakens, it begins to work. It has a unique energy. There's no place for slackers here. It only prefers workers. Your work is valued here. The script is progressing well. More details in the next letter.

Santap

He wrote indiscriminately, day and night. He used the car as little as possible and preferred to walk. From Lokhandwala, via Four Bungalows and Model Town, he would encounter hundreds of acquaintances by the time he reached Seven Bungalows late in the evening. 'How are you, Santap bhai?'

He would accept everyone's greetings. He would not displease anyone. In these moments, he would often remember Sangini. She also used to do the same.

Afterwards, he would meet with the director. His office was always teeming with activity. The director had a penchant for organizing gatherings. He held a court of sorts every day. They would discuss everything under the sun. Hamlet noticed that the atmosphere improved upon his arrival. The chatter would die down and only the script would be discussed when he was around. The 'healthy' director would try to make him stay after ten o'clock, but then recognizing

Santap's exhaustion, he would let him go. It was common knowledge that the director hosted these endless *creative* sessions through the night. Only in the morning did the 'healthy' director go back to his own home and so would everyone else. The next day he would reappear … after lunching and resting heartily through the day, ready for work at five in the evening. That was when Hamlet used to reach the office.

He'd been told that the 'thin' writer was very close to the 'healthy' director. But surprisingly, he'd not seen the writer in any meeting with the director.

He had already received a small advance, which was sufficient for him. He had never even dreamed he would be paid for his writing. The values of theatre were still deeply ingrained and alive within him.

That was his only mistake.

In Delhi, Pandit was both his director and friend. Hamlet held immense respect and affection for Pandit and was fiercely loyal to him. He had envisioned a similar relationship with the 'healthy' director. But Sambal was correct: 'This is cinema, not theatre. And right now, you are working in Mumbai; forget Delhi.'

He could not forget. And the consequence was right there for him to see.

The 'healthy' director would agree to everything Hamlet said. He would praise each one of Hamlet's dialogues. He would applaud Hamlet. And so would the others.

'Sir, the dialogues are mine. Along with that, I am writing the screenplay too.'

'Totally, totally. The entire screenplay is yours.'

'Sir, my agreement hasn't been done yet?' he would ask in a low voice.

'It will be done; it will be done. Don't you trust me? You are now my house writer. This won't be the only film you'll write for me. You are going to write manymanymany more.'

And the very next day, he took Hamlet along and flew all the way to Hyderabad.

In Hyderabad, he introduced him to some people from a famous production house in Ramoji Rao Studio. They were making the Ramayana, in three parts.

'But I am writing Bhagat Singh.'

'Arre, you are a computer, yaar. I trust you. Forget about the other film for a few days. This film is bigger than that.'

He had sent this news to Jiya as well.

Jiya was an uncomplicated girl. She was more practical than he was.

'Did you get the agreement done?'

'It will be done, yaar. I am working so hard. This guy is trustworthy.'

Then, on one of the days after he had returned to Mumbai, he reached Seven Bungalows in the afternoon. There he saw the 'thin' writer coming out of the director's office. He was suspicious. Then he thought that it was a misunderstanding.

'What is he doing here?' he asked the watchman.

'He comes here every day in the afternoon. He is an old friend of director sahab's.'

He went to meet the 'healthy' director.

'Sir, please get my agreement done. The script is complete.'

'I am just waiting for my last film to be released. There's some complication there and I am completely engrossed in that issue these days.'

And before the director's last film could hit the silver screen, he got a call from Jiya from home.

'Satbir chacha is no more.'

He took the next flight and arrived in Delhi. Satbir chacha's body lay before him. The poor man had passed away after living a long and lonely life.

He cremated him. He had to stay in Delhi for the duration of the thirteen-day rituals. But he found some solace in the fact that they were all going to move to Mumbai now. Life would finally strike a balance. The whole family would stay together.

When he returned to Mumbai, a car took him directly from the airport to the producer's office. Upon arriving, he discovered that the entire film crew had assembled for a big meeting. Representatives from all departments, including production, direction, costumes, camera, set and more were present. He learned that it was the day of the final script narration. He took out his script and held it in his hands. Everyone was seated inside. The 'healthy' director started …

'As you know, four films about the pre-independence era are being produced. Major production houses are occupied with their respective scripts. But we are confident that no one will have a script like ours.'

Hamlet placed his script on the table nearby and opened it.

'This script has been written after much hard work and research. A significant amount of labour has gone into it. Now, I will request the scriptwriter to perform its first reading in his own voice in front of all the departments.'

Hamlet held the script tightly. He looked at the 'healthy' director, waiting for his cue to start.

'The writer of this script is …' The *thin* writer leaned forward and opened the script to read.

Hamlet was stunned. His hard work of a year and a half was in front of him, but it had someone else's voice and face. His eyes popped.

The reading concluded. Everyone clapped. The gathering dispersed. Everyone parted ways. Hamlet caught up with the 'healthy' director outside.

'Sir.'

'Yes. Tell me, tell me.'

'This script is mine.'

'Have you ever written a screenplay in your life? You brought a play. Is there any connection between my film and Bhagat Singh? This is professional writing we are dealing with here. The processes here are completely different.'

'But I have been working with you for a year and a half.'

'Then take the money for doing that much.' The 'healthy' director quickly looked around. There was no one to be seen.

'Come to my office tomorrow. We can discuss things there.'

'I don't want money. I won't give up my credit.' His face hardened.

'Do you have any agreement? On what basis are you asking for credit?' The director's voice turned harsh in turn.

'You know. Your office people know. Your conscience knows.'

'Discuss this high-spirited issue of conscience in your Delhi. I am giving you a fair deal. Come to the office tomorrow. Take whatever money I am offering. And leave the credit.'

'I will take the credit I deserve!'

'Try. Maybe you will succeed,' he said and left Hamlet behind.

Hamlet stood there, stunned.

That night, he bought a bottle of rum. While drinking that night, the faces of Jiya, his mother and Josh flashed before his eyes.

The next morning, his eyes were bloodshot. After bathing, he went straight to Sambal Bhardwaj's office in Oshiwara, where he saw Nadeem Shah sitting inside. Nadeem had come to get a song for his play recorded. It was a poem by Faiz Ahmad Faiz, composed to music by Sambal and to be sung by Surekha.

'Santap Trivedi!' Nadeem's roar echoed.

'Yes, sir.'

'How come you are here?'

'To write.'

'What?'

'About pre-independence India.'

'Four films set in that era are already being made. For whom are you writing?'

Santap mentioned the director's name. A smile spread on Shah's face.

'Is his *thin* writer still with him?'

'Why?' Hamlet lifted his eyes.

'You won't get the credit.'

'How can I not get it?' Hamlet's voice grew bitter.

'Try it, by all means.'

'You tried it. You didn't get it. Does that mean I won't get it either?' Now Hamlet's voice was harsh and loud, too.

Nadeem remained silent and kept staring at Hamlet. Sambal was speechless and Surekha was frozen. Nadeem was a renowned figure in the industry. Equally well known for his short temper. But Hamlet was not worried. The last year and a half flashed before his eyes, accompanied by the faces of Jiya, his mother and Josh.

'I worked so hard for a year and a half. I put in my blood and sweat. Why won't I receive the credit for it?' His eyes welled up with anger. His throat seemed to be choking.

Nadeem stayed silent. After a moment, he asked, 'What will you do?'

'I will do whatever it takes. If I cannot do anything else, I can at least jump into his office with a bomb tied to my chest.'

Nadeem continued to stare at him. Sambal and Surekha were astonished. Hitesh Sonik remained quietly bent over the recording table.

'I am going to leave.' Hamlet stood up abruptly and stepped outside. No one attempted to stop him.

After coming out, he called up the 'healthy' director.

'Fine. I will meet you in the office at three in the afternoon tomorrow.'

'Comecomecome.' And the phone was hung up.

Hamlet stepped out of Oshiwara. His eyes were red and his face was searing with fury. The rugged and raging Santap Trivedi of Delhi had been jolted awake. He headed straight to the liquor shop.

'Half Signature. One Bisleri too.'

He took half of the whisky and poured it into the Bisleri bottle while standing in a corner. Then, he drank it in big gulps. He hadn't had whisky in a long time, especially not in such a quantity and with such urgency. It hit him hard. In an instant, his thoughts, behaviour, belief, morals and values, everything changed.

'If I must live in the muck, then I will live in the muck and figure out ways to survive here.'

At three o'clock the next day, he was in Seven Bungalows.

The 'healthy' director was waiting for him in his room on the ground floor. Hamlet entered the room.

'Make sure that no one enters this room.' The director instructed no one in particular.

'Yes. Now speakspeakspeak.' The door was latched from outside.

'What?' Hamlet asked.

'Have you had alcohol?' He placed his hand on his nose.

'Not on your father's account, you fatso,' he growled.

'Mind your language,' he shouted.

'I left manners at your Lokhandwala guest house. I am leaving that place. And I'm joining hands with other producers.'

'Which producers?'

'Those who are making films on this subject.'

'Who?'

'There are others as well, who have suddenly developed a taste for reminiscing about that time.'

'What do you mean?'

'It means that I am taking my script, my research and my play to the places where they are needed and respected. Four films are being made about the pre-independence era.'

'You cannot do this. You have heard my script. This will be plagiarism.' He growled.

'Everyone does it.'

'You were working for me!' he screamed.

'Do you have any agreement?' And the director continued to stare at him.

'Is there any evidence that I was working for you?'

'You will be blacklisted in the industry.'

'But I will take you down with me!'

The director was constantly watching him with murderous eyes.

'Whether others' films are made or not, I will make sure yours is not made.'

'Look, listen to me.' He loosened a bit.

'Bye.' Hamlet stood up.

'Looklooklook. The credit for the screenplay has been sent already.' He stood up.

'Where?'

'The writer has locked it under his name.'

'Dialogues? And the play?'

'I will try.'

'I don't have that much time.' And he turned away.

'I am lookinglookinglooking. Listen to me.' He quickly came close to Hamlet.

'It will be done. Believe me.'

'I believed you all this time, you fucker. Tell me, how long should I wait? Until your next plate of bhujia arrives?'

And he took a bottle out of his bag. It was filled with petrol.

'Whatisthiswhatisthiswhatisthis?' The shocked director exclaimed.

Hamlet emptied the entire bottle onto the table while gazing at him with expressionless eyes.

'Whatareyoudoing whatareyoudoing whatareyoudoing?' the director shouted as soon as he smelled petrol.

And then Hamlet took the matchbox out from his pocket.

And then something happened that the film industry still remembers today as the famous—or infamous—Petrol Scandal.

He managed to get the credit at last. Not to the extent that he had thought, but then something was better than nothing. Now, at least the name of his play would appear on the big screen, with special thanks. He was called to the producer's office and an agreement was signed, the documents of which he has kept safely with him to this day. Along with this, he received three and a half lakhs ... no, four and a half lakhs were given. (He had taken a lakh in the name of the Ank Ek group.) Along with this, he also received an air ticket to Delhi.

In Delhi, he hugged Jiya tight and cried buckets that night.

'A year and half worth of hard work is gone. He has ruined everything.'

Jiya kept caressing his head. 'It doesn't matter. Things like these also happen. You have understood Mumbai. What now?'

'What now?'

'What will you do now?' It was a tough one to answer.

He straightened up. He stared into the darkness in front of him.

'What should I do?'

'You tell me.'

'I will go to Mumbai,' he said sternly. 'If I have to live in the muck, then I will learn to survive in the muck. What do you say?'

'I have been saying this for a long time. There is nothing left here. Begin your new innings.' Jiya lovingly caressed his hair.

The next day, he went to 14, Ashoka Road. In those days, rehearsals for Ank

Ek were taking place at the Communist Party's office, where they had been allocated space. He met Pandit and handed him a cheque for one lakh. By that time, he had lost his fire.

'Are you paying me from your own money?'

'I have taken it separately for Ank Ek,' he said in a firm voice.

'Come inside.'

'I am going to leave,' he said as he stepped outside. He understood that their strained relationship would never be the same again. Now, he felt liberated from both Pandit and communism.

He took the next flight and landed in Mumbai.

He had given some money to his family. For Josh, he had bought a children's boxing kit, which was enough to cheer up the little boy. He had not told his mother about the debacle in Mumbai, but upon seeing his face, she had guessed that something untoward had happened.

'If I can't find a house for you today, I will stop calling myself a true blood Old Delhiite,' Manurishi Chaddha had said.

Manurishi Chaddha and Deepak Dobriyal hailed from Delhi, where they were members of Arvind Gaur's Asmita. Both were Hanumans to Santap's Ram.

Finally, he found a house in Mumbai's Model Town. A one-bedroom set. He paid the rent for eleven months, taking comfort in the fact that he would no longer have to wander around at night, hunting for shelter. Having a roof over one's head in Mumbai was very important then and remains so even today.

Hamlet was sitting in his room, lost in thought. No longer did he have a car, nor the guest house in Lokhandwala. Now, he had to struggle like every other common struggler in the world of films. All he had to back himself up with was over twenty years of experience in theatre. He had friends, but they were far away. He realized that everyone had come here to forge their own lives. Each person was

> 'IF YOU COULDN'T CARE FOR YOUR OWN FAMILY, HOW WOULD YOU CARE FOR VIVEKANANDA? ALL THIS ISN'T AS EASY AS YOU THINK. LIFE IS FRIGHTENING! YOU HAVE TO LET GO OF HUNDREDS OF ATTACHMENTS.'

focused solely on their own work. They could share his sorrows over drinks, but they were unable help him otherwise. He had to live his life alone, just like everyone else.

Jiya, amma and Josh were far away from him, in Delhi. They were alone too. He had responsibilities. Amma had lived an empty life until now. Jiya was lonely too, and little Josh, just four years old, was too small to understand the meaning of life.

Now, he recalled his initial inclination: spirituality. He attempted to meditate but suddenly felt a sharp pain in his head. He contacted Vishnoi.

'Leave it at once. Otherwise, the consequences will be fatal. It's unimaginable to practise spirituality while you are tied to alcohol. You always put your hands in flowing poison. You had somehow landed a job, but couldn't even do that properly.'

Hamlet narrated the entire story to him.

'Arre, I don't want to listen to anything, yaar. What are you talking about? Meditation? If you couldn't care for your own family, how would you care for Vivekananda? All this isn't as easy as you think. Life is frightening! You have to let go of hundreds of attachments. First, sort out your life. Then move in this direction.' And he hung up the phone.

He didn't know how to *struggle*. Where should he go? Whom should he talk to? Auditions were not popular at that time. New work was found on the basis of previous work experience. His reputation too had taken a beating because of this pre-independence film. It was a small industry. The news didn't take long to spread. On top of that, the 'healthy' director was there to ruin his meagre chances. His opinion mattered and he milked that authority by defaming Hamlet: 'He is unprofessional, arrogant and ill-mannered.'

'If this situation persists, finding work in the film industry will be difficult,' Sambal Bhardwaj said rather seriously one day.

ANIKET KASHYAP

'I am Aniket Kashyap, sir. I am a filmmaker. I have written and directed Paanch.'

Hamlet had arrived at Prithvi Theatre for the eleven o'clock morning show. The play was titled *Sir Sir Sarla*. It was written and directed by Makarand Deshpande, featuring Aniket Kashyap, Sonali Kulkarni and Rajendra Gupta.

Hamlet and Makarand were both theatre enthusiasts and by that shared affiliation, also friends. Hamlet had heard much about him while in Delhi. He could not decline Makarand's personal invitation.

The play was good. After watching it, he had come to Prithvi Cafe for a cup of tea when a boy approached and took the seat in front of him.

'I am Aniket Kashyap, sir. I am a filmmaker. I have written and directed *Paanch*.'

'Good. You were in the play, right?'

'Ji, sir.' His eyes were brimming with emotion.

'Good.'

'Sir, you …' The boy felt a lump in his throat. 'Please come to my office. It is opposite the Marriott Hotel. North Bombay Housing Society.'

'What will I do there?'

'You can sit there just as you would anywhere else.'

'Arre? Unnecessarily?'

'Not unnecessarily, sir. I have watched *Jab Sheher Hamara Sota Hai* twice, along with your other plays. I was in Delhi during that time. I am from Hansraj College, sir. And you are my …' his voice was caught up again while speaking. '… and you are my God.'

This friendship was destined to last long. After Pandit, this was his most intense and creatively fulfilling relationship.

They were sitting in the North Bombay Housing Society that night. Old Monk was flowing freely.

'I have made a film, sir. *Paanch*. The screening is tomorrow. Will you come to see it? In Town?'

'First of all, stop calling me sir-sir. My name is Santap. Santap Trivedi.'

'Okay, Santap bhai. Will you be coming tomorrow?'

'I will come. Not like I have anything else to do anyway.'

'I am making my next film, *Gulaal*. It would be an incredible honour for me if you could contribute to it.'

'Arre, please don't talk like that, yaar. What can I contribute?'

'Just listen to the script. Share your thoughts. That will be enough for me.'

'Anytime. Just let me know. When would you like me to listen to it?'

The next day, Hamlet watched *Paanch* and really enjoyed the first half.

'It's good. When will you release it?'

'It's stuck because of the producer, sir. But I am going to start working on *Gulaal* right away.'

The next day, Aniket's entire crew gathered in his office. There were young boys and girls, all eager to do anything for Aniket.

The reading of *Gulaal* took place. Aniket read exceptionally well. His voice was deep and his eyes honest. The reading concluded.

'How did you like it, sir?'

'Santap!'

'Sorry. Santap bhai!'

'Yaar, you are unique for sure. You have a contrarian way of thinking. There is something different in your script. It was the same in *Paanch* also.' He stopped. 'What is there in this for me?'

'There is nothing at the moment, Santap bhai. If we manage to find a producer, we will be able to move it forward.'

'Okay.' And he got up.

Then, they both began meeting, mostly over drinks. There was something about Aniket Kashyap. Hamlet had taken a liking to him.

'I have some money, Santap bhai. I am planning to start the shoot. If I can shoot a bit, I will be able to present it to a producer.'

Hamlet could not comprehend all these technicalities. He was so removed from the economics of filmmaking.

'I have thought of using *Kandisa* from Indian Ocean as the film's score.'

'Kandisa' was a huge hit by Indian Ocean. A fantastic title track from their second album.

One day, the two of them were sitting in Aniket's office.

Two music composers arrived. They were struggling to gain a toehold in the industry. They had a tabla and a harmonium with them.

'Yaar, I don't have a requirement right now. My concept of music is different. But if you're here, then go ahead and play something,' Aniket said.

They both started and went along with the same old songs on love and betrayal.

'Okay, I will keep you guys in my mind.'

They were just packing their tabla and harmonium when Santap had a thought.

'One moment. Hand me this harmonium.'

He pushed the harmonium closer to him.

'See, do you want this?' And he started singing—

Yaara o maula ...

The song went on. Aniket kept listening. Then he said, 'Sir, one more, please?' Hamlet sang—

Jab sheher hamara sota hai ...

Aniket sat there, overwhelmed.
'Sir, one more, please?'
'How many will you listen to? I have many. The entire day will not be enough.' He sang once again—

Beedo dooji thali ka lage bada masala man bole chakmak

Aniket kept looking at him, completely enchanted. Then he said, 'Sir, you are doing the music and lyrics for my film. I will give you an advance tomorrow. In cash. Fifty thousand.'

And the news spread everywhere quickly. Aniket had a bad habit of announcing things prematurely.

The next day, he received the advance money, fifty thousand rupees.

He informed Jiya. But he spoke to Aniket the very next day.

'Look, I haven't gotten used to Mumbai yet.'

'What do you mean?'

'Would you mind if I composed these songs while I am in Delhi?'

'I wouldn't mind at all. When would you like to leave? Baggaaaa?' He called out. And his ticket to Delhi was ready. Along with it, a new harmonium.

He flew to Delhi.

The next afternoon, he sat by the fountain in Mandi House with his new harmonium. This was where he had composed all the songs for his plays. There was noise from cars, autorickshaws and buses all around. This place was familiar, the fountain next to Omi's Fruit Chaat on Bhagwan Das Road. His personal haven.

> **HE SAT BY THE FOUNTAIN IN MANDI HOUSE WITH HIS NEW HARMONIUM. THIS WAS WHERE HE HAD COMPOSED ALL THE SONGS FOR HIS PLAYS.**

And sitting there, he started creating music. Lyrics too. He used to compose music while writing.

He improvised a few of his old songs and gave them a new form. Some other songs he composed entirely from scratch.

In seven days, the music for eight songs was ready. He called Aniket in Mumbai.

'The music is ready. When should I come?'

Aniket was not surprised. He was never surprised by anything that Santap said or did.

Hamlet took the very next flight back to Mumbai. And went straight from the airport to the North Bombay Housing Society, in front of the Marriott Hotel.

A bottle of rum was kept in the office. He began to sing.

Aniket sat there, listening intently. Then, he dialled a number.

'Would you like to listen to *Gulaal*'s music? Come to the office if you'd like.' He called countless people and delivered the same message. By eight o'clock in the evening, the office was packed. Aniket was quite popular and had a large circle of friends. People were in awe of his filmmaking calibre, even though none of his films had made it to the screen as yet. That evening, a huge crowd had gathered in his office. They had lost count of how many bottles of Old Monk they had downed. Everyone seemed to be stuck on the same song.

'Once more, Santap bhai.'

And Hamlet would start singing—

आरम्भ है प्रचंड बोले मस्तकों के झुंड,
आज जंग की घड़ी की तुम गुहार दो

The beginning is terrific, the crowd of heads announces
The hour of war is upon us, they herald its coming

The very next day, Hamlet's music for *Gulaal* became the talk of the town. Music for a film which had not even been made yet.

'Santap, let the film get made first. Then celebrate. Aniket's kismet is a bit jinxed,' Sambal had said seriously.

What he had said indeed proved to be true. *Gulaal* was released seven years later.

The first shoot took place in Jaipur. Then, the schedule went for a toss.

When Santap reached Aniket's office, an ominous silence enveloped it. Everyone was sitting quietly with their hands folded.

'What happened?' he asked.

'Sir, we ran out of money. The film has been stopped,' Aniket said.

'Have you shared the rushes of everything that has been filmed so far with the producer?'

'I showed it to him. Everyone says it's an experimental film. It won't work. They have pulled back from the project.'

'Music?'

'Nobody understood it. They said it is heavy. Lyrics also.'

'What will you do now?'

'I will make the next film. The script is ready.'

'You can't find a producer to back this one and you're talking about the next film?'

'The producer for this new one is ready. Mid Day is backing it.'

'What is this film about?'

'Based on a novel by S. Hussain Zaidi. *Black Friday*.'

'The one based on the 1993 bomb blast?'

'Yes, it's the same, sir. Will you write the lyrics for this one?'

'Who is composing the music?'

'Indian Ocean!'

'I will write the lyrics. When do I start?'

Hamlet went on to compose the most profound song of his life—set to the music of Indian Ocean:

अरे रुक जा रे बन्दे,
अरे थम जा रे बन्दे,
कि कुदरत हँस पड़ेगी हो

O man, stop a while
O man, hold on
This universe laughs at you

Aniket was indeed born with bad luck. The film was banned. The case went to court. Santap was again out of work. Unemployed.

PIYUSH MISHRA

A-303 LINK PALACE

'I AM TIRED TODAY. LET'S CHECK OUT THE HOUSE TOMORROW,' JIYA SAID while tossing her luggage into the Model Town house. Little Josh was also nearby. This was the year 2002.

Jiya had left amma with mausi. Mausi lived in R.K. Puram.

'If we have to live here, we will need to buy a house here, won't we? Why don't we start trying for it right now?' Jiya was extremely intelligent and practical.

Tigmanshu Dhulia lived in Goregaon East. He noted that a few buildings were under construction in his neighbourhood. Hamlet and Jiya had gone to see these buildings in various societies and liked one society particularly, Link Palace, where construction was ongoing.

'The society is good. Let's figure out how to shore up the funds to purchase a house here,' Jiya said.

'Check out the two-bedroom, yaar. The three-bedroom is beyond our budget.'

'The three-bedroom faces the Aarey forest. There's plenty of space, which will be convenient for guests as well.'

'Who has the money, Jiya?'

Jiya stared at him for a moment before saying, 'I have saved some money without telling you. We will loan the remaining amount.'

'Who will give us a loan? *Gulaal* has been shelved.'

'Arre, won't you earn more now that you are here in Mumbai?'

'I don't have any work, yaar. I have no hope of finding work in the near future either.'

Jiya explained, 'At this moment, we only need to deposit the booking amount. That much can be managed. After that, we will figure out how to arrange the rest.'

And the booking amount was paid. A-303 Link Palace, Sai Baba Complex, Goregaon East.

Jiya left the next day. Now he had to earn money. Before leaving, she kissed Santap's lips and said, 'Don't worry. If we're unable to pay, we'll sell it. I've done a survey. People live in such odd rooms here. We'll also find a place to live. In the meantime, I will do the backend work to sell the Delhi house. And …' she paused. Her eyes filled with tears. 'Look, please cut back on your drinking. It has become excessive. We still have a long life to live with amma and Josh. Please.'

Life went on. The dreams of working in Mumbai had come crashing down, along with the hope of accomplishing something significant. Everyone here was preoccupied with their own work and no one was concerned about anyone else. Each person had to arrange for their own food and accommodation. Deepak and Manu lived in Itkar Society, sharing their space with many others as well. Strugglers were scattered throughout Mumbai. Vanrai Society, located in front of the Hub in Goregaon East, was where most of the strugglers were clustered. The living conditions there were quite challenging. Their bed and kitchen shared the same room. Commuting was another significant issue. But when they received a call for work, their readiness to troop out was inspiring. Travelling in an autorickshaw was a dream, since affording the fare was not always feasible. Yet, everyone managed to keep living. Somehow.

One day, he was enjoying a drink at Adarsh Bar when Deepak Dobriyal came running up to him.

'Santap bhai, come with me. My father is here from Delhi.'

'Arre! So what will I do?'

'He has come to take me home. He has seen my room. He is saying that it is better to go to Delhi than live like stray dogs here. If nothing has happened here till now, then nothing will happen in the future either.'

'Arre yaar!' He was in a fix. 'What will I tell him?'

'They will only listen to you, Santap bhai. You are the oldest among us and the only one who is a renowned name here from Delhi's theatre circuit. Please, Santap bhai.'

Hamlet arrived at Deepak's home, still confused about how to address the situation. His father calmed down a bit upon seeing him.

'Look! You tell me. Is this a way to live?'

'I won't say much to you, Dobriyal sahab. I'm just asking for one year for him. Please grant him this single year. If he fails after that, you are free to take him with you.'

He finally agreed, but it was with incredible difficulty. Then *Omkara* was released and after that, there was no looking back for Deepak Dobriyal. He never had to return to Delhi.

This was not an isolated case. The same scene played out in everyone's home. People would come to him with their sob stories, and he would lend them his ear. Santap would offer them booze, sit and drink with them.

LIFE WENT ON. THE DREAMS OF WORKING IN MUMBAI HAD COME CRASHING DOWN.

Everyone would forget their sorrows for a while, but life would begin anew the next day.

Everyone in that city was on the lookout for a break.

MAQBOOL

'I will appear for the audition, yaar. I'll do whatever it takes. I need this film.'

'Look, yaar. You won't get money here either because even if you land the role, this will be your first major screen appearance after *Dil Se*. And *Dil Se* was a flop,' Sambal told him gravely.

Sambal Bhardwaj was making *Maqbool*. This was his second film as a director. His first was *Makdee*, a children's film.

Sambal's *Maqbool* was an adaptation of William Shakespeare's *Macbeth* set against Mumbai's underworld. The role was of Banquo, renamed in the Hindi adaptation as Kaka. The cast included Shashi Kapoor, Nadeem Shah and Tabu. Kay Kay Menon was in the titular role of Maqbool.

> 'I WILL APPEAR FOR THE AUDITION, YAAR. I'LL DO WHATEVER IT TAKES. I NEED THIS FILM.'

'Arre, it's a role to die for, yaar. I'll fight tooth and nail for it. You just take my audition.'

'Talk to Honey. He's looking after the casting and the auditions.'

He met Honey Trehan.

'Arre, sir! You will give an audition? What are you saying? What right do I have to give you a role? This is the director's job. Don't forget that you were the one who got me a job with Sambal ji.'

'I really need work, yaar. I have already bought a house.'

And he auditioned for the role. This was the biggest role of his career in cinema so far. The perfect role, to his liking.

William Shakespeare, *Macbeth*, Banquo.

All the pent-up agony inside him burst forth. It had been a while since he had acted. Acting, the passion he had lived for. Acting, the skill he had dedicated thirty years of his life to hone. Acting, the dream for which he had left Delhi and come to Mumbai. This role had everything. Everything that he needed, along with the best co-actors, a great script and an excellent cameraman.

He had auditioned for the role.

Before heading to the studio, he had prayed with his eyes closed. The biggest test for him that day was whether the craft to which he had dedicated his entire life would serve him well. He understood that this city was ruthless and that only good work would lead to more opportunities. It was here that he had to dig for his roots and grow like a tree.

Honey was more nervous than him.

'Sir, please give me the courage to conduct your audition.'

'Stop talking nonsense, yaar. In this city, everyone is only focused on their own work. This isn't Delhi. I've understood this much.' After the audition, he stepped out. Nadeem Shah walked out of the lift and headed inside without even looking at him.

He let out a sigh. Perhaps he was still holding on to that day's anger.

'I'm really worried, yaar. There are issues from the producer's side. Kay Kay is working elsewhere. He has grown a beard. I don't want a beard. Shashi Kapoor ji isn't fitting the role of Abba ji.'

Santap raised his eyes. He was looking at him with curiosity and a question in his gaze.

'I understand the glint in your eyes, yaar. Your audition has reached me. But I cannot take a call until I finish the entire casting process. Ultimately, Nadeem will have the final say in this audition.'

Hamlet's heart skipped a beat. He left the office.

That day, he went to Prithvi. There, he met both Kay Kay and Aniket.

'It's just a matter of a beard, yaar. How can I shave it off now? I'm in the middle of shooting someone else's film.'

'Can't you ask them to wait a little longer? It's just a matter of three months,' Aniket said.

'Sambal is unwilling to budge. Santap will tell you more.' He looked at Santap.

'I don't know, yaar,' he sighed. 'It's difficult to say anything until Sambal's own problem is resolved. My casting is stuck too.'

Casting in Mumbai, particularly for such a role, was a matter of life and death—much like NSD. Actors were willing to sacrifice everything to audition for this film.

'I won't be paid, but life will change for the better. My thirst of a lifetime will be quenched. The role is amazing.' He was speaking to Jiya on the phone in a slurred voice.

'Keep your fingers crossed. I will also pray for you.'

The situation became more complicated. There was no end in sight. Sambal felt worried. And then an explosion happened. Tigmanshu Dhulia organized a press screening for his first film, *Haasil*.

Sambal met Santap outside the press screening venue. His face was beaming.

'Maqbool has been found. Now, Irrfan will take on this role. Abba ji's issue has also been settled. Nadeem suggested Padam Kapoor for this part. He insisted that it is impossible to find a better actor than him anywhere in the country.'

'And the witches? I mean the Pandit-Purohit?'

'Nadeem said he will speak with Som Puri. They will be collaborating on a film after a long time. He has taken it upon himself to persuade Puri sahab for this role.'

A robust cast was ready. Padam Kapoor, Nadeem Shah, Som Puri, Tabu and Irrfan. Banquo—Kaka—remained. Santap looked at Sambal with a pounding heart. Sambal understood the unspoken question in his gaze.

'Meet me in my office tomorrow. Let me think about it through the night. Once I agree, it means the film will not be made without you.'

Santap had a dark night. He dreamt that William Shakespeare was laughing at him and making fun of him.

The next morning, he was in Sambal's office on time.

Sambal looked at him and smiled.

'Don't worry. You are playing Kaka.'

Hamlet felt as if he might collapse right there and immediately start dancing out of joy.

'What are you saying, yaar?'

'Nadeem has said that if I can handle you, then I can take you on. What do you think? Will I be able to handle you?' He smiled.

Hamlet did not utter a word. His eyes moistened.

'Go and prepare for your role. We will conduct a workshop in Matheran—Nadeem will supervise.'

The next day, he drank a lot at his regular joint, the House of Food in Andheri.

He left there sloshed at ten o'clock at night. A car approached from the front, its headlights flashing. 'Abey, get lost, bey ...' A scream followed. And then a loud crash ...

The next day, he was in the hospital.

THE FIRST ANGEL

HE OPENED HIS EYES SLOWLY WHILE LYING ON THE BED. HE COULD HEAR the doctor's voice.

'Thankfully, there is no fracture, and the injury is not serious either. However, you will need to stay in the hospital for three days.'

He deliberately kept the news from Sambal. He could not risk losing his first role. He didn't call Jiya either. It was only a matter of three days. He would manage, regardless.

And it was here that he met his first angel, Evan Rebello.

'I had come to the alcoholic ward to see someone. I found out that you were admitted here. So I came to see you. Did this accident happen after drinking alcohol?'

Hamlet disliked this unsolicited conversation. It was intrusive and too personal. 'Yes. So?'

'My name is Evan Rebello. I am a recovering alcoholic. Do you drink too much?'

'I did yesterday. But how does it matter to you?'

'I am concerned about every single alcoholic,' he said calmly. 'Once you are out of this place, come and see me. I live in Malad West.' He handed Hamlet his card. Hamlet took it quite reluctantly.

'You might be thinking that I am attaching myself to you unnecessarily or out of force. But if you drink every day and consume too much alcohol, then you have fallen victim to the most dangerous disease in the world: alcoholism. According to the World Health Organization, this is the deadliest disease globally, even worse than cancer and heart disease. Doctors do not have a cure for alcoholism. Its medical reference number is A-303. If you consider it appropriate, please get in touch with me. Have a good day.' He turned and left. Hamlet realized that there was no faff in what he spoke. Every word was measured.

PIYUSH MISHRA

DEEPER INTO ALCOHOLISM

The workshops for *Maqbool* started. Then the shooting, too.

In the middle of the shoot, Jiya landed in Mumbai on 28 March 2003. With bag and baggage. Amma and Josh in tow. The house in Delhi had been sold. The instalments for the new house had been arranged, but it was still under construction. For the interim period, they had moved to a one-room flat in Sai Baba Complex—B-3, Sai Milan.

Hamlet realized that his drinking was indeed out of control. It was abnormal.

He would not remain the same person after drinking. He would change. Before drinking, he was controlled and behaved like a normal person. But after having the first peg itself, his psyche would transform and his thoughts would change. He noticed others drinking and everyone seemed to be enjoying themselves. Their humour would be heightened. They would be having fun. However, for him the feeling of drunkenness was different.

Once, after a drinking session, he called Dr Dinesh Sharma in Delhi. He was an ardent audience member from his theatre days and also a respected friend.

The next day, he received a call from the doctor sahab. 'What wrong have I done to you that you abused me so much on the phone? How much older am I than you? My wife was sitting next to me and listening to everything.'

Hamlet had no memory of the event.

In the mornings, he would receive calls from girls. They would all be crying.

'We respect you so much, Santap sir. Don't make such dirty calls to us. Please.'

Hamlet would scratch his head. 'What is happening to me?'

He vomited after drinking alcohol in someone's room. He urinated in someone else's living room. Everyone respected him ... but gradually, everyone had started objecting to his behaviour.

Despite all this, his acting skills were flourishing anew. He had been given the opportunity to work with the finest actors in India.

Nadeem and Som were old friends. They

> **HE VOMITED AFTER DRINKING ALCOHOL IN SOMEONE'S ROOM. HE URINATED IN SOMEONE ELSE'S LIVING ROOM. EVERYONE RESPECTED HIM ... BUT GRADUALLY, EVERYONE HAD STARTED OBJECTING TO HIS BEHAVIOUR.**

had found a chance to collaborate for a film again after a long time and that too in a city like Bhopal. (*Maqbool* was filmed entirely in Bhopal.) Moreover, both were terrific actors.

Tabu was regarded as a profound and serious actress in cinema. She had proved her acting mettle in *Maachis*.

Padam Kapoor was a veteran actor from NSD. *Maqbool* gave him a more prominent role alongside Nadeem and Som for the first time. He was eager to prove himself.

Irrfan was playing the lead role in a film for the first time in his life and that too alongside Tabu. This also marked his first significant role after arriving in Mumbai. It was a do-or-die situation for him.

Overall, *Maqbool* was a World Cup where every team was desperate to win.

But Hamlet's personality was becoming weaker every day. Alcohol was feasting on him.

Nadeem had called him an 'absolute bastard' with a venomous growl.

'I will remember that.'

And he always remembered that.

Padam Kapoor asked him, 'You do everything—music, lyrics, song, script and acting?'

'Ji, sir. In fact, I am doing it all in *Gulaal*.'

'Yaar, have you done everything in your life?' His voice was tinged with sarcasm. A mocking smile spread across the faces of those who were listening to this conversation.

Despite the truth in his words, he had not been able to prove his skills until then. In the early 2000s, *Gulaal* still had a long way to go. And anyway, it was difficult for everyone to believe the words of a drunkard.

He was no longer taken seriously by the film fraternity. His personality had dwindled. His words felt hollow.

Maqbool was filmed, and then released on 30 January 2004. It was well received.

His performance received a great deal of appreciation. However, surprisingly, the significant figures behind the making of the film did not even acknowledge his contribution. *Maqbool* was a blank for him.

JAI ARRIVED

'Why do I drink so much?'

He was sitting in Evan Rebello's flat in Malad.

'Because it's a disease, Santap bhai. Alcoholism. A mental strain and physical allergy. Twenty out of every hundred people are alcoholics and, sadly, those poor souls often don't even realize it. We drink every day, thinking that today we will drink less. And after drinking, we regret why we had so much to drink.'

'Reason?'

'I don't know the reason. Medical science doesn't understand it fully. Research is ongoing. Doctors don't specialize in this domain because it doesn't offer them a lot of income. An alcoholic approaches them after losing everything. No one considers an alcoholic to be sick. Instead, everyone sees them as simply antisocial. Indeed, the alcoholic is an object of pity, because he himself does not understand why he drinks so much.'

> 'I WILL DO ANYTHING, YAAR. I JUST DON'T WANT THIS ALCOHOL ANYMORE.'

'Any solution?'

'There is. Spirituality. If you can trust me, then go ahead. Otherwise, death by drinking is certain. There are only two ends to this. Either an early death or a slow descent into madness.'

Hamlet recalled his behaviour after drinking.

'I have every reason to live, my friend Evan. I want to live. Free me from this disease.' Tears filled his eyes.

Evan placed his hand on Hamlet's.

'The programme is simple enough, Santap bhai. But don't think it is easy. You will need to sacrifice everything. Thoughts that pervade your mind right now, your current mindset and your current beliefs ... A completely new person will emerge within you. Are you willing to try?'

'I will do anything, yaar. I just don't want this alcohol anymore.'

'Meet me tomorrow. I will take you somewhere.'

The very next day, Hamlet received an offer from Yash Raj Films.

'Shaad Ali is making a film. *Jhoom Barabar Jhoom*! The shoot is in London. You have to fly tomorrow. What do you think?'

And Hamlet flew to London the very next day.

The same year, little Jai was born.

Shaad was Mani Ratnam's assistant during *Dil Se*. He got along very well with Hamlet. In *Jhoom Barabar Jhoom* he had been offered a chance to share screen space with Abhishek Bachchan and Preity Zinta. Amitabh Bachchan was in the role of the sutradhar—narrator.

The shoot went well. But Evan Rebello's words kept echoing in his mind all the time.

Upon his return from London, he learned that he was writing another Yash Raj film. It was Madhuri Dixit's comeback, *Aaja Nachle*. The climax of the film required an opera based on the legend of Laila–Majnu—he wrote and composed the sequence in just four days.

The third film was brought to him by Samar Bajpayee. 'This is Amrit Sagar, Ramanand Sagar's grandson. He has returned after studying at the New York School of Film and is making his first film, *1971*. You have to write the story, screenplay and dialogues.'

The film revolved around Indian soldiers from Bangladesh who had been imprisoned in Pakistan. In the film, some soldiers attempt to escape. Despite reaching the border of India, however, none of them succeeds in passing through. Samar Bajpayee was playing the lead role in the film.

This was one of the best scripts of his life, but the film did not receive a proper theatrical release—no good cinema halls were arranged.

All three films tanked. Hamlet was devastated by the consecutive setbacks. And then that same year, his mother passed away. This was in 2007.

'My name is Sandeep and I am an alcoholic. I started drinking for fun a long time ago. Over time, this addiction grew so much that now I am disgusted by my life.'

He was in a classroom in the Four Bungalows church. There were benches and tables. One person chaired the session while fifteen to twenty people sat around him. After Sandeep, another person had stood up to speak.

Hamlet himself was stunned. He felt as though someone else was narrating his own story. This is where he met Raj bhai.

'These meetings are held almost every day across Mumbai. Attend them. The rest of the programme will also be explained to you soon,' Raj bhai said.

And then it was as if a miracle happened.

A loud and thunderous call came, from Aniket Kashyap.

'*Gulaal* is finally being made, Santap bhai! We have found a producer. Get ready to come to Jaipur.'

And *Gulaal* was made. And it was made exceptionally well. *Gulaal* provided him with everything he had been looking for.

He wrote the lyrics, composed the music, acted, sang and also crafted his own dialogues in *Gulaal*. *Gulaal* was nothing less than a dream for him.

He had been given an all-access licence to vent his frustrations of many years.

He invested everything in *Gulaal*. All his creativity, all his art and all his craft.

He would go to Sambal's studio. The songs were to be recorded there.

Two songs were in Surekha's voice. He sang three others. One was by Swanand Kirkire, one by Indian Ocean and one by Shilpa Rao. Hitesh Sonik was conducting the music.

'Yaar, I can't sing in front of a microphone. You should find someone else to sing.' The recording was in progress.

'Only you will sing, Santap bhai. No one will be able to sing this better than you. Just try to befriend the microphone once,' Hitesh said.

And he was singing:

Yeh duniya agar mil bhi jaaye toh kya hai?

Two songs were recorded in Surekha's sonorous voice, laced with its characteristic *khanak*. Aniket used to call one of them a political *mujra*.

राणा जी म्हारे गुस्से में आएँ ऐसो बल खाएँ
अगिया बरसाएँ घबराए म्हारो चैन।

My beloved Rana ji, he fumes and twists in anger
Rains fire on me; my heart whimpers in fear

The music was ready. Hitesh had done a great job.

Santap was enraptured while shooting in Jaipur. He forgot himself while playing Prithvi. He felt that his theatre days were back.

Indeed *Gulaal* epitomized theatre. Theatre-like moments, theatre-like atmosphere and theatre-like characters. And to top it all, Aniket's enthusiastic direction.

Aniket was a madcap director. And extremely daring.

'Why should we explain everything to the audience? It is their duty to use their own understanding. You will see! This character will be a hit.'

He was referring to the character of Ardhanarishvara, who, painted in many colours, moved-wandered-shadowed Hamlet's character Prithvi Bana in the film. That was the one character people asked about the most afterwards.

Gulaal was released on 13 March 2009. 'Aarambh Hai Prachand' became a smashing success, not only in India but also internationally. Unfortunately, the film proved to be a dud at the box office, but it took the internet by storm. *Gulaal*'s songs played on every college campus. People were swaying to 'Beedo'. Hamlet found everything he had sought for so long in Mumbai. Stardom, recognition and acceptance.

And he decided to celebrate it in America with his family.

BRAIN STROKE

Jiya's brother Sanjay lived in the US and it was here that an incident occurred, which strengthened Hamlet's faith in spirituality.

His family had already left; he was alone at home. He had a flight scheduled for the night of 18 May. While he was at home, he had begun to sense that something strange was happening to him.

On the day of his departure, he arrived at the airport and discovered he couldn't even fill out the immigration form properly. The right side of his body felt lighter than the left.

His flight took off. He was staggering while going to the toilet.

His flight stopped in Abu Dhabi for a four-hour layover. He found it difficult to even walk through the airport.

His flight arrived in America after twenty-four hours. His legs wobbled as he deboarded the plane. He felt as if the right side of his body had ceased to exist—as if it had vanished.

Jiya was overjoyed to see him. But then was immediately alarmed to see his condition up close. Still, she did not suspect anything amiss. Everyone was basking in the joy of the newfound success.

The next twenty-four hours also passed.

The fame of *Gulaal* had reached all the way to America as well. Thanks to the rage about the film on the internet. People started coming to meet him. One of them was Dr Sudhir.

The doctor looked at Hamlet carefully.

'Take him to the hospital. The symptoms don't look good.'

He was rushed to Jimmy Collins Hospital, where the doctors discovered that he had suffered a brain stroke forty-eight hours ago. In the time since then, his condition had deteriorated a lot. He remained in the hospital for three days. His treatment continued and the doctors concluded that the stroke was serious. Half of his body had become useless. And he would never be able to walk or speak properly. The biggest shock for him was the realization that he would never be able to act again.

'I will undergo physiotherapy, doctor. I still have a lot of work to do,' he said, almost sobbing in his raspy voice.

'I apologize, gentleman. This cannot be cured.'

He returned from America as a disabled person.

Upon his return, he consulted a local hospital in Bombay.

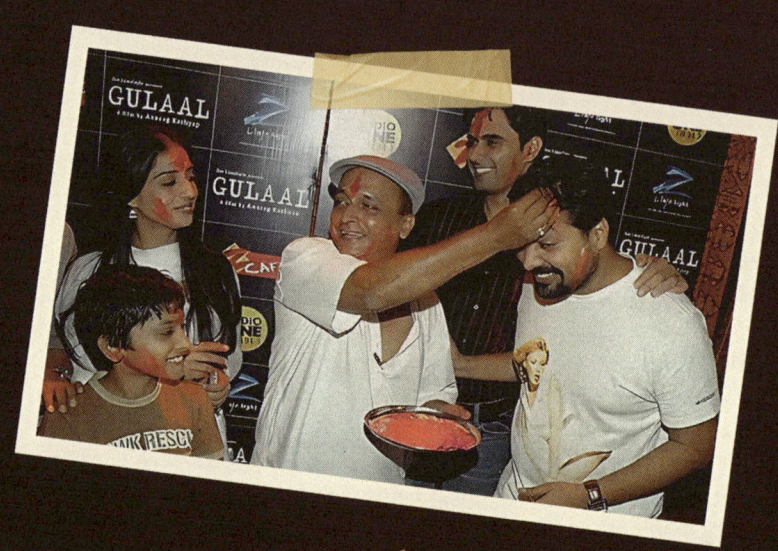

'Now you won't even be able to speak properly. Let alone walk on your own.'

He was sitting quietly in his study in A-303 Link Palace. The world and his life in it seemed to have come to a tragic end. Now he would have to sit in a chair for the rest of his life.

THE SECOND ANGEL

'There are many energies around us that we may not fully understand. You should consider pranic healing. There is a doctor at the Gokuldham Medical Centre. Her name is Anju. I have a personal rapport with her. Perhaps something good will come of it,' Sambal Bhardwaj said.

He underwent pranic healing for a month. Anju di would have him lie down in front of her and gesture with her hands in the air. She would make some indistinct sounds with her mouth. He often drifted off to sleep during the process.

After a month, he was back on his feet. He was walking, talking and waiting for the shooting of *Gangs of Wasseypur* to start. Aniket Kashyap's next film.

The episode made him realize that life is more than what we see with our own eyes. What we cannot understand, we label as a miracle. We often forget that miracles also occur in this world itself.

'Go for Vipassana. You will find relief in it,' Vishnoi said on the phone.

And he enrolled in a ten-day Vipassana camp in Igatpuri, where he met his second spiritual guru. Shri Laxminarayan Goenka.

When he returned from the Vipassana centre, he was a different man altogether, ready to take life head-on once again.

'Will you do my film, Santap bhai?'

Imtiaz Ali asked him this at the Barista in Seven Bungalows.

'But I am working on *Gangs of Wasseypur*.'

'That will be completed later. Mine will be ready before that.'

Imtiaz Ali was an old friend of Ank Ek, and a fan of Hamlet's.

'What is the name of your film?'

'*Rockstar*.'

'Who else is working on this one?'

'Ranbir Kapoor.'

This friendship also lasted long.

Eventually, he found that he was nearly addicted to Vipassana meditation.

Propounded by the Gautam Buddha, Vipassana was a method of meditation, which is also mentioned in the *Rigveda*. This knowledge had been lost for a while. Then Shri Satyanarayan Goenka brought it to India from Burma. Since then, it has been quite popular in India. By practising Vipassana, one's internal disorders begin to diminish. We are all afflicted by two things fundamentally—excessive attachment and excessive hatred. In other words, craving and aversion. Both issues often fade when we gain control of our breath.

> **WE ARE ALL AFFLICTED BY TWO THINGS FUNDAMENTALLY—EXCESSIVE ATTACHMENT AND EXCESSIVE HATRED. IN OTHER WORDS, CRAVING AND AVERSION.**

Alcohol formed the core of his excessive attachment. He began practising Vipassana and sitting through long meditation sessions. Gradually, relief transpired. His fear began to fade away quite unexpectedly.

Evan said, 'Now go to Raj bhai, Santap bhai.'

'Take a pen and paper. List all the sins you have committed in your life. In black and white. Do not hesitate. Every sin. Those hidden things you do not want to confess even to yourself. The ones no one else knows except you. If you have touched a small girl's body, then blurt it out on the paper. If you have ever beaten your wife, then write about that too. Make a comprehensive list. The rest we will discuss later,' Raj bhai said.

He made the list and took it to Raj bhai. Raj bhai read it and tore it up. 'I said *every single thing*. Clean every corner of your heart. Come clean on paper. Be naked, shameless and brutal, and vomit all of it out of your system. Nothing should remain inside you. This is the programme. Have you ever prayed?' he growled.

'I used to sit and pray at times.'

'Pray. Not to god, but to a higher power beyond yourself. Visualize it. Speak to it. It will happen. It will surely happen. That higher power will help.'

Hamlet started praying. It felt weird at first.

'I am unable to do it.'

'Have you made a list? Of the people you've hurt?'

'I am making one.'

'There are so many obstacles between us and our higher power. There is so much trash in between. First and foremost, clear this filth. Only then will your prayers be heard.'

Hamlet began to make a list and soon realized that this exercise was slowly driving him crazy. Had he really done all of these horrific things? And all these wrongdoings were buried inside him? He scratched his wounds. Scraped and rubbed hard at them. He hid nothing. He blurted out everything. The list included every girl he had slept with. Every person he had betrayed. Every individual he was angry with.

The list was ready.

And after completing it, he felt disgusted with himself. He was troubled by so many deplorable ailments. So hateful, damnable, *disgusting*.

But there was at least one upside. The accumulated muck inside him had been spilled out of his being. The wounds had been burst open. He had started to feel lighter already, and was determined to complete the programme. He went to Raj bhai again with the list.

'Okay. Now, share all of this with someone respectable you know. Don't hide anything. You will find relief right away.'

Hamlet was stunned.

'But these are my secrets. This is me, the real me. I would not want to share these things with myself. How can I share them with anyone else?'

'You will have to tell them. If you want relief.'

Hamlet remained silent. Then he said, 'Who could be more respectable than you? Let me tell you.'

'Alcohol is merely a symptom. The true disease lies deeper within you. It's a spiritual disorder. Address it, and everything will be fine.'

And Hamlet began reading out his list. And he kept going at it. Raj bhai listened attentively to him. Hamlet realized that he was himself responsible for most of his misdeeds.

Gradually, the memory of Nadeem Shah's 'absolute bastard' faded. Sambal's omission of his name in the promotion of *Maqbool* melted away. The 'healthy' director denying him his rightful credit for the film he wrote began to disappear. And he realized he was crying uncontrollably. He wiped his tears.

> 'ALCOHOL IS MERELY A SYMPTOM. THE TRUE DISEASE LIES DEEPER WITHIN YOU. IT'S A SPIRITUAL DISORDER. ADDRESS IT, AND EVERYTHING WILL BE FINE.'

Raj bhai was silent. Then he said, 'Come now. You already have the list. Apologize to everyone you have hurt or troubled. For now, the programme ends here.'

Hamlet stood there silently, listening intently.

'Strive to live your life anew without harbouring ill will towards anyone. And remember, these disorders will resurface. There is a lot more of life ahead for you. You will have to make this purging an annual event. Keep your inner self pure. Life will stay balanced.'

When Hamlet returned home, he was flying in the air.

Rockstar happened. He found a friend in Ranbir.

And after that, *Gangs of Wasseypur* took him over the moon and beyond. The film was a huge success. So was his role.

One night, he wrapped his arms around Jiya. Jiya caressed his head. Then smiled.

'Are you very happy?'

'I feel very happy. Everything feels good. There were so many wonderful people around me. I was unnecessarily holding on to anger towards everyone.'

'Who are you talking about?'

'People around me. Sambal gave me a new life. Nadeem gets angry, but if you look closely, he doesn't do anything too damaging. Which is fine. Every time I ask him questions about acting, he responds. Manurishi and Deepak are ready to sacrifice their lives for me. Samar ... he got me such a big film to write. What if that film flopped? And Aniket, well he has given me everything.'

'Is this the result of your going to Raj bhai?'

'And Evan Rebello. They are saintly souls. Such people can only be found by luck.'

'These days, you are drinking in moderation. As long as it stays under control like this, I will have no objections.'

'You have endured a lot. It's a blessing that the children were spared from witnessing that side of me. Now, I am ready to repose faith in life once again.' Just then, his mobile rang. He answered the call.

'Hello.'

> **'I AM READY TO REPOSE FAITH IN LIFE ONCE AGAIN.'**

There was silence on the other side. He spoke again—'Hello.'

After a moment of silence, a voice came from the other side—'It's me.'

Hamlet was stunned. The voice was familiar.

'Sangini?' He had nearly forgotten how to speak.

'How are you?'

'I ...' He could not muster the words. 'How are you? Where are you?' The person on the other end had probably smiled.

'I am fine.'

'How did you get my number?'

'You are not a common man anymore. I have watched *Maqbool*. *Gulaal* too. And *Gangs of Wasseypur*.'

Hamlet was silent at first. Then he spoke.

'How are you?'

'I'm fine. Ramakant Vishnoi's niece is getting married in Gwalior. I'm coming, will you also join?'

He stayed silent for a moment.

'I am coming.'

'Okay. See you.' And she hung up.

He put the phone down, bewildered. Jiya asked him—'Who was it?'

'Sangini.'

'Arre, how is she? Where is she?'

'She is coming to Gwalior for Ramakant's niece's wedding. She has invited me to join her there as well.'

'Then go. Convey my regards.'

Santap stared at her. Then he asked her, 'Don't you feel bad?'

'What?'

'You know my feelings towards her.'

'I knew about your attraction towards Urvashi too. And in her case, I know it went beyond attraction.'

Hamlet looked at her with his eyes wide, alarmed.

'You didn't come home at night back then. I had investigated. You had started living with her.' She spoke in a flat voice. Hamlet maintained his silence.

'A woman's heart is a treasury of secrets. If you peek into it, you will discover the depths of the ocean. I had no objections then and I have none now.'

'I did not share the same relationship with Sangini.'

'I understand. There's no need to explain. Relationships shouldn't need explanations. Doing so diminishes their significance. When should I book the tickets?'

And he was aboard the next flight to Gwalior.

LONG-LOST MEMORIES

Rinku's wedding arrangements were made in a dharamshala in front of Vishnoi's house in Didwana Oli.

All day, the place buzzed with a flurry of wedding-related activities. In the evening, Sangini said, 'Now we will leave, Ramakant.'

'Where?'

'Arre, home.' Sangini laughed. 'We can't stay here forever.'

'Will Santap also come along?'

'Of course! she laughed.

They stepped out of the venue. The same traffic in Sarafa Bazar. Tempos, autorickshaws, scooters. It was seven o'clock in the evening. Dusk had fallen.

They started walking towards Gast Ka Tazia.

'Where are you staying?'

'At Vrinda's place. And you?'

'City Centre. At Central Park Hotel.'

Both were walking.

'Gwalior has changed a lot.'

'But you are the same as before. How is Jiya?'

'You know about Jiya?'

'About Josh and Jai too. Now, nothing about you is private. Everything is available in the newspapers.'

Both were silent. They had crossed Gast Ka Tazia.

'How is your mother? And Chandni?'

'Mother passed away. Chandni got married. We are meeting after twenty-five years,' she spoke in a flat voice, 'I teach at an NGO. I live with a few children. Some plants and trees, a cat and a puppy that I have just adopted, and an empty house.'

Her voice seemed to be coming from a distance while saying this.

> 'I REMEMBER EVERY MOMENT SPENT WITH YOU. BUT THE FURTHER YOU LOOK AT A MEMORY FROM, THE BETTER IT APPEARS.'

'I did not marry. Vishwas got divorced. Prabha separated from him. He tried to propose again, but by then a lot of time had passed. I decided that life would remain like this. The whole day is spent with the children. Then it is evening and I return to my room. Some old memories stay with me and I relive them. Then I eat and sleep. The next morning, the same old routine. Is this what you wanted to know?'

'You have become a little bitter.'

'I have not become bitter. I have accepted life as it is. And now the memories do not come to haunt my mind that much.' Her voice seemed to have drowned.

'Don't you miss me?'

'Of course, I do. I remember every moment spent with you. But the further you look at a memory from, the better it appears. Isn't it?'

The question was unfinished, and then she asked:

'Have you cut down on your drinking or not?'

'Did Vishnoi tell you?'

'Now I know everything about you. Reduce alcohol. You still have a long life ahead.'

'Give me your Bhilai address. I will come.'

'What will you achieve by coming? I have retreated into myself. I will not come out.'

They had crossed Patankar Market.

'You have my phone number. You can call me sometimes. Anyway, I don't have much to talk about now.'

They had reached Ghoda Chowk.

'You must be wondering why I haven't giggled yet. I've locked that giggle in a box and have tied it with the pallu of my sari. Whenever I need it, I open the box, just as I am going to do right now.' And she giggled aloud. But it was hollow.

> 'I MISSED YOU A LOT. BUT IT WAS EQUALLY IMPORTANT FOR ME TO FORGET YOU. MEMORY HURTS A LOT WHEN YOU ARE TOO CLOSE TO IT.'

They had reached Vrinda's house. It was eight o'clock in the evening. It was darker now.

They stood beneath the house. Santap recalled the days when he used to ride with her back to her home on his bicycle.

She turned. Her face was hidden in the darkness. Then her lips moved.

'Life is not always the same. I have learned this from life itself. To meet someone and be parted from them is the rule of the world. Embrace this rule. No sorrow will approach you. No grief will touch you,' but her voice choked. 'I missed you a lot. But it was equally important for me to forget you. Memory hurts a lot when you are too close to it.' Her voice trembled. 'Live your life. Achieve fame. I will watch you from a distance and cherish the memories we shared. I'll leave now.'

She turned and kept climbing the stairs of the house.

Hamlet stood there. The darkness had engulfed the surroundings. He moved then, turned and began to walk. Suddenly, he remembered everything. A knot rose in his throat. He wiped his eyes and shouted, 'Auto!'

'How was the wedding?' Jiya asked as she opened the door.

'All okay!' He came in, kept the luggage aside and sat on the sofa.

'What's the matter? Are you feeling okay?'

He hugged Jiya tightly, his eyes welling up.

'What's the matter? Did you talk to Sangini?' Jiya turned his face towards her.

'Nothing,' he said, wiping his eyes. 'Vishnoi was very happy. Told me you are on the right path. You will find peace now.'

'Did you bring a mantra from him?' Jiya laughed, sensing Vishnoi's spiritual knowledge.

'The mantra is that I have recognized my life at last. Have Josh and Jai gone to school?'

'Yes.' Suddenly, she was startled. 'Hitesh called. He asked me to ask you to call him immediately.'

He dialled the number. Hitesh's voice came from the other end.

'Santap bhai, will you sing "Husna" for me? For Coke Studio Season 2?'

'Arre, there will be a live recording there. I am afraid of live recording.'

'Arre, you have already done *Gulaal*. You have already sung "Ik Bagal". Now what's there to fear? I will be there, anyway. I am doing the music programming as well.'

Hamlet stayed silent for a moment. Then he replied, 'Alright. But all the responsibility will fall on you.'

'You don't know anything about your voice.'

He didn't know that this song would take him to the remotest corners of the world.

A year later, Hitesh called again.

'One more. This time, "Ghar". This one's for Coke Studio Season 3.'

He also sang 'Ghar'. What happened next is not known.

Hamlet pauses here, takes a breath. He has travelled far and lived a long life. Now, he needs to rest.

And so, Hamlet concludes his story. Anyway, it has become quite lengthy already.

PIYUSH MISHRA

AND FINALLY: THE PRESENT

Imtiaz Ali reached out to him.
  'I am doing another film. *Tamasha*.'
  'What do you want me to do?'
  'The role of an eighty-year-old man.'
  'Yaar, don't get me typecast.'
  'No one can typecast you. You do diverse roles.'

His lust for diverse roles has either been satiated or is being satiated. Be it *Matrubhoomi* or *Maqbool*; *Rockstar* or *Tamasha*; *Gulaal* or *Gangs of Wasseypur*; *Tere Bin Laden* or *The Shaukeens*; *Revolver Rani*, *Happy Bhaag Jayegi*, or *Pink*. Doing diverse roles had always been his wish and his goal.

While working with India's—and perhaps the last century's—greatest actor, Amitabh Bachchan, Hamlet had the opportunity to observe him up close. What a brilliant and dynamic personality he possesses. So much is hidden within the lean, six-foot-tall Bachchan sahab.

See, Robert De Niro, I can shake hands with you now. Many moons ago in Gwalior, I changed my name from Priyansh Sharma to Santap Trivedi. I had a burning desire that someday I would be able to look into your eyes and talk to you. Today, in your own land, America, in your own language, English, with actors from your own community, despite being the only Indian in the group, I am playing the lead role.

He did *Playback Singer* in Los Angeles.

Nadeem Shah does not respond well to disagreements even today. He enjoys intimidating others. However, Hamlet is no longer afraid of him. His fear has nearly dissipated, thanks to Vipassana.

ACTING IS THAT GRAVITATIONAL FORCE UPON WHICH NOT NEWTON BUT EINSTEIN APPLIES. ACTING IS A BATTLE IN WHICH BOTH SIDES WIN.

OTT platforms have arrived on the scene. Invitations are pouring in. He has appeared in *Illegal*, *Matsya Kaand*, *Salt City* and *Anarchy*. All diverse roles. And he will continue.

Acting is not a force but a field. The actor reigns supreme. He does not need a co-actor to react to his actions. Both action and reaction stem from within the actor. Solo acting serves as living proof of this idea. Acting is that gravitational force upon which not Newton but Einstein applies.

Acting is a battle in which both sides win.

Acting is *with* your co-actor ... not *against* them.

No profession in the world allows one to make money more quickly than acting in cinema, as long as the person knows how to ace the game.

Nadeem had once said, 'An actor should never shed tears on stage.'

Hamlet does not agree.

Nadeem had also said, 'While delivering dialogues, we often forget to take a breath in between. This spoils the speech.'

Hamlet agrees. His speech has become quite good now.

Pandit had said, 'Change your attitude in every dialogue. This will allow you to perform longer.'

Hamlet has done it. Today, he is performing for longer periods.

Today, there is no dearth of money. He can live comfortably. Now, he will only do what he desires.

He enjoys visiting small towns. There, he meets with local theatre groups. He inquires about their activities and discusses acting with the members. His heart flourishes when he conducts theatre workshops.

He is a regular acting instructor at the M.P. School of Drama. The National School of Drama does not give a fuck about him. However, each year he diligently hosts a party for the first-year students there. The second- and third-year students invite themselves on their own to drink excessively.

All of the songs he wrote for the stage have been published in the collection *Mere Manch Ki Sargam*. Another collection of his poems and shers has been published too. *Kuchh Ishq Kiya Kuchh Kaam Kiya*. Many of his old plays have

been published as well.

He has taken up *Gagan Damama Bajyo* with the Tamboo banner. His theatrical productions have been quite successful.

He has found a valuable and reliable friend in his manager, Rahul Gandhi, and a close advisor in Nishant Agarwal—they manage his professional life very well.

He has formed his own band, Ballimaaraan. There is no better way to honour Ghalib sahab and Delhi.

He is now going on tour to Europe with his band.

One day, Jiya had cried a lot.

'One should always marry according to their parents' wish and consent.'

Today, she reigns as the queen of his house. 'The Undisputed Queen'.

Marathe had said—'You cannot stay with someone for long.'

'Look, I'm still with Jiya.'

'Not because of anything you did, this is because of her graciousness, you fucker.' And Marathe had laughed out loud.

Today, he has control over his alcohol. Raj bhai was right. Alcohol is just a symptom. The root cause of this disease lies somewhere else. A spiritual disorder. He is trying to put it in order for himself.

Josh and Jai are growing up as good kids. Hamlet wishes them the best in their lives always.

Vishnoi is not here today. He left this world during the pandemic. Pravesh and Evan Rebello had already departed before him, but all of them gave Hamlet a lot. He thanks them all, every day.

Today, he visits Gwalior often. He likes Gwalior a lot. The old memories have faded away. Santosh Gupta, Arvind Bhadauria and Jaiveer Singh Yadav take great care of him.

He wishes to relive the experience he had in front of the convent school once. It hasn't happened again as yet, but it will. He remains hopeful.

His curiosity about himself has diminished, as has his restlessness. Today, his mind is balanced. It no longer runs away from him. Nor does he entertain negative thoughts about anyone. Now, he has begun to understand life a little better. He has rediscovered his personality, which he had lost in his childhood or perhaps in a past life. He is immensely satisfied with this rediscovery.

He remembers Pandit, from a distance. He remembers Sangini, up close. Living alone somewhere with her memories for company.

He regularly calls some friends. Dr Dinesh Sharma, Ajit Lahane (Marathe), Prashant Dubey (Pramad Dubey), Raj Bharat, Desai sahab, Mukesh Chhabra, Dr Vivek Shukla, Arun Kalra, Sai Kabir, Mitul Dixit, Rabia Naziki, J.B. Singh,

Nikhil Verma, Arvind Babbal, Ritu (Reva), Abha Narayan Lamba, Bhavna Upadhyay and the other Tamboo companions. Old times, old memories.

Hamlet has written many scripts. *The Legend of Bhagat Singh*, *Agneepath*, *Yahan*, *Shuddhi*, *Ghajini*, *Shamshera*.

And songs too.

Surekha Bhardwaj keeps telling him about new ways of doing riyaaz.

He still doesn't understand communism. The Russian Revolution occurred in 1918. Czar Nicholas II, his wife Alexandra, and all five children were imprisoned. Two of the children were very young. A meeting of the Bolshevik Party (which later came to be known as the Communist Party) was held to decide whether only the Czar should be executed or his entire family. In the end, the Czar and his entire family were killed—brutally stabbed with bayonets. And these communists claim Sardar Bhagat Singh to be their comrade—calling him one of their own—who regretted killing Superintendent Sanders all his life. Revolution comes not with ammunition but with ideas. In fact, Bhagat Singh deliberately threw a bomb in the assembly at a spot where there was no one present. Yet, the images of Sardar Bhagat Singh Sandhu, Sukhdev Thapar, Shivaram Hari Rajguru, Batukeshwar Dutt and Pandit Chandra Shekhar Azad Tiwari are displayed prominently in every communist party office.

Today Hamlet has received a letter from Urvashi Thakur.

> Sir,
> I cannot write everything in an SMS, which is why I am sending a letter. I am in Dharamshala, Himachal Pradesh, where I meditate in the refuge of Lord Buddha. You can refer to me as a Buddhist nun as well.
>
> There is peace now. I don't know how long it will last. I lose myself while roaming in the valleys here. Sometimes, when I think of Delhi, I suddenly remember you and the days spent with you. And I remember watching your performance in *An Evening with Santap Trivedi*. I wish I could fly and be near you in an instant, but this mind must be kept on a leash. It is the mind that creates problems.
>
> I pray in the morning and the evening. I live in the hope of achieving a cycle of simple living and high thinking. Old habits no longer bother me. Now, men do not matter to me. You are different. You are special to me.
>
> If you ever come to Himachal, please remember me. Actually, your visit will not be a discreet affair anymore. I will come to meet you myself whenever you're here.
>
> I hope Jiya di is doing well too. Please send my love to Josh and Jai. Everything about you is in the newspapers as well as on Wikipedia.
>
> Charan sparsh!
> Your disciple,
> Urvashi Thakur

Fear. It comes. It comes menacingly. It comes bursting. No one is spared from its arrival. Fear comes and then clings to your being.

The reason? We don't know. We must know.

Express your fear to someone. Shamelessly.

The fear will leave. It took Hamlet a lifetime to perform this simple gesture. It seems that even now, Hamlet hesitates to take the stage and perform.

That, too, will go away. Someday. On its own. Amen!

Fear. It comes. It comes menacingly. It comes bursting. No one is spared from its arrival. Fear comes and then clings to your being.

The reason? We don't know. We must know.

Express your fear to someone. Shamelessly.

The fear will leave.

EPILOGUE

My life has been one big commotion—ferocious, tempting, salty, groaning, occasionally sprinkled with witticisms and guffaws. Then it was also about brawls, then troubles, then despair, then light, then half-baked answers, and finally, intoxication. In other words, not knowing where I was headed. But overall, it's been holistic ... or should I say, wholesome? Indeed, I can't really complain.

I was jolted to consciousness solely because of devotion. It provided me with balance and brought me stability. I may not have discovered answers to all my questions, but my hope and faith have significantly increased. Loneliness, which once felt like a curse, now seems like a blessing. I have fallen in love with silence, tranquillity and quietude. Despite searching for a reason, I struggle to understand why I should meet people unnecessarily. The rest revolves around yoga, meditation and Vipassana. Zindabad.

First, a torn childhood; then, a disorderly youth; then, ravenous theatre; then, alluring cinema, and in the end, prayer.

The search for what lies ahead continues. The only lesson I have learned from life is that one should *accept* everything. Including one's own sins and those of the others. Acceptance brings peace.

Life is about action. Persistent and unattached action. Once an action is taken, it will reap its fruit for the doer; it cannot be undone before that cycle is completed. The Bhagavad Gita as well as Vivekananda convey this principle.

Acting zindabad, theatre zindabad, cinema zindabad.

As for the question of where we are headed or where we are supposed to go—it is being talked about intensely and loudly all the time.

And Hamlet ends now by quoting an extract from a poem from Badal Sarkar's play *Evam Indrajit*—

TUMHARI AUQAAT KYA HAI, PIYUSH MISHRA

जीवन के उस स्वर्ण-प्रात में
मुक्त-हृदय निर्द्वंद्व भाव से
दीक्षा ली थी पदयात्रा की
सतत तीर्थयात्रा करने की।
जीवन की संध्या में पहुँचा
मन मेरा ये भूल न जाए
दीक्षा के उस मूल मंत्र को
तीर्थ नहीं, है केवल यात्रा
लक्ष्य नहीं, है केवल पथ ही
इसी तीर्थ पथ पर है चलना
इष्ट यही गंतव्य यही है।

In the golden dawn of life
with a liberated heart and a detached mind
I took the vow of a journey on foot
to undertake a persistent pilgrimage
I arrived at the dusk of my life
May my mind never forget
The essence, the root of that vow
that it's not a pilgrimage, but only a journey
not a goal, but only the path
It is on this pilgrim's path that one must walk
This is the true wish; this alone is the destination.

Inquilab zindabad!

ABOUT THE AUTHOR

Piyush Mishra is an actor, poet, music director, lyricist, singer, script and dialogue writer, and a well-known theatre director and playwright. He spent his early life in Gwalior, where he received his education.

After his graduation from the National School of Drama, he started his career as a professional theatre artist and went on to write and direct several critically acclaimed plays. He has also featured in many Bollywood films and has contributed to them as lyricist, music director and script and dialogue writer as well.

ABOUT THE TRANSLATOR

Shillpi A Singh is an award-winning communications professional, journalist, and translator with over two decades of experience. She has worked with *The Asian Age*, *The Times of India*, *Hindustan Times*, and *India Today*, as well as with TERI and NABARD during India's G20 Presidency.

As an independent journalist, her writings have appeared in leading Indian newspapers and magazines. She has also managed publicity for acclaimed films and books. As a translator, she has worked on Namwar Singh's *Doosari Parampara Ki Khoj* for Dr Akhilesh Kumar.

HarperCollins *Publishers* India

At HarperCollins India, we believe in telling the best stories and finding the widest readership for our books in every format possible. We started publishing in 1992; a great deal has changed since then, but what has remained constant is the passion with which our authors write their books, the love with which readers receive them, and the sheer joy and excitement that we as publishers feel in being a part of the publishing process.

Over the years, we've had the pleasure of publishing some of the finest writing from the subcontinent and around the world, including several award-winning titles and some of the biggest bestsellers in India's publishing history. But nothing has meant more to us than the fact that millions of people have read the books we published, and that somewhere, a book of ours might have made a difference.

As we look to the future, we go back to that one word—a word which has been a driving force for us all these years.

Read.

Image, left, Deepit Badani